Business Information

Business Information

Technologies and Strategies

Richard Thomas and Mike Ballard

Stanley Thornes (Publishers) Ltd

First published in 1995 by:
Stanley Thornes Publishers Ltd
Ellenborough House
Wellington Street
Cheltenham
Glos. GL50 1YW
UK

A catalogue record for this book is available from The British Library.

ISBN 0 7487 1922 9

Typeset by
Northern Phototypesetting Co Ltd, Bolton
Printed and bound in Great Britain by
Redwood Books, Trowbridge, Wiltshire

Contents

Preface

This book has been written to address two needs. The first is to provide students with an introduction to the use (and abuse) of information and information systems in business. The study of information, how it is defined, collected and used to advantage in business is comparatively recent. It has grown in parallel with the emergence of information technology and the potential it has provided to gather and manipulate data on an unprecedented scale. However, the result has often been a glut of the wrong kind of information and a poor return on investment in IT. If information is to give business competitive advantage, whether in identifying customer needs more precisely, informing decision-making more fully or controlling costs more effectively, it needs its own framework of management. Indeed, it can even require the transformation of the business itself.

The second need is to introduce students to the main information technologies available. This need can only be fully met by placing IT within the broader context of information management. As many companies have found to their cost, simply investing in the latest technology and leaving its management to technical staff is not sufficient. This book both emphasises the practical issues related to choosing and deploying IT and how it can be fitted into a broader information strategy.

The book is divided into four parts. The first analyses information and information systems. Parts 2 and 3 look at the main technologies. Part 4 looks at developing an information strategy and the place of IT within that strategy. At each stage, there is an emphasis on real-life illustrations and case study exercises to consolidate understanding.

Part I
Business information

1 Decision-making and information

Objectives

By the end of this chapter, you should be able to:

- define the difference between data and information
- understand the nature and types of decision-making
- describe the role of the manager
- distinguish between strategic, tactical and operational decision-making
- list the key requirements for effective management information
- understand how information provides competitive advantage
- answer the range of questions at the end of the chapter.

Introduction

Information is the lifeblood of business – without it a business cannot plan or make decisions. Despite this, many businesses have been traditionally very poor at handling their information needs. Many managers complain they are swamped with information they do not require, and starved of what they do need, or that what they get has come too late and in an inappropriate format. Behind this predicament often lies a failure to plan for the information needs of a business. As recently as 1990, surveys suggested that as many as 25% of UK businesses felt that the provision of information was secondary to other management issues and that only 34% of firms had a formal information strategy (Cashmore and Lyall, p. 198). In these circumstances, the growth of information technology, with its huge capacity to multiply the volume and range of business information, only serves to worsen the situation, choking the business with redundant information which it is expensive and time-consuming to produce, circulate and assimilate. Information becomes a burden rather than an asset.

This book is about the need to treat information as a key **business resource** and to plan properly for its use. If done effectively, a business may then turn information from a burden into a major source of competitive advantage. To begin this process, we need to start with a clear understanding of the nature of information itself.

What is information?

This seems a deceptively easy question, but consider the following scenario.

Illustration 1.1: Drallab Limited

You are the new production control manager in Drallab Limited an engineering company, and you receive the following 'information' on budget variances in your department:

(a) Unsorted		(b) Sorted alphabetically		(c) Sorted in numerical order	
Milling	87	Drilling	23	Purchasing	−11
Grinding	58	Grinding	58	Invoicing	−7
Presses	34	Invoicing	−7	Turning	0
Purchasing	−11	Milling	87	Drilling	23
Drilling	23	Presses	34	Presses	34
Invoicing	−7	Purchasing	−11	Grinding	58
Turning	0	Turning	0	Milling	87

Which columns would you see as **raw data** and which would you see as useful **information?** How would you define the difference between the two?

Looking at each column, you might see column (a) as raw data because it is unsorted and difficult to make use of. Column (b) is at least arranged in a way which would help you to locate one item quickly. However, if your job is to control production against budget targets, column (c) is likely to provide the most helpful information – here you can see immediately where there is a problem that needs action.

Returning to the question of the difference between information and raw data, you can begin to see how you are distinguishing between the two. Your most basic questions are:

● What do I need to know to make the right decision in my job?
● What is it that meets this need?

The answers to these questions tell us about the nature of information:

1. Information begins with a *business need* – here, for example, the need to control production against budget targets.

2. That need springs from a requirement to make a *business decision* – here the need to spot and correct any variances against budget.

3. The need also determines how *raw data* is converted into *information*, i.e. sorted into a form which allows the manager to make a decision. As we can see, without *data processing*, it cannot be used.

This gives us a working definition of information in business:

> '**Information is raw data converted into a form to enable the user to make a decision in response to a business need.**'

This process is represented in Figure 1.1. In most instances, the stimulus for collecting data has been the need by a manager, supervisor, or employee, to make a decision about a situation. The process through which the raw data will go again depends upon the needs of the prospective recipient as well as the way in which the final information is presented. Let us illustrate the process at work in a second scenario.

Figure 1.1   The data conversion process

Illustration 1.2: Smith Limited
A computer numerical controlled (CNC) lathe produces components 500 mm in length. Some of the items produced are not within the designer's specification. The manager responsible knows that components must be between 494 and 509 mm to be usable and has been asked to find out what proportion of components are wasted. The manager can then decide whether to have the machine refurbished, or buy a new machine that can work within the designer's tolerances, or possibly change the designer's specification.

STEP 1 Define the business need and the resulting decision that needs to be taken. Here the decision is very clearly defined. As a result, the manager knows the kind of information needed, the way it will need to be processed and the outcome required. As precise a definition as possible of a decision need is essential in the effective use of information.

STEP 2 Define the data required. Here it has been decided to record the lengths of 60 items produced during one hour's production. The results are shown here:

Component length measurements: raw data					
505	492	510	505	504	487
482	491	502	481	496	492
500	512	503	499	498	511
488	486	502	503	510	501
498	492	496	521	505	490
482	522	513	518	520	516
501	512	501	498	492	498
476	490	510	500	495	482
511	496	498	490	485	499

Whilst neatly tabulated, it is not possible to draw any conclusions from the table; it remains raw data.

STEP 3 Process the data into information. A first step might be to rank the data into ascending order as shown. As you can see, we now have crude information on which a decision could be made.

Component length measurements: ranked data					
476	490	496	501	505	512
481	491	498	501	507	512
482	492	498	502	507	512
482	492	498	502	508	513
482	492	498	503	509	516
485	492	498	503	510	518
486	494	499	504	510	518
487	495	499	504	510	520
488	496	500	505	511	521
490	496	500	505	511	522

STEP 4 We can use it to isolate the precise information needed, as follows.

	Quantity	Total (%)
Under 494 mm	11	18.3
494 – 509 mm	37	61.7
Over 509 mm	12	20.0
Total	60	100.0

The manager and process planner would now be in a position to decide if the machine needs to be altered or replaced.

A common theme can be identified in this example. The problem has started with the need to make a decision about a situation and therefore the requirement for information has been identified. Knowing what is wanted enables the correct raw data to be collected and after some rearrangement the data becomes more meaningful. An additional feature to the seven-stage model of Figure 1.1 is shown in Figure 1.2. Often the making of a decision leads to the need to make another. The cycle is repeated.

This definition of information in terms of business decision-making is fundamental. If information is not generated specifically to help make a decision and tailored to make that decision easier, it is a potentially wasted asset. It becomes data floating around the business, its value as information still locked up. As we shall see, many businesses generate huge quantities of so-called 'information' in this way because they do not assess its value in terms of the decision needs of managers. As a result, information in the business becomes divorced from the real decision needs of its recipients. The business that invests time in defining the decision needs of its managers, and engineers the production and flow of information within the business to meet those requirements, is able to turn information into an asset which will work for rather than against the business.

Figure 1.2   Feedback in data conversion

Information and decision-making

In reality, of course, the decisions that most managers have to make are much less clear-cut than this example. To illustrate this point, consider Illustration 1.3.

Illustration 1.3: The Insurance Business

You have just been appointed as the national sales manager for the division of an insurance company dealing with commercial insurance for businesses. Your main clients are smaller manufacturing businesses, especially in the North East where the company has traditionally been strong, though there is now a small group of policies directed at retail businesses. Your responsibilities include your own sales territory, plus a small sales team of four, with two covering the North, one the South East, and one the South West. There is a separate customer services department which handles claims.

On arrival, your Managing Director tells you that the number of clients has been falling steadily and that the division is becoming increasingly unprofitable. He wants you to find out why and reverse the trend. He suggests you start by cutting one of the older sales reps and raising premiums. In your first week, you encounter a range of problems. An irate policy holder in your territory rings to complain about the delay in dealing with a claim. You find that claims tend to be dealt with by whoever happens to be free at the time in customer services, with the result that mistakes and delays occur which then have to be sorted out by the over-worked customer services supervisor.

Speaking to your sales team, you discover that they are spending only about 20% of the time actually dealing with clients. Much of the time is spent chasing up queries on policies for new clients, in adapting them to meet their needs, or claims for existing customers. They never know who to contact in customer services, with the result that there is significant duplication, misunderstanding and delay. Other time is spent in compiling detailed weekly reports on their activities. As a result, they are seeing fewer and fewer new customers. Finding new business has always been a difficult area with reps telephoning potential new customers largely at random when they have the time, generally with limited success. Because of previous cuts, the division is doing less and less direct mail and advertising.

In this case, you are positively bombarded with differing pressures, perspectives and information. To make sense of this kind of situation, and in order that you can isolate your key decision and information needs, we need a different set of tools to analyse the nature of the **decision-making process** in more depth. In other words, before we can consider information, we need to understand managerial decision-making first.

How can one isolate the key decisions one needs to make as a manager? In this section, we will look at the nature of decision-making, how it relates to the role of the manager, and the way managerial decision-making fits in with operational, tactical and strategic decision-making in a business.

Simon identified three key stages in the decision-making process illustrated in Figure 1.3.

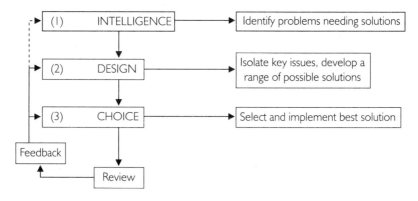

Figure 1.3   The decision-making process (H.A. Simon)

In the first stage, a manager may become aware of some aspect of the business that is underperforming. She or he will need the right information to provide appropriate **benchmarks** for measuring performance, information to measure the degree of under-performance itself, and information to assist in defining the nature and causes of the problem. The more proactive manager will also seek to anticipate potential problems, for example, using forecasts of future market trends to anticipate possible fluctuations in sales performance.

As sales manager, your main problem is declining profitability as a result of falling income from insurance policies. You need to find some way either of increasing revenue or cutting costs, or perhaps a combination of the two.

What is much less clear are the problems in the business and its market which have resulted in this predicament. Is it because you are over-staffed or because your staff are proving unable to meet the needs of existing or potential customers as well as they should? Is it because your customer base is in decline? Many managers often come unstuck at this **intelligence stage**. If they don't have a clear sense of the problems they face, they will be in a poor position to identify their information needs. Later in this section, we will look at ways of coping with more complex 'soft' decision-making of this sort.

Once they have completed the intelligence stage, many managers overlook the **design stage** of decision-making, seizing on the first solution that presents itself, rather than assessing alternative options to select the most effective. As sales manager, you may well be tempted to take up your managing director's suggestion and implement it straight away as an obvious way of improving the figures in the short term, but what will raising prices and losing your most experienced rep do for your long-term position? Both stages require a flexibility of approach that demands an equivalent flexibility in information provision.

Such flexibility may also be needed to help test particular options at the **choice stage** when a manager comes to choose the best solution and to provide appropriate benchmarks for measuring the effectiveness of the solution. The results of this process may then lead to a review of the design and choice stages of decision-making, and may even lead to a reassessment of the nature of the problem itself.

This process suggests the need to allow managers to control access to and manipulation of information as much as possible themselves. Whilst it may well be appropriate for a business to control some flows of information centrally, catering for common and predictable decision needs amongst managers, effective support of managerial decision-making may well require a decentralisation of other aspects of information provision amongst managers themselves to allow them to cope with less easily predicted problems and to tailor information to their personal circumstances. We will investigate ways of achieving this kind of information provision in Part 4.

Self-assessment questions

1   Choose one decision that you made in the last week and identify the intelligence, design and choice stages involved.

2   How many alternatives did you come up with? What information did you use to make your choice?

'Hard' and 'soft' decision-making

How can you cope with the kind of complex decision-making raised in your predicament as sales manager? Simon identified two basic kinds of decision-making, as shown in Figure 1.4.

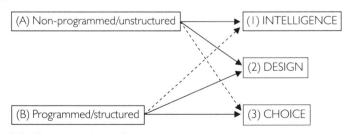

Figure 1.4   Simon's two kinds of decision-making

Non-programmed or **unstructured decisions** are those where issues and outcomes are not clear, where there is a good deal of uncertainty and few rules to follow. This 'soft' kind of decision-making is most likely to occur at the 'intelligence' stage in Simon's model of the decision-making process. It is difficult, for example, to create a system of rules which automatically isolates the range of potential problems a manager might face. At this stage, thinking needs to be more creative, flexible and intuitive. Decisions are likely to be qualitative rather than quantitative.

Programmed or **structured decisions** are those where issues and outcomes can be clearly defined and there are rules to follow. An obvious example is the processing of an invoice from a supplier. The decision on whether to pay is determined by a clear set of rules: is there a copy of the original order, has it been authorised by the department that received the goods or services, do the amounts match, etc. In making these decisions, choices are often between a simple 'yes' or 'no', moving in a structured sequence towards a final outcome. This 'hard' kind of decision-making is likely to fit most easily with the 'choice' stage in Simon's model where, for example, clear targets may be set for measuring implementation. Such targets are often quantitative more than qualitative.

Self-assessment questions

1 List some of the decisions that you have made during the day.

2 Separate them into those that might be classed as structured decisions and those classed as unstructured.

Structured ('hard') decision-making

These two types of decision have led to two differing models of the decision-making process. The 'hard' system, structured approach is outlined in Figure 1.5.

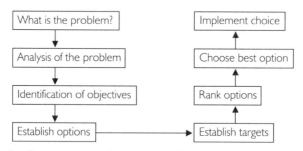

Figure 1.5   The 'hard' systems approach to decision-making

This approach, which develops Simon's basic stages in decision-making, assumes a structured progression through each stage. It assumes problems can be more precisely defined, objectives and targets are clear, options can be clearly identified and compared against each other and the key objectives, and that a clear choice can then emerge.

This kind of approach can be demonstrated in **decision trees** which show the systematic analysis of options leading to a final choice.

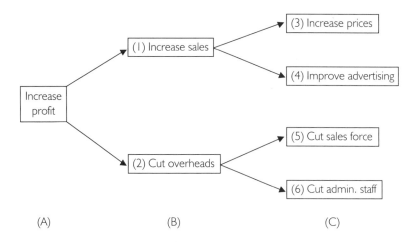

Figure 1.6   A decision tree

In the example given in Figure 1.6, (A) relates to the identification of the problem and objectives and (B) to establishing options, whilst (C) illustrates the process of investigating the consequences of a particular option choice. In this case, option (1) is seen to involve alternatives (3) and (4). Both of these may be seen as high risk if there is evidence that higher prices might reduce sales and the market may not respond to any change in advertising. Option (2) also has potentially high risk consequences: a cut in the sales force may reduce sales, whilst a cut in the level of administrative staff may help profits in the short-term, but impair the firm's longer-term efficiency.

Self-assessment question _____

1   Construct a decision tree for the decision points and options for your further study and career pattern.

As far as you can see, structured decision-making can be very helpful in following through the consequences of particular options. However, the problems you face as sales manager, for example, are less easy to pin down in this way.

Unstructured ('soft') decision-making
In reality, many problems and options are not so easily defined and compared, and managers are often less structured in their decision-making. The soft systems approach (Checkland and Scholes 1990) was developed by Checkland in the 1970s to reflect the reality of decision-making for non-programmed, unstructured 'soft' decisions. The seven-stage model is shown in Figure 1.7.

STAGE 1 The problem situation identified. A problem is apparent to the people in the workplace, but each person has their own perception as to what it is about. There

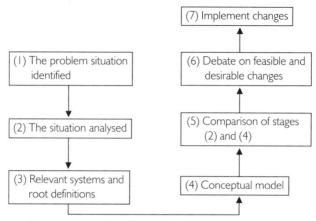

Figure 1.7   The 'soft' system approach to decision-making

are a range of definitions. As sales manager, one of your first actions may well be to talk to all those involved, whether customers, sales reps or customer services personnel, to get a number of different perspectives on what the problem is and the variety of issues involved.

STAGE 2 The situation analysed. A **'rich picture'** is developed that will include all the factors that people think are involved in the problem. The analyst or group then attempts to identify key 'issues' and tasks on which everyone can agree. A second step in solving your sales problem might be to gather together those involved to talk through and agree key issues, for example, the speed of responsiveness to the customer.

STAGE 3 Relevant systems and root definitions. The 'rich picture' identifies all those involved and key issues on which they are agreed. You must now sort through and link up key issues to produce one or more root definitions of the problem and systems which describe it. As sales manager, you may decide that a root definition of the problem is customer focus (or the lack of it) in all the relevant systems which have some impact on the customer.

STAGE 4 Conceptual model. A schematic model of the problem and its solution, based on the root definitions and relevant systems, is developed. This will illustrate the 'transformation process' needed to solve the problem and the key tasks needed to achieve the transformation. In your sales role, you may well develop a model of how effective customer service can be delivered, against which you can assess your current operations.

STAGE 5 Comparison of stages (2) and (4). As the name of this stage implies, the conceptual model developed in stage (4) is compared with the 'rich picture' at stage (2).

STAGE 6 Debate on feasible and desirable changes. All the people who were originally involved with establishing the 'rich picture' are brought together to debate the situation and decide possible changes that are feasible and desirable. An outcome of this stage is an 'agenda for change'.

STAGE 7 Implement changes. The agreed agenda is put into effect.

Whilst many managers claim to follow a 'hard' approach, in practice they follow a 'soft' systems model which is often more appropriate for more complex and 'fuzzy' issues. If we return to Simon's model, a soft approach may be the best way of tackling the 'intelligence' stage of decision-making, allowing a range of opinion and insight out of which key issues will emerge.

These two types of decision-making have profound consequences for the handling of information. The information requirements of structured decision-making can be more precisely predicted and defined. The information itself is often quantitative and can be used within a strictly-defined and rule-bound system. Decisions are likely to be relatively automatic, routine, frequent and short-term.

The information requirements of non-programmed or unstructured decisions are likely to be unpredictable and more *ad hoc*. A manager may require qualitative and quantitative information from a range of sources and to be able to assess such information in a variety of ways. Information needs may well evolve as investigation begins to isolate key issues and new areas arise. There is a greater emphasis on manipulation. Because these decisions are less easy to define, many businesses have not seen it appropriate to try to provide information for such soft decision-making, concentrating instead on such clear-cut areas as budgetary control. However, it is often these softer decisions which are more important to the growth and health of a business. As we shall see in Part 4, IT may still be a valuable resource in tackling soft issues as well as more formal 'harder' decision-making.

The value of this analysis of decision-making is that it allows decision-making to be broken down into stages which makes it more likely that key issues and problems will be correctly identified. As a result, managers will be able to define more clearly what information they then need to assist them and to be able to make more considered and effective decisions. Some of these skills will be applied in the case-studies at the end of the chapter.

Decision-making and the role of the manager

Decision analysis is a key managerial skill and an essential prerequisite to isolating a manager's information needs. However, it needs to be set in the context of the managerial role as a whole. If we look at your position as sales manager in the above illustration, you are faced with a range of demands, from day-to-day queries through to leading your sales team and longer-term planning. Where do you start?

At the turn of this century, Henri Fayol identified the main activities carried out by a manager. Since then, many others have elaborated on his analysis and this section contains a consensus of current views. All managers, no matter what status they have in an organisation, carry out the activities shown in Figure 1.8, but the mix of each depends on their level of responsibility and authority.

Every manager plans his/her own work and the work of others, organises himself/herself and others, directs others as to what to do, and motivates them, exerts control over situations and other people. The results of these are fed back to the planning process to modify future plans. All of these primary activities involve the use of information in different ways.

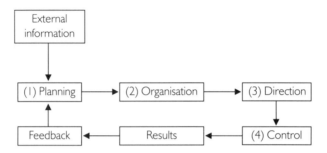

Figure 1.8   Everyday activities of a manager

As Figure 1.8 shows, **planning** is, potentially, the most important part of the manager's role. In the example of the sales manager discussed in the last section, his/her key role would be less in doing any direct sales work with customers, which might be delegated elsewhere, than in planning the overall sales function and how it could meet customer needs better. It provides the framework within which organising, direction and control are defined and can then take place. Planning involves the issues shown in Figure 1.9.

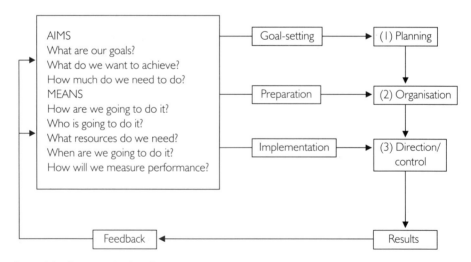

Figure 1.9   Issues involved in planning

As we can see, planning is central to information. In setting out **aims,** it defines the needs of the manager or the decisions he or she must take. In the planning process, agreement and setting of goals then allows the manager to consider the **means** of achieving his or her aims. The second stage of the planning process involves organisation, agreeing resources and how they will be used. At the same time, aims will generate **targets** to be met. Once this preparation stage is complete, the manager can move to **implementation.** It is at this stage that the directing and control elements in the manager's role come into play, setting objectives for staff, leading and motivating them, and measuring progress towards fulfilment of business aims. This process produces **feedback** which may modify any of the earlier stages.

At each stage, information needs will be generated. If each stage is clearly defined and thought through, these information needs will also be clearly defined. However, failure to complete any of them, especially the first key planning or goal-setting stage, will lead to a loss of direction and purpose in a manager's role and, if translated across the business, to a loss of direction in the business itself. This lack of definition also means that there is no framework of decision needs against which to determine what information a manager requires. Without this framework, information flows are likely to be unproductive and haphazard. The major challenge for a manager or, indeed, a business, in making effective use of information is a clear set of goals established at this planning stage and the commitment to shape information flows around the decisions required to fulfil these goals.

Although a proper planning framework should make it clear what key decisions a manager needs to take, and the information he or she will then need, these requirements can be confirmed by the use of various techniques. One representative example is the **critical success factor** method. This requires a manager to assess what factors are critical to successful fulfilment of his or her job. It has the added benefit to the manager that focusing on the key aspects of his job may clarify his role and make him more effective. The critical success factor method was first developed at the Massachusetts Institute of Technology in the late 1970s and can be applied both to the performance of an individual manager or to an organisation as a whole. In any organisation, between three and six factors can usually be identified as crucial to the performance of the organisation. The factors might include a good distribution system, the ability to listen and respond to the customer, a successful research team and consistently effective advertising. Just as an organisation has its own particular success factors, so does an individual manager.

To determine the information needs of a manager by using the critical factor method requires the information provider to act as an analyst and to carry out several interviews or sessions with the manager. This process was described in 1979 by John Rockart (the director of the Center for Information Systems Research, Massachusetts Institute of Technology) as taking place in the following way.

In the first session, the manager's goals should be recorded and the critical success factors that underlie these goals should be discussed. The interrelationship of the goals and critical success factors should then be discussed in order to clarify the position and possibly to combine or eliminate some of the latter. Then an initial attempt should be made to determine the specific pieces of information or measures needed to achieve the goals and their underlying critical success factors. The second session should review the results of the first after the analyst has had a chance to work on them and should then go on to consider the specific measures and possible reports in detail. A third session might be necessary in some instances.

After studying the critical success factors, the analyst should then study the existing reports received by the manager to compare the current information supplied with the information determined by the critical success factor interview. Any major discrepancy between current and required information should be investigated before the new system is put into practice.

Self-assessment questions _____

1 Apply the critical success factor approach to your role as sales manager.

2 What information needs are generated?

Strategic, tactical and operational decision-making

At the level of the business, the distinction between the planning activities of the manager and the way they feed through to the organising, direction and control elements of his or her role is reflected in the distinction between strategic, tactical and operational decision-making. The following lists define examples of key decisions at each level.

Strategic decisions: Time-frame 3–5 years

- What business and markets are we in?
- Where will our markets be in 5 years?
- What do our customers want now/in the future?
- What threats do we face?
- What do stakeholders want?
- What is our competitive advantage?
- What resources will we need?

Tactical decisions: Time-frame 1 year

- What specific products or services will we provide?
- What competitive advantage do they have?
- What resources do we need to provide them?
- How will we market our products or services?
- What financial objectives should they meet?

Operational decisions: Now

- Can we fulfil a customer's order?

- Have we enough resources to sustain production/marketing?
- Are we producing our product or service to its specification?
- Is it continuing to meet its financial objectives?
- How is the current marketing campaign going?

Strategic planning

Strategic planning concerns the nature and direction of the business as a whole. Its perspectives are long term and directed at the future of the business and the markets it is in. They are directed outwards towards the expectations of the stakeholders and towards changes in the markets in which it operates. It sets overall objectives for the whole organisation which then determine tactical and operational planning. Long-term may be, as the figure suggests, five years or more for a large business. In a small business such as an owner-managed restaurant, for example, it may be as little as $1\frac{1}{2}$–2 years. A simplified picture of the strategic planning process is shown in Figure 1.10.

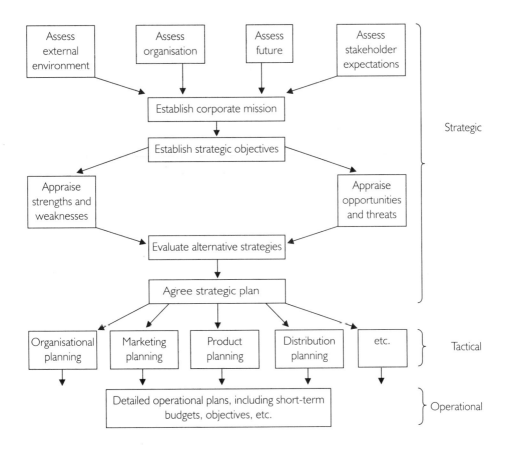

Figure 1.10   The strategic planning process

As the process suggests, strategic planning emphasises the intelligence and planning side of decision-making. The issues it faces are complex, qualitative and fuzzy and decision-making is consequently more unstructured and 'soft' in approach. Objectives may be a mixture of 'softer' objectives (e.g. to achieve higher levels of customer satisfaction) and specific 'hard' targets (e.g. to achieve a certain level of return on sales or market share).

It is beyond the scope of this book to look in detail at the strategic planning process, since it is a subject in its own right. We can only summarise some of the key issues. The most easily defined part of the process is often the financial. Most businesses are either subsidiaries of larger organisations or financed directly by a group of investors, for instance, those holding shares in the company. These **stakeholders** will require a certain level of return on their investment which will be translated into overall profit targets for the company. In turn, these will suggest a certain level of sales performance, investment and productivity to achieve this return.

It will usually be within this framework of strategic **financial objectives** that a business will concentrate on the less easily defined strategic issue of 'how' these objectives will be fulfilled. This issue will involve an assessment of a businesses identity, perhaps through identifying its core processes or its customers and the reasons they buy its products. From this basis, the business can then identify its strengths and weaknesses in, for example, 'adding value' to its products or satisfying customer needs. This analysis can then be set against an assessment of the environment in which the business operates, including, for example, future changes in market behaviour and size, levels of competitive intensity and trends in the costs it faces. Contrasting the two allows a business to gauge how it must develop to grow its position to fulfil the financial objectives it has been set. Many companies now try to crystallize the qualitative side of this process into a **corporate mission statement** which sums up its identity and key tasks in a way the workforce can easily recognise and subscribe to. Beneath this will be a series of more specific targets for each part of the business, for instance, to achieve a certain level of profit or performance as its contribution to the company's mission and the overall financial objectives it has been set.

Tactical planning

Beneath strategic planning lies **tactical planning,** in which overall targets are translated into detailed action plans for each part of the business. As an example, company growth targets will need to be broken down into specific sales and profitability targets for individual products split between the existing range and those new products required to meet overall growth requirements. These action plans will need to be monitored through budgets against which costs, sales and profitability can be measured. Supporting these targets will be plans to ensure that the right resources are available to support product development, for instance, in the planning of the appropriate level of human resources, marketing activity or plant capacity, at the right level of cost to ensure profitability.

For most businesses tactical planning operates within a yearly cycle and is typically expressed through a series of budgets monitoring the timing, cost and resulting performance of the relevant activities. Within this framework, the business moves down to operational planning in which individual employees or units will have specific objectives and targets to meet on a monthly, weekly or daily basis in ensuring that tactical plans keep to their broader targets. A distribution manager will, for example, be required to control stock levels on a daily basis to reduce the level of risk to the business whilst allowing the rapid and cost-effective movement of goods to meet market demand.

As we move down the planning cycle, the scope of decision-making narrows within the boundaries of the agreed strategic plan. It becomes easier to quantify options and set specific, detailed objectives. Although there remains a significant need for softer decision-making, there is a stronger emphasis on the 'design' and 'choice' stages of decision-making and on organisation and control within planning. Information requirements become much more internally-focused and more clear-cut, focused frequently around 'hard' budgetary targets.

The quality of the strategic planning process is critical to effective business decision-making and the framework it establishes for information provision. If a business has a clear sense of strategic direction, perhaps crystallised in its corporate mission statement, and this direction is effectively translated into a set of specific tactical and operational goals, individual managers will have a clear framework for their own planning activities. Decision-making, and the information which supports it, will be focused around the firm's strategic requirements and can be judged according to how well they support those requirements. A clear strategic framework both provides an agenda of the information needed to answer the specific questions it raises and a benchmark by which to judge the value of information circulating within the business.

We can see this by referring back to the use of the sales manager discussed earlier. If the company had a strong sense of its mission to its customers and stakeholders, a clear picture of its markets, customers and competitive advantage in relation to its rivals, it is likely that the managing director would have been able to give you a much more focused brief backed up by specific targets, and that you would have had a ready-made framework for isolating and correcting potential problems in the business. The lack of this strategic focus may well be the root cause of the crisis you have been called on to tackle.

From decisions to information

Once a manager or business has a clear sense of the decision issues it faces, it can then isolate the information it requires. An illustrative example of the range of information needed across the differing business functions and stages of the business plan is provided in Table 1.1.

The success of a business will depend, to a large degree, on how well it can match the right kind and type of information to the appropriate decision need of a manager. At the strategic level, for example, much of the information required will be external and future-orientated. It will involve building a picture of a businesses market using a wide range of data, including Government sources or market research, to complement what can be gleaned from a company's own sales and customer data. It will also be concerned with using this data to create models with which to project estimates of future trends. Since many of the issues are 'soft' and unpredictable, a premium will be placed on giving managers access to as wide a range of information as possible and the capacity

Table 1.1 Business information needs

Functional area	STRATEGIC	Information needed	TACTICAL	Information needed	OPERATIONAL	Information needed
Marketing	Where will our markets be in five years?	● Forecasts of population trends ● Changes in consumer spending power, etc.	On which products should we concentrate most promotional activity?	● Past sales histories ● Feedback on customer preferences ● Growth trends in individual markets	How well is the current campaign doing?	● Sales performance against budget ● Customer feedback via sales reps.
Production	Can we keep our costs of production competitive?	● Forecasts of raw material costs ● Likely supplier behaviour ● Potential competitor costs	Is our present capacity sufficient for this year's production requirement?	● Forecasts of total production requirement? ● Estimate of current capacity	When do we reorder a component?	● Estimated level of future production ● Current stock level ● Supplier delivery time
Finance	How will we fund long-term capital investment?	● Estimates of investment needed ● Sources and cost of finance	What financial targets should each product meet?	● Average gross margin ● Return on investment, etc. needed to support business	Are we on budget this month?	● Sales performance and gross margin to date ● Overhead costs to date
Human resources	Is the current organisation right for the business?	● Number of support staff compared with those directly concerned with product development ● Level of overhead compared to sales performance	What resources will each department need this year?	● Estimate of future workload ● Estimate of current productivity ● Audit of training requirements	Which IT training course do we choose?	● What training priorities employees have ● What courses are available ● How will they meet needs? ● How much do they cost?

to manipulate it in varied ways. At the operational end, however, a customer services clerk will want a fairly limited range of precise information delivered quickly and clearly in an easily recognised format: What is the price of product 'X'? Do we have enough stock to fulfil an order? Does the customer have an account? Is the customer in credit? What discount do I give?

In matching information successfully to a particular decision need, a business needs to be aware not only that the information itself will be different across level and function, but also that the kind of information and the way it will be used may also differ. Table 1.2 illustrates some of the differing information requirements by strategic, tactical and operational levels.

As the table illustrates, strategic planning, for instance, may well require a wide range of information, but with a relatively low level of detail and not necessarily in huge volumes. In projecting future sales for the company, for example, it will not be necessary for the managing director to have weekly sales for each product line calculated to the last pence. He or she may well require summary reports from differing parts of the business, perhaps rounded to the nearest thousand and divided monthly or even annually for past years' performance. The information will only be of value if it is presented in the right format appropriate to the kind of decision need.

The requirements for effective information

Once a business has made the decision to focus its information provision around its key decision needs, especially at strategic level, it must consider the criteria for effective information. Information will only be valuable if it is communicated in the right way to the user. This section reviews the essential characteristics of such information.

Value adding Unless the information actually contributes something new and useful to the user, it is a waste of resources. A report merely confirming what is easily available elsewhere takes value out of the business.

Relevance Above all, of course, information for managers must be relevant to their needs. The impact of many reports is often damaged by the amount of irrelevant material they contain, wasting a manager's time as he or she sifts out useful material.

Accuracy and reliability Information should be sufficiently accurate for it to be relied upon by the manager and for the purpose of which it is intended. There is no such thing as absolute accuracy and raising the level of accuracy, whilst it increases cost, may not necessarily increase the value of information. The level of accuracy must be related to the decision level involved. At operational levels, information may need to be accurate to the nearest pence, pound, kilogram or minute. A sales invoice, for example, will be accurate to the penny. On the other hand, a Sales Manager at the tactical level will probably be best suited to information rounded to the nearest £100, whilst at the strategic level rounding to the nearest ten thousand pounds or higher are common.

Table 1.2 Strategic tactical and operational information

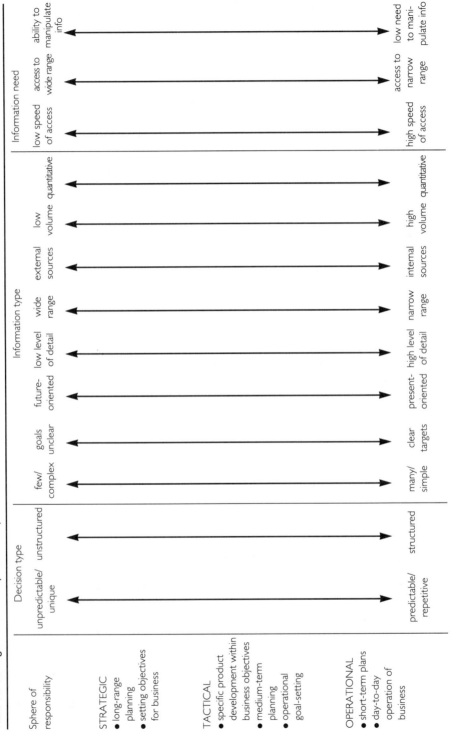

Sphere of responsibility

STRATEGIC
- long-range planning
- setting objectives for business

TACTICAL
- specific product development within business objectives
- medium-term planning
- operational goal-setting

OPERATIONAL
- short-term plans
- day-to-day operation of business

Decision type
- unpredictable/unique ←――――――――→ predictable/repetitive
- unstructured ←――――――――→ structured

- few/complex ←――――――――→ many/simple
- goals unclear ←――――――――→ clear targets

Information type
- future-oriented ←――――――――→ present-oriented
- low level of detail ←――――――――→ high level of detail
- wide range ←――――――――→ narrow range
- external sources ←――――――――→ internal sources
- low volume ←――――――――→ high volume
- quantitative ←――――――――→ quantitative

Information need
- low speed of access ←――――――――→ high speed of access
- access to wide range ←――――――――→ access to narrow range
- ability to manipulate info ←――――――――→ low need to manipulate info

Accuracy should not, of course, be confused with precision. Information may be inaccurate, but precise, or vice versa. If the information is based on a particular set of sources or assumptions, or is an estimate of some kind, this needs to be made clear in assessing what weight a user should put on it.

Completeness Ideally, all the information required for a decision should be available. In the real world, of course, this never happens. What is required is that the information is complete in respect of the key elements of the problem. This means that there must be close liaison between information providers and users to ensure that the key factors are identified.

Direction Information should go directly to the right manager for whom it was intended. Incorrectly directed or poorly addressed information, or information supplied at the wrong level to a line-manager who fails to pass it on, becomes redundant.

Cost-effectiveness Information has no value in itself. Its value derives from the change in decision behaviour caused by the information being available minus the cost of producing the information. An elaborate, costly and time-consuming report on a minor operational matter, whilst it may meet a decision need, would be a potential waste of resources.

Timeliness Good information is that which is communicated in time to be used. To an extent, the need for speed can conflict with the need for accuracy although modern processing methods can produce accurate information very rapidly. Delays in data gathering, processing or communication, can transform potentially vital information into worthless waste paper. The timing of regularly produced information is also important. Information should be produced at a frequency which is related to the type of decision or activity involved. Too often reports are produced routinely at quite arbitrary intervals – daily, weekly, monthly and so on – without regard to the time cycle of the activity involved. At operational levels, this may mean a requirement for information to be available virtually continuously – say on a VDU screen – but at other levels much longer intervals are likely to be appropriate which should not be determined merely by the conventions of the calendar.

Level of detail Information should contain the least amount of detail consistent with effective decision making. Every superfluous character means extra storage, more processing, extra assimilation and possibly poorer decisions. The level of detail should vary with the level of the organisation: the higher the level, the greater the degree of compression and summarisation. Although information, particularly at lower levels, often has to be very detailed to be useful, the general rule of as little as possible consistent with effective use must always apply. Because of the need to be concise and to direct attention to where it is needed **exception reporting** is frequently used for control information.

Comprehension If information cannot easily be understood, it loses its value to the user. Whilst some users find it easier to understand a column of figures, others find graphical presentation or a written commentary easiest to absorb. Effective communication takes into account the abilities and preferences of users.

Illustration 1.4: Information overkill

One senior executive in a UK company reported that he received no less than 97 reports in the course of a month. Almost all of these were originated by someone else who felt that he should be receiving this 'vital information'. Presumably it would take most of the month to read and digest the 97 reports; and if this were done little time would be left for running the business.

This may be contrasted with Lord Weinstock of GEC – famed for his control methods – who reported that he receives all the basic information he needs on three sheets of paper from which he can tell immediately if anything is seriously wrong with the company (Cashmore, p. 67).

A systematic approach to information

As we noted at the beginning of the chapter, there are still many businesses that do not plan systematically for their information needs. This would not be a problem if managers were always clear about their key decision needs and, at the same time, had instant access to exactly the information they required. In practice, information provision in many businesses has fallen short because neither of these elements was present. Many managers have, traditionally, been poor at understanding and articulating their requirements. This situation has been summarised by one analyst as follows:

> 'Managers are to information as alcoholics are to booze. They consume enormous amounts, constantly crave more, but have great difficulty in digesting their intake.' (Robert Heller quoted in Cashmore: p. 5)

At the same time, many businesses have traditionally focused their information provision around their immediate, short-term priorities. On a day-to-day operational level, information requirements are driven by the requirements of fulfilling orders and sustaining production to maximise income, controlling and limiting expenditure to protect profits and cashflow, and accumulating the data required for financial reporting. This emphasis was strengthened by the role of IT and accounts personnel in organising the collection and ordering of this data to fulfil these requirements and in the preparation of budgets to monitor this kind of operational activity. Unless a conscious attempt was made to move beyond these immediate requirements and to canvass the broader decision and information needs of other managers, formal information channels remained limited and unresponsive to these needs.

A major challenge for any business is to develop ways of helping managers to define their decision and information requirements clearly. This chapter has outlined various ways in which this can be achieved, particularly through the clarity and rigour of the strategic planning process and the analysis of the individual components of decision-making. The second essential link in the chain is the effective linking of information providers and information users. This may be achieved by periodic meetings between the two to review information flows or the appointment of an information manager to co-ordinate flows of information across the company, both to determine whether the right information is flowing to the right people to meet their decision needs, and that it is being communicated in the best way to be effective.

Information and competitive advantage

As we have seen, companies have traditionally emphasised the use of information in the control and operational element of management. Attention was focused on 'hard' operational targets, usually numerical, and information gathered to test periodically if these targets were being achieved. Information-gathering was concentrated around measuring this kind of internal operational performance, for instance, changing levels of sales against budgetary targets with the simple aim of highlighting discrepancies, whether positive or negative.

Information is now seen less as solely a mechanism of control and much more as a strategic weapon. Professor Itami, for example, has distinguished two types of assets that businesses possess (Cashmore, p. 6). The first are **visible assets,** whether the goods a business produces, the technology and buildings it owns, or the people it employs. The second are **invisible assets,** based on:

- the kinds of information resources a company possesses
- the accumulated production experience and expertise of the workforce
- the company's reputation and image in the market place
- the accumulated understanding of customer needs or market trends.

Whilst it is always possible for a competitor to copy or buy a visible asset in time, it is less easy to identify and reproduce an accumulated understanding of customer behaviour and preferences, for example.

The recognition of the value of this kind of market-orientated information as a source of competitive advantage has meant that information provision now focuses much more around the broader, strategically-focused, decision needs of managers. Information is now used to help managers to understand, anticipate and fulfil market needs more effectively, for example. If the whole range of decisions required in a business, particularly those at strategic level, can be made on the basis of the best information available, that business is likely to put itself in a stronger competitive position in the future. In Part 4, we will look in more detail at how information and IT may be used by companies to secure competitive advantage.

Summary

This chapter has identified the following key themes:

- Business information is defined by the decision-making needs of managers.
- There are a range of stages in and types of managerial decision-making which requires information at differing points.
- The clarity of decision-making is determined by the clarity of the strategic process and the way it feeds down to tactical and operational decision-making.
- There are a range of criteria which need to be satisfied if information is to be useful for decision-making.

- If information is collected and used to support the decision-making needs of a business, it provides competitive advantage.

In the next chapter, we will look at how the way business organisations evolve, and how the way they are structured helps or hinders the effective flow of information to decision-makers.

Now, using the range of skills outlined in this chapter, answer the following.

Questions for discussion

1   What differentiates information from data?

2   The owner of a large DIY store has decided to open another store in a nearby town. Discuss what information he needs to make such a decision and where he might find it.

3   List all the external organisations with which a company needs to communicate with. Discuss the types of communications that need to take place between a company and outside organisations.

4   Information is a vital resource for performing all of the functions of management. Discuss the role of information in these activities.

5   What is the difference between operational and tactical information within a chain of grocery stores?

6   What is the difference between tactical and strategic information for the owner of a small group of restaurants?

7   Discuss the differences between structured and unstructured decision-making.

8   What is the difference between the 'hard' and 'soft' systems approach to decision-making?

9   Discuss the levels of decision-making that will employ the soft systems methodology.

Problems

1   The management of a chain of fast-food restaurants is examining their information

needs. They are considering expanding into Europe. Discuss the information that they will need in order to make this decision.

2   Acme Manufacturing make a range of washing machines, dish washers, etc. Recently the management have been getting feedback from customers about the out-of-date style of some of the products. Discuss the information needs for the company to make a decision about whether or not to restyle their products.

3   Acme Manufacturing has redesigned the first product in a range. Discuss the tactical decisions that must now be made to implement the change.

4   The headquarters of your company is moving to a different location. Discuss the differences between the information needed to make the move, the information to find a new location and the actual moving of offices.

5   The marketing department of a large company makes use of a great deal of information. List the information that it needs to function effectively and indicate if it is strategic, tactical or operational.

Case-study 1.1: Your role as Sales Manager
Look back to Illustration 1.3 at the beginning of this chapter. Using the stages in decision-making and the 'hard' and 'soft' methods outlined earlier:

- diagnose the key problems behind the decline in profitability
- put together a draft report to the managing director with your recommendations for action
- list the information you will need to test your diagnosis and carry out your recommendations.

In considering the issues, you may find the following questions helpful:

1   Should you be concentrating on immediate cuts to help profitability, or on reorganisation and investment for the future? What information do you need from your managing director to answer this?

2   What sort of things might customers be looking for in measuring good service? How can you check?

3   Where is the company failing to provide that service? What reasons are there for this failure?

4   What initial suggestions do you have for solving the problems? Is there a case for reorganisation of some sort? Who could help you analyse these problems better?

5   Is it sensible to rely on your current customer base? If not, where could you expand? How could you target new customers?

Case-study 1.2: Operational, tactical and strategic decision-making: South Hampshire Restaurant

The owner of the South Hampshire Restaurant (SHR) recently installed a mini-computer-based information system that will help in improving operations and providing control over day-to-day operations of the business. The system consists of a systems box, stored in a cupboard in the owner's office, nine terminals and a number of printers.

When an order is taken, the waitress enters it directly via one of the four terminals located in the dining facility. The order is stored on the computer's database and is transmitted to one of four printers for processing; the cold-item printer for salads or sandwiches, the hot-item printer for hot plates or dinners, a beverage printer for ice-cream, soft drinks, coffee or take-away, and a bar printer for spirits or beer. There is a terminal by each printer and one in the owner's office.

- The printed check lists the items ordered and prices, eliminating the waitress's handwritten order.
- If a menu item should be sold out, a message is immediately displayed on the screen.
- The customer is then asked to place another order.
- A unique feature of the software is that it breaks down meals by food and labour costs.
- It also produces daily reports, showing the order rate of each item on the menu.

The software was programmed by one of the part-time waitresses who was working on a computing degree at the local university. In designing it she interviewed and worked closely with the nine full-time waitresses and the two chefs. Acceptance of the system by the staff was favourable and customers noticed the clarity of the bill and improvement in service.

In managing a restaurant such as SHR:

1   What information is necessary for strategic, tactical and operational decisions?

2   How does the system contribute to each level of decision-making?

Case-study 1.3: The requirements for effective information: Carryseat
You are a product manager for Durban Limited, a manufacturer of a range of baby
and children's products. As part of its strategy, the company has declared its mission
statement to be:
  'to meet our customers needs better and more profitably
  than our competitors'.
Your particular responsibility is for the baby car seat, the Carryseat, which Durban
has had on the market for one year. The car seat is manufactured with three types
of pattern cover and the company has also experimented with a higher price version
(in the pastel shade only) which includes a facility to convert the seat into a rocker
for use in the home. Your responsibilities include controlling stock levels whilst
ensuring continuity of supply, putting in orders for new stock which take, on average, two months to fulfil. You are also responsible for a planned upgrade of the
range next year and have been given a budget which includes one potential pattern
change, correcting any minor faults, extending the rocker facility throughout the
range, if needed, and adding one other new feature. Any change needs to be justi-
fied in terms of its likelihood to increase sales.

You currently have the following information supplied to the accounts department
to help you in your job:

- budget printout for the year showing the total budgeted monthly sales by
  number of units sold and income
- a printout for the previous year of total monthly sales by income only
- a monthly report on actual unit sales (see below).

Product line	Jan.	Feb.	Mar.	Apr.	May	Current stock
Pastel	230	401	302	417	503	1905
Tartan	103	223	111	257	302	1117
Springtime	203	411	320	512	607	2250
Rocker	201	312	322	412	512	1512

At present, you are aware that there have been a number of complaints and suggestions coming through the sales team and the customer service department with calls
from shops and the field (individual customers). These are fed through on a haphazard basis. So far, the list includes the following complaints and suggestions:

- difficulty in fastening buckle
- tartan shade runs when washed
- handle does not lock in right position
- add storage box
- add 'summer' pattern
- add facility to attach to supermarket trolley.

Bearing in mind the company's overall strategy, suggest ways you can improve the current flow of information to assist you in carrying out your responsibilities. In doing so, consider the following questions:

1   Identify the key decisions and information you need to decide when to reorder stock.

2   Amongst this information, what is missing from the reports you currently receive?

3   How would you redesign the reports you have to provide one source enabling you to make a decision on stock ordering easily and quickly? Could reordering be carried out automatically?

4   Compare your redesigned report against the criteria for effective information discussed earlier in this chapter and suggest any further improvements.

5   Suggest how you might redesign a report to assist you in deciding on what pattern changes, if any, might be appropriate and whether the rocker facility could be extended throughout the range.

Further reading

Cashmore, C. and Lyall, R., *Business Information: Systems and Strategies*, Prentice-Hall, 1991

Checkland & Scholes, *Soft Systems Methodology in Action*, John Wiley, 1990

Curtis, G., *Business Information Systems*, (Chapter 1) Addison-Wesley, 1989

Gray, I., *Henry Fayol's General and Industrial Management*, Pitman, 1988

Simon, H. A., *The New Science of Management Division* (revised edn.), Prentice-Hall, 1977

Wisniewski, M., *Quantitative Methods for Decision-Makers*, Pitman, 1994

2 Organisations and information

Objectives

By the end of this chapter, you should be able to:
- understand the growth phases of organisations
- understand how information needs change as organisations grow
- be able to diagnose potential information problems within organisations
- be able to answer the self-assessment questions and case-study at the end of the chapter.

Introduction

So far, we have looked at what defines information and its relationship to decision-making in business. As we have seen, information is defined by the decision needs of a business. A business's information requirements are determined most essentially by the goals it sets for itself at the strategic, tactical and operational levels. Those goals may include the use of information itself as a weapon of competitive advantage. Further information requirements are then generated for each manager. The previous chapter concluded by analysing the types of information required and outlining specific examples of information needed by differing managers.

In this chapter we will look at the way these information needs change as organisations grow and how their approach to information develops, or lags behind, in matching these requirements. This chapter will emphasise the ways in which attitudes to information need to grow to fit evolving needs and the consequences of failure to do so. At the end of the chapter, you should be in a position to analyse the growth phase of an organisation and its potential information characteristics and problems in comparison with its key decision-making needs. As we shall see later in Part 4, IT can have a major impact on a company's organisation, generating new pressures and possibilities for the right organisation to achieve competitive advantage. We will look at this theme in Chapter 10.

Organisational theory

Before we look at the way organisations develop, we need to review briefly some of the basic concepts in organisational theory to put our analysis of organisational change in context.

An organisation may be defined as a group of people combined to achieve specific objectives. Organisational theory is concerned with the inter-relationship between these three essential ingredients:

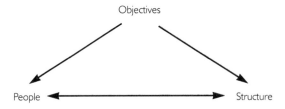

It is specifically concerned with analysing how structures enable people to act effectively in fulfilling an organisation's objectives. A company's goals, defined through the strategic planning process, provide the starting point for assessing its organisational needs. In reality, as we shall see, organisations often fail to adapt to the changing needs and goals of a business. The wrong structure can make it very difficult for employees to achieve company goals or to identify and acquire the information they need. It can undermine understanding of real company needs and even the quality of decision-making and goal-setting itself.

Organising horizontally: functional specialisation and beyond

One of the starting points of organisational theory has been in the concept of *functional specialisation*. Business requires the use of specialised skills such as marketing, production, finance and human resource management. These may be deployed in various ways in different organisations. For instance the small business may require the use of several such skills within one individual. Alternatively a larger business may decide to concentrate a particular set of skills within one part of the business. Such businesses develop an organisation structured around functionally-specialised units or departments. A typical example for a manufacturing company is given below:

Figure 2.1

Such a structure has the advantage of concentrating skill and experience in one area. It has the disadvantage of encouraging the functional units to understand and consider only their own specialised roles and needs within an organisation. Information flows between some of these units may become effective, for instance in the day-to-day good links between production and purchasing. However, other links which may be significant to company success, for example, the flow of information between Research and Development and Sales and Marketing in the development of successful customer-driven product, may be actively inhibited by such an organisational structure. If business objectives require a high degree of flexibility and creativity between a number of functions, alternative methods of organisation may need to be developed. An example is a matrix structure, illustrated in Figure 2.2 for a firm manufacturing office machinery.

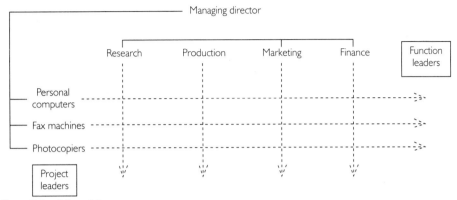

Figure 2.2   A 'matrix' structure

In this structure, an employee reports to two managers. A management accountant working under the Finance Director may be seconded to work for the Project Leader for personal computers, who will gather a team from the various functional units to achieve a specific business goal. Such a structure may allow a much more direct focus on the goal with smoother information flows across the company. However, this is a more fluid and complex structure which, if not managed effectively, can lead to conflicts of leadership and communication as functional and project lines of responsibility intersect.

Organising vertically: tall and flat organisations

A second fundamental issue in organisational theory has been how decision-making and authority are delegated vertically within an organisation. Traditional organisational theory emphasised precise definitions of levels of authority and status. The result of such an approach is a 'tall' hierarchical structure with strong central control and decision-making delegated in progressive stages down the chain of command. An example of this kind of organisation is given below:

Figure 2.3   A 'tall' organisation structure

Such organisations have the advantage of clear definitions of job function and degree of responsibility. On the other hand, this kind of organisation has been criticised as rigid and inflexible. With levels of responsibility precisely defined, there is, potentially, little scope for initiative, especially in the more junior posts. Decision-making tends to be a one-way process determined from the centre. Information flow up and down the organisation can also be disrupted by having to operate through so many layers of management. Such organisations can, therefore, be slow to respond to changes in business needs and conditions, with those taking decisions remote from customers and those closest to customers remote from any significant decision-making .

If they are associated with large-scale manufacturing operations in particular, such organisations can also be characterised, especially at lower levels of responsibility, by broad *spans of control*, that is the number of employees reporting to a manager. A broad span of control suggests a relatively formal structure directed towards routine, repetitive tasks with prescriptive one-way flow of information. More unpredictable activities requiring a flexible response to, for example, changing market conditions, point both to smaller groups and spans of control, and to greater flexibility in dialogue and decision-taking between line managers and staff.

A contrast to the kind of 'tall' structure just outlined is the flatter organisation illustrated below:

Figure 2.4   A flat organisation structure

In this type of organisation senior management delegates responsibility much more widely to junior management who, in turn, allow much more scope and independence to their staff at the operational level. Shorter chains of command and information flows may encourage greater initiative, feedback of information and, therefore, a more rapid response to changing conditions. This may be combined with short spans of control, perhaps by organising junior staff into small groups under a team leader..

Formal/mechanistic versus informal/organic organisations

This initial discussion has pointed to a contrast between two organisational types. On the one hand, there is the more formal organisation defined, horizontally, by elaborate functional specialisation and, vertically, by a tall structure with precise graduations in authority/responsibility. On the other, an alternative, more organic organisation may be characterised by a flat structure allowing more equal levels of responsibility and a horizonal matrix approach mixing changing project-specific groups across functional boundaries.

This contrast points to a key issue in business organisation: the need to retain flexibility of approach, especially in response to changing business needs and goals, and to develop an organisation appropriate to the scale and type of business, as well as the potential of the people within it. A mature, large-scale manufacturing business may well require, and benefit from, a good deal of functional specialisation and a relatively elaborate chain of command at this stage of its growth. However, even it may find the parallel use of a matrix structure with independent groups concentrating on specific projects helpful in developing new practices or products. As we have seen, the two contrasting organisational types each have major implications for the way information is handled. Within too rigid a structure, information flows become static and increasingly divorced from real business needs. Within too informal and organic a structure, information needs may be poorly defined and information flows chaotic and misdirected.

Self-assessment questions _____

1   Define an organisation.

2   Draw a functional organisation chart of a business you are familiar with or the Business Studies School at which you study. What improvements would you suggest?

3   Outline the information strengths and weaknesses of 'tall' organisations.

The growth of organisational and information needs

To understand the way organisations and their information needs evolve, we shall make use of a model adapted from the work of Larry E. Greiner on American companies in the 1970s. Greiner identified various phases of development in business organisations as they grew in maturity and size, together with the organisational characteristics and problems associated with each phase. His work is updated here in the model shown overleaf to include later developments in the 80s and 90s and some of the specific issues associated with each phase.

Phase 1
Phase 1 represents the setting up and early years of a small business. At this stage it may consist of a single owner or partnership with, perhaps, a few employees at most. There may well be a business plan, but the main focus is operational, creating the product or service, attracting and sustaining initial market growth. There will be little time to set up comprehensive control systems. Many of the business's operations will be relatively unplanned, responding to immediate market needs to ensure survival and growth. The structure of the business will be informal and organic, evolving to fit circumstances with little attempt at specialisation of functions. The management structure is, by definition, flat with informal communication and a short span of control – the workforce isn't yet big enough for the large-scale supervisory responsibilities which define a broad span of control over a significant number of employees. A major tension in further

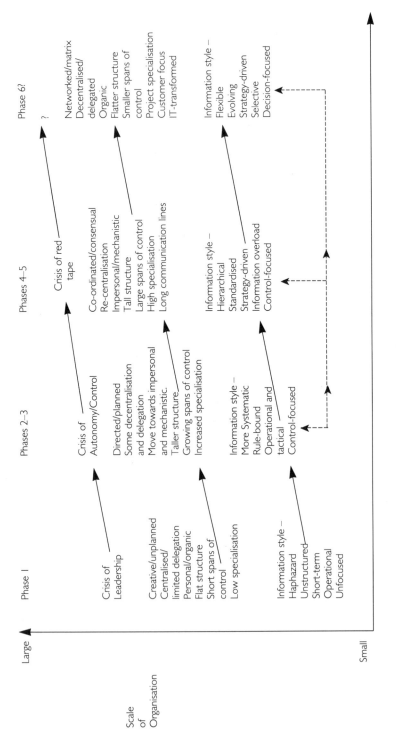

Figure 2.5   Developments in organisation characteristics (Greiner)

growth will be in the ability of the original ownership to relinquish strong initial control and delegate as operations become more complex – this will determine the shift to the next phase of Greiner's model.

The information style of such a company is also informal. Decision-making is unstructured and short-term. There is likely to be significant reliance on verbal communication and on memory, since the volume of information is low and information flows relatively simple. However, even at this stage, there are significant pressures towards a more conscious, planned, approach to information. Financial reporting requirements will dictate the storage and processing of relevant information. Operational pressures will grow with sales activity and it will become increasingly necessary to set up systems for order processing and stock control, for example. The resulting systems may well be relatively *ad hoc* reactions to immediate pressures rather than a planned approach. Such a failure to step back and think through information needs may then become a serious obstacle to a firm in later phases of growth, as indicated in the following illustration.

Illustration: Phase 1   Bill Giles

Bill Giles started his business 15 years ago and it has gradually grown in size until he now employs 48 people. As time has gone on and Bill has grown older, he has found it more and more difficult to control. When the business was smaller, he could carry all relevant information in his head, as could the people he employed as supervisors. Gradually, a traditional departmental structure has evolved. Such a structure has been fine for most managerial activities. However, there have been occasions recently when co-ordination between sections has been lacking. For example, the product designer retired recently and his replacement, who had very good references, has produced mould designs which, after they had been manufactured, were found to exist already in the tool stores. Another example is the accounts section where invoices have been paid, only for it to come to light much later that the batch of components had been returned due to a faulty part.

Phases 2–3

Phases 2 and 3 relate to the growth in business from small to medium size. The single owner or partnership is likely to have given way to a broader senior management team chaired by a managing director. Functional specialisation will have become well-established and there may well be a tension between the strong central control characteristic of the small business and the need to delegate more to tactical managers. This tension is characteristic of firms moving from Phase 2 to 3 in Greiner's model.

Operational systems will have become both more elaborate and more formal to cope with the volume of activity in such areas as production, stock control, order fulfilment, credit control and financial reporting. At the same time, there will be much stronger emphasis on tactical and operational control, with target-setting backed up by budgets and variance reporting. Similarly, as products and markets diversify beyond the niche established by the founding business, increased choice, competitive intensity and pressure for longer-term growth will force a much greater degree of strategic planning.

It will be at this stage in the company's growth that it will begin to experience the tension between the relative merits of a formal organisation with precise definitions of function and authority and a more fluid structure adapting more organically to changing conditions. At the same time, it may also begin to face tensions in the provision of effective management information for its key decision needs. If a conscious decision is not made otherwise, a business may well inherit the early *ad hoc* approach to information, overlaying it with basic tactical and operational control systems. Such systems, geared to the immediate requirements of order processing, finance and stock control, for example, may well be poorly suited to the broader tactical and strategic needs of other managers, or to the broader use of information for competitive advantage. The degree of functional specialisation may both add to the complexity of informational flows and deepen the problem, with limited communication and understanding between the processors and providers of information, concentrated in the finance and IT departments, and other managers. One commentator has summarised the position within firms of this kind as follows:

'data from operational and transaction systems, such as accounts, is religiously aggregated, summarised and presented, but most of it never gets read because it is internal, divided into inappropriate time periods and often out-of-date. As one executive puts it, they are "damage reports that you get after you've hit the iceberg, rather than the radar systems that steer you around it".'[1]

The same failure to define the real information needs of a business, and to structure information flows accordingly, is also likely to typify the firm's overall use of IT in both meeting information needs and giving the firm competitive advantage. This is a major theme to which we will return in Part 4.

Illustration: Phases 2–3   The presentation of financial information

Many accounting information systems are geared primarily to satisfy the legal requirements of the Companies Act for published accounts. Under these requirements, stock of any product is valued at production cost, i.e. according to the direct costs of manufacture, plus a proportion of the general manufacturing overhead. No account is taken of, for example, the research and development, sales and marketing, or distribution costs that a particular product may have incurred. These are accounted for separately in the balance sheet as a general company overhead.

Detaching these other costs from a product makes it potentially difficult to assess the relative profitability of one product over another. Compare products (a) and (b).

	Product (a) (£000)	Product (b) (£000)
Turnover	250	200
Direct manufacturing costs	40	35
Manufacturing overhead (5% turnover)	12.5	10
General company overhead (including research and development, sales and marketing, etc: 30% turnover)	75	60
Net result	122.5 (49%)	95 (47.5%)

On these figures, product (a) looks to be the most profitable. However, if we attributed the relevant research and development, sales and marketing and distribution costs directly to each product, we would get a very different picture.

	Product (a) (£000)		Product (b) (£000)
Gross profit*	197.5	Gross profit*	155
Research and development	15	Research and development	5
Sales and marketing	20	Sales and marketing	10
Distribution	10	Distribution	5
Storage	1	Storage	1
Direct product profit	151.5 (76.7%)		134 (86.4%)

* (after deduction of direct manufacturing cost and manufacturing overhead)

Since the costs of research and development, marketing and distribution are relatively high for product (a), product (b) is the more profitable.

Industries such as retailing, where manufacturing costs are much less significant (goods are bought from suppliers) than those of storage, distribution and marketing, have moved over to **direct product profit** (DPP) as a more helpful way of presenting information for their decision needs on individual projects. They have realigned the provision of information from the accounting function *to fit the decision needs of their managers* rather than just the internal needs of the original provider.

Phases 4–5

In Phases 4 and 5, the business grows to substantial scale. At this stage it may consist of a number of subsidiary businesses, perhaps sub-divided again by location or product/market specialism. A simple example of an engineering company, Vickers PLC, is illustrated below.

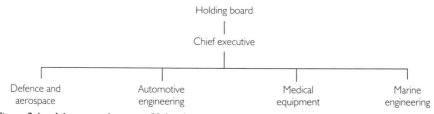

Figure 2.6   A large conglomerate (Vickers)

In the case of Vickers, each of its principal product areas incorporates a number of operating companies with their own product niches. Co-ordination becomes a major issue in retaining a coherent identity, momentum and competitive advantage (in the economies of scale a major business can command over suppliers, for example). A particular danger at this point is the imposition of too much central control at the expense of the flexibility needed by individual companies within the group to react appropriately to their own market conditions. The opposite danger, represented by the Phase 5 organisation, is to allow too much consultation between subsidiaries, leading to a growing bureaucratic inertia.

If there still remains a failure to react flexibly and creatively to the essential information required for key decisions inherited from Phases 2–3, the existing system will become even more elaborate, unfocused and unwieldy. Earlier problems of information overload and waste are likely to be amplified, and the application of IT will only add to the momentum. The result may well be the capacity to collect a wide range of information, of which much may be unhelpful or unnecessary to the real decision-making needs of the business and its managers. This situation of information over-capacity has been effectively summarised by Lester C. Thurow:

> 'I am often shown the computer on an executive's desk and proudly told that the Chief Executive could use the computer to get the inventories in his Singapore facility if he wished. I am always tempted to ask four questions:
>
> - first, when did you last ask for the inventories at your Singapore facility?
> - second, if you have to ask, don't you have the wrong person managing your Singapore facility?
> - third, if you did ask, is there any way that you can use the answer to make your company run better?
> - fourth, how much does it cost to have the capability of moving inventory information from Singapore to Headquarters?'[2]

An alternative scenario within such a large-scale business, again inherited from earlier phases of growth, is an inflexible information system geared primarily to operational and control requirements, with standardised reports arranged to a predetermined pattern by the holding company, illustrated below.

Illustration: Phases 4–5   STC in the 1980s
During the 1980s, STC, the telecommunications company, had an information system geared primarily to the control requirements of senior management. Information was supplied according to a set of ten predetermined schedules. Once keyed in, the information was 'locked' into the system so that it could not subsequently be altered. Although ideal for control purposes in this period, the predetermined scope and content of the information made it less easy to manipulate to meet other requirements. The system was also potentially vulnerable to changing conditions and information needs which would leave the format potentially redundant. This approach may be contrasted with more modern database methods which allow managers to access and manipulate information in a wide range of ways to meet local and evolving needs.

Phase 6
Many firms encountering problems at various stages from Phases 2 to 5 have sought to break out of what are seen as rigid traditional organisational structures, often emphasising functional specialisation and a linear hierarchy. They have done so by stepping back from the accumulated structures and practices of the past and redefining their key

decision needs. In many cases this has meant loosening central control, devolving responsibility to individual business units which are closer and more responsive to market conditions and customer needs. One solution has been to reorganise the Phase 4–5 organisation around a matrix/network structure, illustrated below:

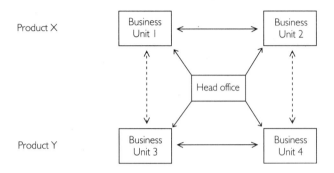

Figure 2.7   Matrix/network structure

The overall business is broken up into separate, self-contained business units defined by, for example, product specialism and linked by a corporate network. Head Office sets overall strategic targets and goals, but the individual units retain considerable independence in how they operate within their product and regional areas to fulfil those goals. Head Office restricts its day-to-day role to ensuring maximum synergy between units, for instance in the sharing or joint purchase of resources. As one senior executive sums it up, such a structure 'balances the need for central co-ordination of resource allocation with the need for local initiatives in differing market environments.'[3]

An alternative solution for some organisations has been to 're-engineer' their business processes by abandoning functional specialisation in favour of groups organised around each key stage in the production process creating the product or service for the customer. The latter is defined as both external (the customer buying the product or service) and internal (the colleagues and process groups on either side of you in the process chain). This kind of structure is illustrated below.

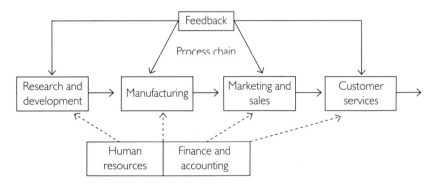

Figure 2.8   A re-engineered organisation

Such an organisation becomes, potentially, much more focused around the key decision needs of the business: those concerned with meeting the needs of the customer. Larger organisations may well try to combine the two approaches, creating 're-engineered' business units within a broader matrix structure.

Within either of these solutions, information flows are radically transformed. In a matrix structure, communication channels are more complex and unpredictable. There is a premium on maximum flexibility both for communication in the network and in the manipulation of centrally stored information by business unit clients. In the process-driven business, information flows need to be flexible within the groups responsible for each stage and between those groups and support services. As we shall see in Part 4, IT has played a major role in giving businesses the flexibility and incentive to re-engineer in this way.

Most fundamentally, benchmarks for determining the value of information in each case become focused around measuring value added to the customer at each stage in the production process. Just as the organisation may now be more closely geared to the decision needs of the business, so information needs may be more consciously thought out. As an example, within the re-engineered business, units in the process chain may now determine the kind and timing of information from the finance and accounting support unit, rather than face the mismatch of information discussed in the phase 2 organisation. Operational and tactical control needs will be balanced by more strategic, market-driven information needs. Information flows may become more selective and more varied with information providers reacting to rather than dictating requirements. Similarly, such organisations will be more selective and responsive in their use of IT. A major theme of Part 4 will be this flexibility of response which, in some cases, can lead to a business being transformed by its use of IT.

Illustration: Phase 6   The matrix structure at Shell

In the 1990s Shell has become an even more diversified multinational, extending its traditional product range from oil, gas and petrochemicals to include other minerals. It has sought to create coherence from this diversity by adopting a four-dimensional matrix structure. Alongside the traditional network of operating companies, Shell has split its operations into functions (for example research or finance), regions and sectors (whether gas, chemicals, metals, etc). Each unit within the operating company is able to link up with its partners elsewhere in the matrix. As an example, the research unit within the chemicals sector of the East European region can link up to its counterpart in the Middle East or to the health, safety and environment function in the metals sector in Australasia to discuss common requirements and issues.

Illustration: Phase 6   Business process re-engineering at Dataform

Dataform is a £30 million business manufacturing hi-tech communications equipment. In response to the increasing pressure from Japanese competitors, the company has been rethinking its strategy, including the development of a more streamlined organisation to cut waste and improve the quality and speed of its service to customers. The existing structure emphasised traditional functional and departmental specialisation, illustrated below:

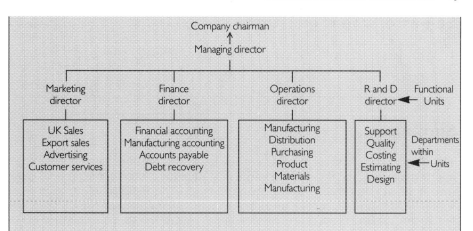

By identifying its core activities as research and development, product marketing, manufacturing and distribution, and streamlining the business around them, Dataform developed the new structure illustrated below:

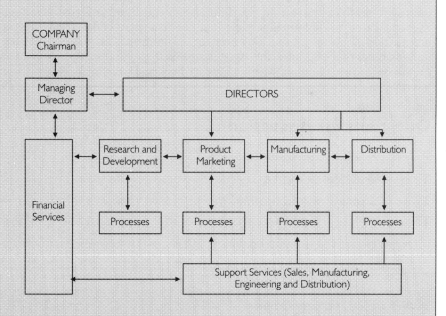

The marketing and finance units were condensed into two integrated departments and buying and materials management integrated into Support Services. The results were a 35 per cent reduction in support service staff which, together with other savings, reduced the cost of non-value added processes by an amount equivalent to a 24 per cent increase in contribution.[4]

Self-assessment questions

1   What information style might you associate with a Phase 2 organisation?

2   Describe how you might re-engineer a Phase 3 business.

Summary

This chapter has discussed the way organisations, and organisational growth, affect information needs and flows within business. Within the context of the previous chapter, it illustrates the tension between the broad range of decision-led information needs within business and the more limited information systems that can evolve in practice, in response to particular kinds of organisational growth and the pressures they generate. In the early years of an organisation, such systems may evolve in a relatively unplanned way. As a result, even when the organisation has grown, the system may only meet immediate operational and tactical control needs of a business rather than its broader strategic requirements, and neglect the full exploitation of information or IT as a competitive weapon in its own right. It is important to be aware of the way information systems may evolve in practice before we can consider how to make the most of the information resources of a business. Similarly, the way businesses are organised can have a profound impact on how information is defined, collected, disseminated and used. Part of any information policy must be an analysis of the effectiveness of the organisation in meeting the decision needs of the business. This dialogue between the decision needs of the business, the way it is organised, its information needs and use of IT will be discussed in more detail in Part 4 when we discuss the development of an information strategy.

Questions for discussion

1   Why does a functional structure develop?

2   In what circumstances might an organisation use a matrix structure?

3   Discuss alternative organisational strategies to help information flow more effectively.

4   How might a large scale organisation structure itself to respond quickly to the market?

5   Discuss the advantages and disadvantages of 'tall' and 'flat' organisation structures.

Case-study 2.1: Country Ceramics

Country Ceramics is a small business employing 25 people. It has a turnover of £1.5 million from producing White Horse ware from its factory in Wiltshire. Sales are currently through a network of shops visited by the firm's two reps and, more recently, by direct sales through advertising.

The structure of the firm is as follows:

White Horse has been on the market for five years and sales are beginning to drop for the first time. Derek Allen, the MD and production director, is facing various other problems:

- His production director, Neil Harris, is getting frustrated in his current role. Neil has set up some excellent new systems which, together with the growing experience of the two supervisors he appointed, means that he needs to get involved less and less in the day-to-day operations. Derek is anxious not to lose Neil because he is bright, a first-class organiser, has lots of ideas for new lines, and has very good contacts with all the major suppliers in the industry, including the two major suppliers of a new glazing process he thinks Country Ceramics should use.

- Derek is also facing pressure from his sales and marketing director, Lyn Beaty, to develop new products. One of her reps is picking up a range of suggestions from retailers which she would like to explore. So far, neither of them has had the time to consider them. Derek thinks that Neil's idea for the use of a new glaze could be a winner, but Lyn is anxious to find out whether any major competitiors are using it and to do more research on customer preferences. Lucy, the promotion executive dealing with direct sales, has suggested making use of her database of customers.

- Finally, Derek is aware that, as the business has grown, there are increasing problems in information coming from Finance. In the first place, there was little prior analysis of the profitability of the White Horse line when Country Ceramics first started. Now that overheads are significant, Derek is aware that a more rigorous costing exercise will be needed than Country Ceramics is used to. As a further example, Derek is concerned that, whilst they bring in plenty of turnover, direct sales may be less profitable than sales to shops once advertising and distribution costs are added in. However, these costs are dealt with as a general overhead in the accounts, making it difficult to assess the final contribution of direct-sales activity. Some of these problems have been solved on an *ad hoc* basis by a recently appointed management accountant with whom David is very impressed. However, there is a need for a comprehensive review of the needs of each function to provide a longer-term solution.

Derek has asked you to write a brief report on how he might proceed. Using the knowledge gained in the last two chapters, diagnose what problems he faces and what solutions you might suggest. It may be helpful to consider the following questions:

1   What key decision does Country Ceramics face?

2   What information is needed to make this decision?

3   What sources of information (including providers of information) are there in Country Ceramics to help?

4   Does the present organisation help or hinder collecting this information?

5   How might you change the organisation, address the key decision needs of the business and improve the flow of information?

Case-study 2.2: The Insurance Business
Look back to the case of the sales manager for the insurance firm (Illustration 1.3).

1   In the light of what you have learnt in this chapter, describe the organisational problems faced by the manager and suggest how the current organisation might be improved.

References for this text

1   I. Meiklejohn, *Computing Matters*, in *Management Today*, September 1989
2   M. Scott Morton, *The Corporation of the 1990s*, 1991, p. vii
3   C. Cashmore and R. Lyall, *Business Information: Systems and Strategies*, 1991, p.60
4   J. McManus, *An Implementation Guide on How to Re-engineer your Business*, 1994

Further reading

Birchall, David and Lyons, Lawrence, *Creating Tomorrow's Organisation Today*, Pitman, 1995

Coulson-Thomas, G. and Coe, T., *The Flat Organisation*, Institute of Management, 1991

Handy, C. B., *Understanding Organisations*, Penguin, 1993

Pugh, D. S. and Hickman, D. J., *Great Writers on Organisation*, Dartmouth, 1993

Shafto, T., *The Foundations of Business Organisation*, Stanley Thornes (Publishers) Ltd, 1991

Towers, S., *Business Process Re-engineering*, Stanley Thornes (Publishers) Ltd, 1994

Wilkens, Peter, *The Ascendant Organisation*, Macmillan, 1995

3 Systems and information

Objectives

After completing this chapter, you should be able to:

- identify the components of a system
- understand the control mechanisms in a system
- describe a business as a system
- understand the use of some basic tools in systems analysis
- use systems theory to solve the problems and case-studies at the end of the chapter.

Introduction

One way of understanding information flows within a business is **systems theory.** A systems approach is a particularly helpful way of analysing the processing of transactional information and is an essential part of programming, as we shall see in Chapter 11 when we consider systems development.

Anyone, but in particular a manager, who is concerned about obtaining the best results from their area of responsibility, will need to know the concepts of systems theory. Systems theory gives a conceptual framework, tools and techniques which will help decision-making and will assist in the identification of the information needed to exert effective control over the system(s) being examined. Systems theory will also aid in the design of the system and system controls.

What are systems?

The term system is used in many situations these days, but very often the true implications of its use are not apparent. A system is:

'a complex assemblage of things that form a connected whole' *(University English Dictionary).*

Within systems theory, there are two fundamental distinctions. The first concerns the **relationships** within the system and is illustrated in Figure 3.1 overleaf.

The system is made up of a number of interrelated **system elements** each having a relationship with some of the other elements in the system. The total system is defined by

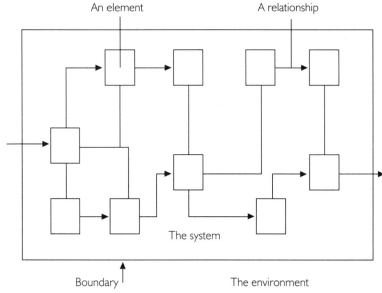

Figure 3.1 Components of a business system

the **system boundary**, setting it apart from the **system environment** in which the system operates.

The second key distinction concerns the **system process.** Most systems are **dynamic systems** – they work towards a particular goal. Such systems can be illustrated as shown in Figure 3.2.

Figure 3.2 Dynamic business system

A simple example is a manufacturing system. Here the inputs are the raw materials needed, the process is the production line and the outputs are the finished goods for sale.

A third key element in considering business systems is **systems control.** The regulation or control of systems is an important activity no matter what kind we are talking about. A simple example of **systems control** is a bathroom shower. Turn on the tap and test the water. Is the water the required temperature? Probably not, so adjust the mixture and test, and repeat until the required temperature is obtained.

Self-assessment questions _____

1   Draw a systems diagram to illustrate the plumbing system in your house.

2   Now label inputs, outputs and control mechanisms.

To exert control over any system, additional elements need to be added. These are illustrated by an enhanced systems diagram shown in Figure 3.3.

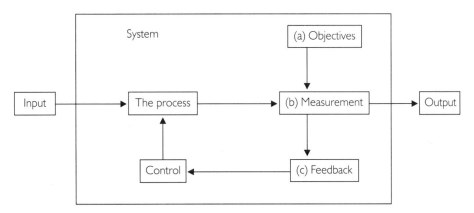

Figure 3.3   Enhanced business system

The output from a business process is a function of the input and four other factors:

(1) **Objectives**   Every system needs to have some sense of direction, like the shower unit where a particular temperature is the aim. As we shall see, **system objectives** will vary depending upon the outcome required of the system. In some circumstances, we will talk of plans, aims or objectives, whilst in others we think of standards to be attained.

(2) **Measurement**   For effective control, the objective must be measurable and there needs to be a way of comparing actual output to the objective. In the case of the shower, we can feel the difference and it can be more precisely measured using a temperature gauge.

(3) **Feedback** and (4) **Control**   Having measured the output and made a comparison with the plan or standard, any variance from that can be fed back either to the controller of the system or the inputs to the system to modify them. If we again look at the example of the shower, our hand has measured the output temperature, communication has occurred with the little grey cells and a decision made to adjust the mixture. We end up with a continuous **feedback loop** where we measure the temperature all the time we are under the shower, adjusting it as necessary.

A major consideration in the provision of feedback is the speed with which it can be given. The sooner feedback arrives at the person who can take action, the quicker the process can be redirected towards the objective or standard.

Self-assessment questions _____

1   Construct a systems model of your job or studies, the inputs/outputs, process, standards or objectives, and feedback.

2   To whom does the feedback go?

3   Who sets the objectives?

The feedback we get from any situation can be of two types, positive or negative. Negative feedback occurs when we want to reduce the effect of the process, whereas positive feedback reinforces the action of the process and adds to it. Some literature will also mention **feedforward** and, in theory, this is possible in some circumstances. However, as there is no obvious application of feedforward in the business world, it will not be developed in this text.

Illustration 3.1: Applying system analysis – the case of Ford
During the 1980s, Ford undertook a major review of its processes to make significant savings. One department investigated was the 500-strong accounts payable department. When they analysed a rival company, Mazda, they discovered that their accounts payable department only employed five people! There was clearly a need to analyse the department's methods.

Ford discovered the following system at work within their company. When the purchasing department issued a purchase order, it sent a copy to accounts payable. When Goods Inwards received the goods, it sent a copy of the delivery note to Accounts Payable. Accounts Payable then matched the purchase order against the delivery note and the invoice which the supplier sent separately to Accounts for payment. If they matched, the department issued payment. Accounts Payable staff spent most of their time on mismatches where the purchase order did not exactly match up to the delivery note and/or the invoice. Whilst investigating these discrepancies, payment was held up and more paperwork was generated.

This system could be depicted in various ways. One model of the system, using the various features just outlined, might look as in Figure 3.4.

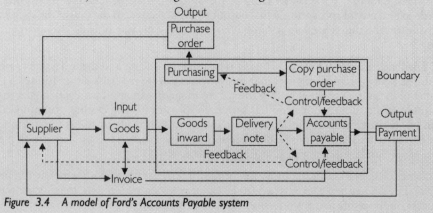

Figure 3.4   A model of Ford's Accounts Payable system

In this case, Systems Theory has been used to isolate each element and its relationship to the others, including input, output, feedback and control. This model now provides a basis for analysis and improvement action which we will consider in Illustration 3.2.

A system process with objective, measurement, feedback and control elements which enable it to regulate itself, continually adjusting output to fit the objectives, is sometimes known as a **cybernetic system.** All the elements of the system should work in harmony, each reinforcing the other. Where they fail to do so, and one or more components disrupts the system (for instance, because the flow of hot and cold water fails to respond to the temperature gauge, or invoice and purchase order do not match), we would describe the system as a **sub-optimal system.**

A further key distinction is between open and closed systems. Most of the systems we are likely to encounter in the business world are **open systems,** i.e. they are influenced by their environment. The business will be subjected to pressures from Government legislation such as Health and Safety, which force employers to behave in a certain way or carry out certain safeguards, whilst other pressures, such as fashion, might mean regular product redesign.

Closed systems are not influenced by the outside environment. Many examples of this type of system exist where machines operate without any outside interference until they switch themselves off, having completed their task. It is difficult in the business context to identify any examples of closed systems as most have some form of input from outside of the operational boundary. Ford's Accounts Payable system is necessarily open, relying on outside suppliers.

Within any one system, there may be smaller **sub-systems** which operate in the same way as the larger system. Sub-systems can belong to more than one system and there is a need to recognise this **systems overlap** and design operations and processes accordingly. The recognition of overlap is particularly important when changes are made in one of the systems which share the same sub-system.

Overlap between large or small systems is often an efficient and economical arrangement. For example, a central purchasing sub-system used by various companies in a group may be able to obtain greater discounts and may aid the standardisation of parts and materials. A centralised computer facility may be shared by all departments within an organisation with a reduction in overall costs. However, such overlaps are likely to increase communication difficulties and may have longer response times. Because of the need to co-ordinate activities and to obtain numerous approvals for change, such structures may be less flexible in rapidly changing conditions.

If sub-systems are tightly connected then close co-ordination, which may be very difficult, is necessary, e.g. exact matching of outputs of one sub-system to the inputs of the next. Resources and facilities need to be finely balanced and there needs to be a good flow of information to keep the system going. One solution is to decouple or loosen the connection so that the two systems can operate with some degree of independence. One way of **decoupling systems** might be able to allow stockpiling of work-in-progress between one production process and another, allowing each to operate at differing levels of performance whilst excess stock lasted.

Decoupling, both in a physical and information sense, allows sub-systems more independence in planning and control. It is likely that with some decoupling, the organisation is better able to deal with unexpected disturbances.

Two major costs are involved with decoupling:

(1) the cost of the decoupling mechanism itself, e.g. the cost of carrying stocks, the cost of the slack capacity, and so on;

(2) the possibility that the sub-systems may act in their own interests and not that of the organisation as a whole: this is the problem of sub-optimisation.

Thus, decoupling has benefits, but also incurs costs. Whether the systems should be tightly or loosely coupled is an important management decision with far-reaching consequences. Ford's system is quite tightly integrated – as we shall see, some decoupling and simplification of the number of feedback and control mechanisms had quite dramatic results.

Illustration 3.2: Simplifying systems at Ford using systems theory
Looking back at the systems chart for Ford, one can see a clear duplication of **control/feedback mechanisms** within Accounts Payable. The system required the matching of the delivery note from Goods Inwards to the supplier's invoice and the copy of the purchase order from Purchasing. Any discrepancy from just one of these three independently-generated sources would involve a protracted search to locate where the error might be. In Ford's case, the situation was compounded by the complexity of the forms with 14 separate items to match to each other.

Ford redesigned and simplified the system to cut out unnecessary paperwork and scope for error and wasted time as illustrated in Figure 3.5.

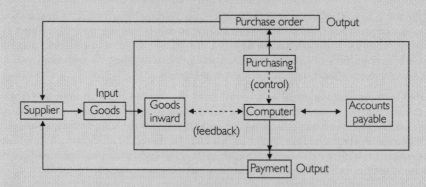

Figure 3.5 Improved business system of Accounts Payable

When the purchasing department initiates an order, it enters the information into a database system and does not physically issue the purchase order to anyone else. When the goods arrive, the receiving clerk checks the database to see if the goods correspond to a purchase order. If they do, the goods are accepted and the transaction recorded on the database. If they did not match, then the goods are not accepted and are duly returned to the supplier. In this case, the use of IT was particularly important in reducing paperwork and simplifying the system so that Goods Inwards became the main source of control/feedback, checking goods automatically against computer records as

The whole business as a system

We have seen how systems theory can be applied to a particular process. It can be applied to a whole business. Figure 3.6 shows an illustration of a business as a system.

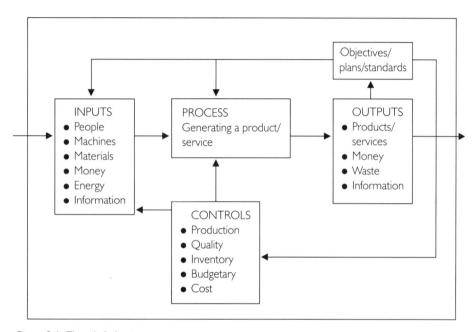

Figure 3.6 The whole business as a system

All of the inputs to the business are identified along with the outputs. The standards or plans can be established so that output can be compared with them. Then feedback, with regard to output variances, will be arranged so that the managers of the process and of each input can be informed. They can then take any corrective action, if necessary, to try to ensure that the output from their system is to plan or standard.

Self-assessment question _____

1   Should the list of inputs include the buildings in which the system operates? Why?

Most parts of a business operate on these basic principles. A representative example is **materials control** as depicted in Figure 3.7.

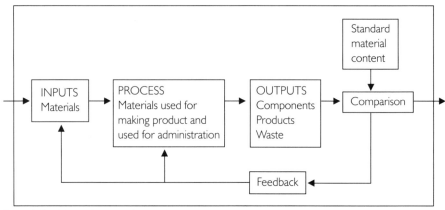

Figure 3.7   Materials use and control system

Materials are purchased to be converted into the company's products or for use during the running of the business. The figure illustrates how materials are bought into the process to be converted into components or products. An unwanted output is waste material. The comparison process is between the standards established by the design and engineering section and the actual output from manufacturing.

A **usage variance** is fed back to the supervision of the process whilst **cost variance** goes to the Purchasing Department. The departments involved in the use of materials are Design, Engineering, Production or Manufacturing, Accounts, Stock Control or Stores or Goods Inwards and Purchasing. Much time and effort is spent in companies controlling materials in this way.

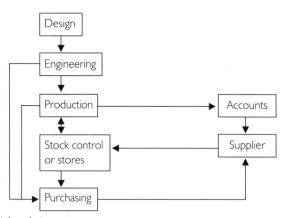

Figure 3.8   Materials ordering system

Figure 3.8 illustrates the information flow that can be expected to support the purchase of materials. The process starts with a requisition coming from Stock Control or Stores, or from Administration into Purchasing. The raising of the requisition will have been prompted automatically by stock levels falling below a predetermined level (re-order level). Purchasing contacts suppliers to order the goods. Accounts will be informed of the expected expenditure. When the goods are delivered, they come with a copy of the suppliers delivery note. This is usually countersigned at Goods Inwards (or Stores) so the driver can prove that the goods were delivered. The copy of the delivery note left with the goods will go to the Accounts to be filed with a copy of the requisition to await an invoice from the supplier requesting payment.

Decision trees and dataflow diagrams

This general introduction to systems theory illustrates one means of analysing information flows within a business. However, as we shall see, systems theory has a specific application to software design which we will encounter in Part 4. As well as providing a general tool of analysis for businesses and systems, it provides a bridge for translating those systems into a form which can be written as software which can then, as Ford did, be used to automate relevant parts of the business.

This relationship between these roles is reflected in Figure 3.9, adapted from C. West Churchman, which illustrates the hierarchy of systems approaches.

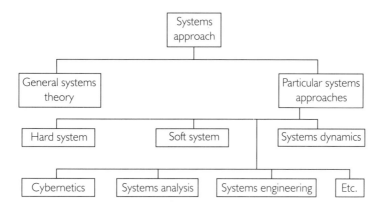

Figure 3.9   Overview of systems approaches

It is not necessary for a manager to have a detailed knowledge of the more specialist branches of systems theory. However, it is helpful to have some understanding of the way systems analysts seek to model business processes. They do so by using a range of tools, including decision tables, data flow and entity diagrams. Understanding these allows a manager to discuss his or her requirements with a systems analyst and to construct a **systems model** appropriate to the businesses decision needs, especially at the operational level.

Decision tables

A decision table provides an outline of the primary decisions made as a result of a number of conditions. A decision table is separated into a number of parts, including:

(1) **Condition section:** includes a list of possible conditions which may affect any deci-

sion that is made. For example, when receiving an order, does the customer have any credit facilities?

(2) **Action section:** contains all the possible 'actions' or decisions that could be made resulting from the conditions described. In general, if a particular condition is satisfied, then this decision will be made. For example, if the customer dos not have any credit facilities, then a decision might be made to reject the order.

(3) **Rules section:** contains a number of columns each providing a unique combination of conditions and thus showing the appropriate action in each case. A range of rules could be built up depending on the customer credit rating, value of order received, and previous dealings with the customer.

Figure 3.10 shows the typical layout of a decision table, including the condition, action and rules sections.

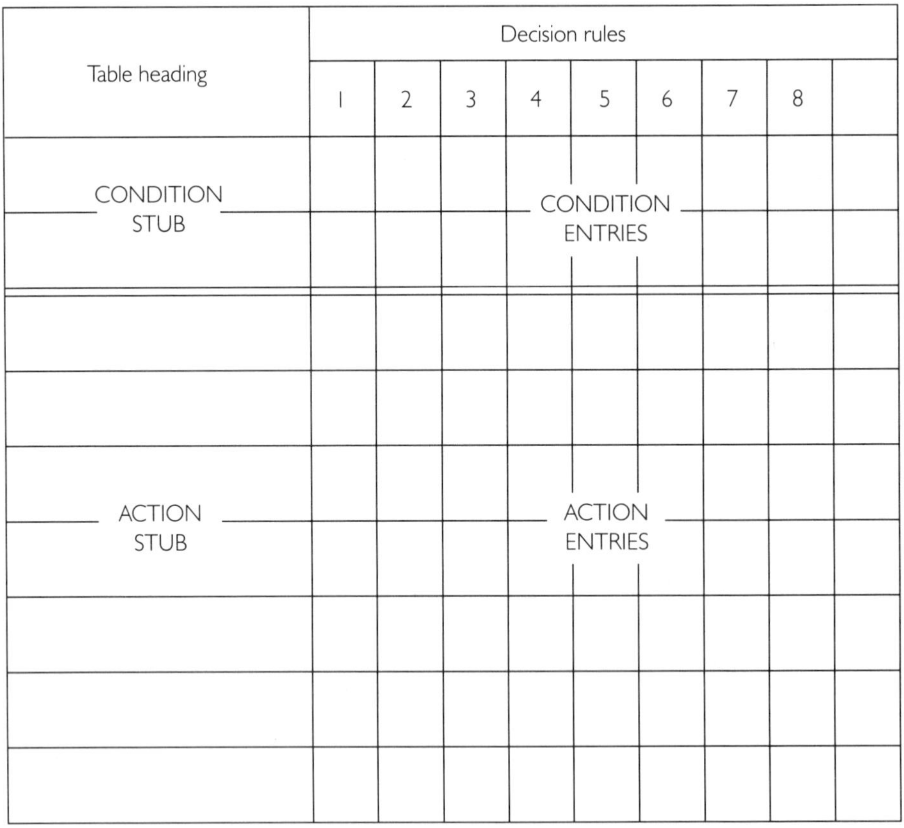

Table heading	Decision rules								
	I	2	3	4	5	6	7	8	
CONDITION STUB				CONDITION ENTRIES					
ACTION STUB				ACTION ENTRIES					

Figure 3.10 Layout of a decision table

A decision table would be used to record a given situation showing the rules for current decision-making. Figure 3.11 illustrates a specific decision table relating to the decisions made following receipt of an order from a customer.

	1	2	3	4
Credit worthy	Y	Y	N	N
Not credit worthy	N	N	Y	Y
Items ready	Y	N	Y	N
Items not ready	N	Y	N	Y
Send items	X			
Send apology		X		
Reject order			X	X

Figure 3.11 Decision table on order processing

The decision table illustrated in Figure 3.11 shows that if the customer is credit worthy and the items are available for delivery, then the ordered items are sent. Alternatively, if the customer is not credit worthy and the customer owes for previous orders, then the order is rejected. All possible combinations of conditions with their corresponding actions are illustrated. This type of table is useful to illustrate in a very simple way how decisions are made. However, the table becomes unwieldy in complex decision-making situations, such as those involving many conditions and a wide range of possible outcomes.

Data flow diagrams

A data flow diagram (DFD) can be used to illustrate the flows of data through a system. Thus DFDs can show how information (or data) currently flows around an organisation. This provides an easy tool to allow the systems analyst to illustrate the current situation and it also provides a good way of discussing current procedures with the staff involved. Figure 3.12 shows one method of notation used in DFDs. A DFD basically contains four different types of elements. Three different shaped boxes are used to illustrate the main components: Process, Source (or Sink) and File. The fourth component illustrated by arrows shows the flow of data between the other elements.

In a DFD a **process** is the action used for handling data. For example, typical processes would be 'checking an order', or 'comparing the items required against a stock list'. A **source** is where the data has originated from. For example, a customer is the source of an order received. A **sink** is where the data are sent to. For example, a copy of the order form may be sent to the Production Department. In such a case, the Production Department is the sink. A **file** contains any required information for later use. For example, a file containing customer details would be kept for future reference.

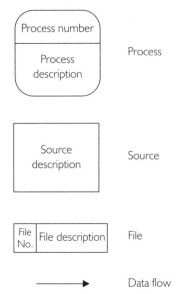

Figure 3.12 Data flow diagram elements

Figure 3.13 illustrates a data flow diagram showing how orders are currently processed. Two processes are illustrated. First, the order is compared against the product list to ensure that the items ordered are available. If not, then the order is rejected. The next process is to check the customer's credit rating. If acceptable, then the order is sent to the Production Department and a copy of the order is placed on file. As can be seen in this DFD, the specific items of data flowing between different elements in the diagram can be named if necessary.

The data flow diagram could be used as a vehicle for further discussion with other staff involved. For instance, the diagram displayed could have been obtained from discussions with the Sales Manager. If this is shown to the Order Clerk who actually does the initial processing of orders, then an amended picture may emerge. In this way the DFD is built up to provide an accurate and concise way of illustrating the processes and data flows round the system.

In the design stage, data flow diagrams will be drawn to illustrate the flows of data around the new system. Such DFDs can be drawn with various levels of detail. The first level DFD may illustrate the overall system and show the corresponding general flow of data. Second and subsequent level DFDs will show increasing details in specific areas within the system. Figure 3.14 shows two levels of data flow diagrams illustrating an order processing system, with one of the processes broken down into further detail.

Structure chart

A large information system will involve many different processes and functions. In most design methodologies the total system is split down into a number of parts (or modules). Each module can then be split down into sections. Such a separation of ele-

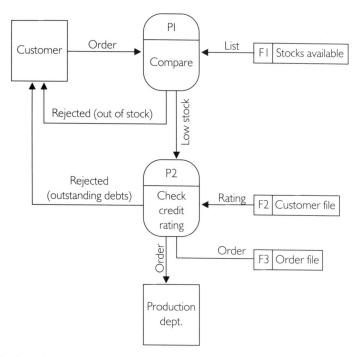

Figure 3.13 Data flow diagram for order processing

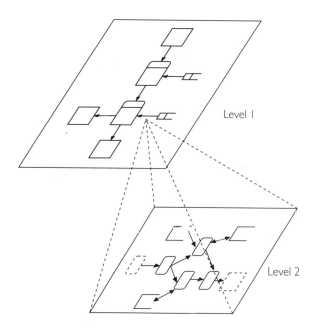

Figure 3.14 Levels of data flow diagrams

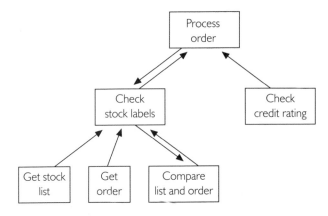

Figure 3.15 Structure chart of ordering system

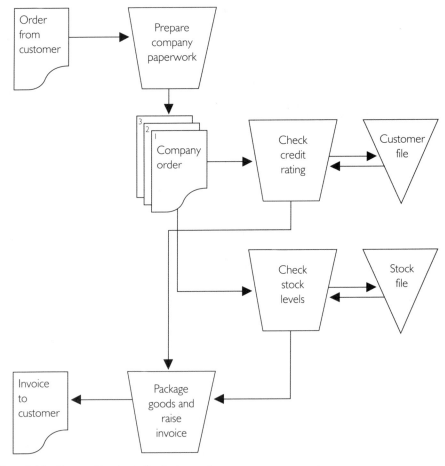

Figure 3.16 Systems flowchart of order processing

ments can continue for a number of levels until the resulting elements are small enough to easily understand and design. This type of structured design approach can be illustrated on a structure chart such as that shown in Figure 3.15. The figure shows an ordering system split down into separate modules, with each module split further where necessary.

This type of hierarchical design approach is referred to as **top-down planning.** In such a case, a global view of the required system may be obtained at the analysis stage from the senior management (strategic managers) within an organisation. Such a view is partitioned into modules, each module being considered by lower levels of management. Further splits take place until manageable units are obtained.

Systems flowchart

A systems flowchart is used to illustrate the flow of information around a system. Different shaped boxes are used to illustrate a variety of processes, input, output and storage media. Figure 3.16 shows a simple systems flowchart illustrating how an order is input into the system and an invoice is produced with reference to the stock and customer data files. Each of the process boxes could be split down further to provide more detail of each stage. The systems flowchart shows the essential inputs, outputs and processes of the system to be designed. Such a diagram could also be used at the analysis stage as described in the previous sections.

Entity diagram

An entity is an object, thing, person, or activity which is important enough to have information kept on it. Thus, in a company involved in processing orders important entities would include customers, suppliers and stock items. The entity diagram illustrates relationships between these entities. In particular, an entity diagram shows whether the relationship between entities is one-to-one, one-to-many, or many-to-many. For example, Figure 3.17 shows the entities involved in the sales process.

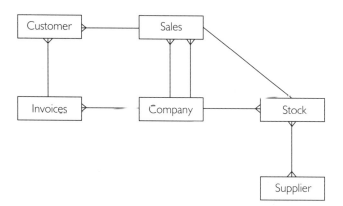

Figure 3.17   Entity diagram

An easy way of interpreting the diagram is to imagine a separate file being kept on each of the entities displayed. The relationship between entities Customer and Invoice is one-to-many, since each customer could receive a number of invoices, though every invoice is sent to just one customer. Other entities in the diagram include Stock (a file containing all items of stock), and Sales (a file of all items sold). The relationship between entities Stock and Sales is one-to-one since every item sold (i.e. in the sales file) has a corresponding item in the stock file. The relationship between entities Supplier and Stock is many-to-many since any item of stock may be supplied by a number of suppliers and any supplier may be able to supply a number of items.

Problems can occur with the interpretation of entity diagrams. They can be very useful, particularly in the design of appropriate data bases for a given information system. However, care must be taken in their use and analysts need to be aware of the difficulty in avoiding ambiguities in such diagrams.

Self-assessment questions

1   Describe the range of diagrams used in systems design.

2   Draw a data flow diagram for processing a holiday booking received by a travel agency.

Illustration 3.3: Applying O&M analysis to Ford
The organisation and methods forms flow chart illustrated in Figure 3.19 shows the movement of paperwork (information) between vendor and various departments within Ford's Material Control, Accounts Payable and Purchasing departments. A further O&M technique, **critical examination,** can be applied to the process taking place, i.e. the purpose, location, sequence, person and means of carrying out the present process is questioned; the reasons for it and alternative ways of doing it. O&M practitioners use a matrix to answer these questions, as in Figure 3.18.

Question	Purpose	Place	Sequence	Person	Means
Present method					
Reason					
Alternatives					

Figure 3.18   Information matrix for critical examination of business processes

This approach would also have assisted Ford in their analysis of their system.

Organisation and methods study

A slightly different approach using some of the ideas of systems theory is **organisation and methods study.** One technique is **O&M analysis** in the forms flow chart which uses columns to represent particular sections or departments so that the movement of information between them can be illustrated and analysed. The result is a similar network of elements and flows which can help us to understand the position at Ford.

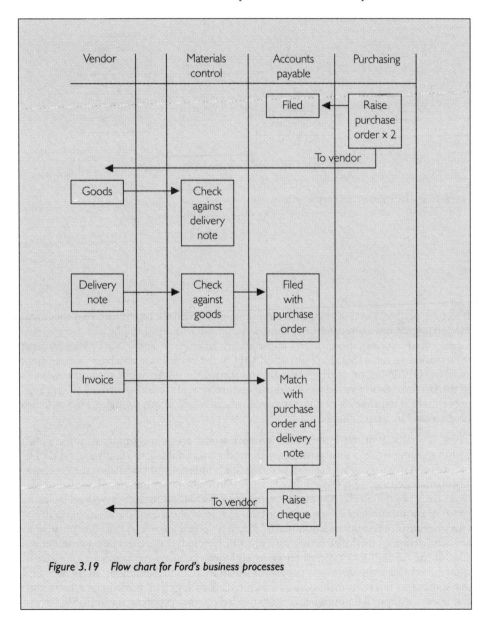

Figure 3.19   Flow chart for Ford's business processes

What is an information system?

Let us apply systems theory to the information within the company. The use of information should start with the 'user' of that information. As we saw in Chapter 1, raw data needs to be collected and processed into information. Upon receipt, the user will decide if it is adequate for their needs and give appropriate feedback to modify the process, if necessary, as in Figure 3.20.

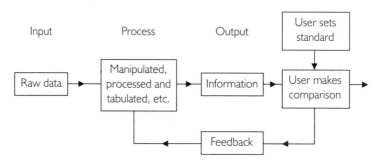

Figure 3.20   Information use control system

If a company has a well developed computer system, then we might find that the information system has been carefully planned. Standards of output might have been established after consultation with appropriate managers and staff. Management information systems (MIS) are discussed later in the book as are database management systems (DBMS) upon which MISs are founded. Developments in computer systems in the last few years have led to Decision Support Systems (DSS) which try to give support to senior managers when they have unstructured decisions to make. DSS will also be discussed in a later chapter.

There is a debate in the information systems' world about the supply of information within a company. It is now possible, with modern technology, to supply a great deal of information in many formats about activities both internal and external to the company. This being the case, who should decide what information any individual needs in order to do their job effectively? Should the supply of information to decision-takers be in the hands of a computing or information systems expert, or should the decision-takers themselves decide on their information needs? There is no real answer to this. It is possible to have the design of the information system to be user led, if the users have some knowledge of the capabilities of computer systems. However, many managers are unaware of what or how the computer could supply information to them and it is not unusual to find that a manager has been making decisions for years with grossly inadequate information and does not appreciate just what is really needed or what is potentially available.

Questions for discussion

1   In what circumstances might the systems approach be used by a manager?

2   What factors should be considered when establishing the boundary of a system?

3   Should there be two aspects to feedback; one to the management of the process, the other to the management of the inputs? Why?

4   Why is it necessary to have a quantitative measure of the objectives or standards that are the justification for the system?

5   What factors inhibit the efficiency of the control mechanism in a company?

6   Should the list of outputs from the business system include the people? They went in and they come out, so what was the process?

7   Which resource that is used by the company has the least amount of control exerted over it?

8   List the five control systems to be found in a manufacturing company. Are they all present in a non-manufacturing company?

Problems

1   Systems that exist in business and commerce are open systems, i.e. they are affected by the environment in which they operate. Control systems exist within the company to try to alleviate the effects of the environment on company activities and obtain conformance to its objectives. (a) List the control systems that you would expect to find in a manufacturing company. (b) Choose one of the control systems and explain the co-ordination between departments that is necessary for effective control to be exerted.

2   'It is essential to determine the standards of performance required in respect of each system as a prerequisite to the effective design and control of the system.' These sentiments were expressed by a consultant who was visiting your firm to advise management on improvement of the company's performance. Choose a control system within the company and discuss the above sentiments in relation to it.

3   Control within an organisation is often based upon the deviation from a planned performance giving the basis for 'management by exception'. Hampshire Mouldings produce a range of boats which are sold countrywide. HM is a traditional boat builder where management control has in the past been exerted by Mr Dent, the owner. All of the senior staff decided to retire at the same time as Mr Dent, not wanting to work under a different regime. On retirement, Mr Dent sold the company and new management have taken over. The new manager has found little in the way of control information and was hoping to make use of 'management by exception' wherever possible. Outline the prerequisites to enable this concept to be employed in the company.

4 'Timely and accurate feedback is said by many to be the main purpose of viewing an organisation as a system or series of sub-systems.' Discuss the other benefits to be accrued when the systems perspective is taken of the firm.

5 You have taken a post at Supaglaze, a company that manufactures double glazing units. The company seems to have an excess of stock on hand and a mixture of odd glazing units and frames that do not match each other. Supaglaze does not seem to deliver on time very often and has trouble with its standard costing system and allocating costs to customers. The first project you are given when you arrive in the new job is to critically examine the lack of control that seems to exist in many areas of the company. Write to your new manager outlining: (a) the controls that you would expect to find in the company, and (b) the necessary feedback to enable control to be effective.

Case-study 3.1: Dorf Supplies
The Director of Purchasing for Dorf Supplies Limited has assigned you the task of correcting several problems associated with the purchasing of and payment for raw materials. The current operation works, as follows:

- Inventory control monitors stock levels of raw material by comparing stock on hand to the stock required to meet the weekly production schedule. This is always available seven working days before the start of the planning cycle.
- Inventory control sends a requisition to Purchasing specifying the raw materials and quantities needed.
- Purchasing prepares a purchase order and sends it to the appropriate supplier. A copy of the purchase order is also sent to Accounts Payable.
- The supplier ships the raw material to Inventory Control, where a receiving report is prepared and a copy is sent to Accounts Payable. The lead time from receipt of the requisition to receipt of the raw materials from the supplier is eight to twelve days.
- The supplier fills the order and mails the invoice to Accounts Payable. The invoice is matched to the copy of the receiving report and purchase order. If everything agrees, a cheque is prepared and sent to the supplier.

Unfortunately, this seemingly simple system has a number of problems. The biggest problem is a frequent shortage of certain raw materials and an overabundance of others. The production schedule must be changed frequently to wait for the raw materials to arrive. The delays in the schedule have been as long as five days. Another serious problem is that suppliers complain of slow payment and the company is unable to take advantage of the two percent discount for payment within ten days. The loss is estimated to be in excess of £100,000 per year. Inventory Control blames the problem on internal paperwork delays in processing the requisitions within Purchasing. Accounts Payable complains that they never get a copy of the purchase order, so that when the receiving report and the invoice arrive, there is no record of what was ordered.

This system is used not only for payment of invoices, but also to supply management with information about cash flow and supplier performance.

Write a report to the Purchasing Director of Dorf Supplies explaining:

1 What approach would you use in solving this problem?

2 Who needs to be involved in its solution?

3 Develop a systems description of the work flow for a solution based on the whole process.

Case-study 3.2: Drallab-O-Mat
The Drallab-O-Mat Laundry Company is a laundry and distributor of commercial cleaning products in the South East of England. Its head office and central laundry is located in Basingstoke. The company also has four warehouse collection points in Southampton, Portsmouth, Andover and Salisbury. The company sells industrial cleaning materials and the four small warehouses and main warehouse at head office act as stores for these articles to provide swift distribution to customers.

The company started in 1979 by supplying and servicing roller towels and have, in recent years, diversified into other hand drying facilities so that they now also sell and lease electric hand driers to customers. The laundry business has expanded into laundering for hospitals and hotels. The vans pick up daily and deliver to the regional warehouse where the laundering is done. There is also a daily pickup/delivery to the laundry in Basingstoke.

As a distributor, Drallab-O-Mat stores cleaning materials centrally at the Basingstoke HQ. In the main, the materials are purchased from international manufacturers such as ICI and Proctor and Gamble. These products are delivered to Basingstoke by the manufacturers in bulk. From there, they are distributed to the regional warehouses by the company van drivers when stocks are falling low.

Customers for cleaning materials are usually school and office cleaning contractors, car washes, small laundries, hospitals, etc. Customers do not like to keep large inventories of these materials on their premises and so only order two to four weeks supply at a time. To do an efficient laundering job, a laundry will need to buy in detergent, brightener, bleach, soap and softener. Therefore, laundry customers will buy in these materials at the same time. A similar situation arises with car washes, where a body cleaner is needed along with tyre, chrome, wheel cleaner and body wax. Experience has shown that if Drallab-O-Mat is unable to supply any one of these items, the customer will go elsewhere for the whole order. Because of this situation, the company has a policy of carrying high safety stocks. For any particular item, the company stocks the products of two or three different manufacturers. Most of the products are carried in a variety of sizes, from five-pound bags to fifty pound drums. This variety of manufacturers, sizes and products means that the inventory is made up of some 500 items.

The small stock of electric hand driers and spare parts are kept at each warehouse and are controlled in the same way as other materials.

The company operates a ledger card system for controlling cleaning materials centrally and at regional warehouses. Orders come in to the Head Office directly, from a salesman, from the regional warehouse or via a van driver. All orders are passed to head office and are transcribed onto company documentation.

The orders then go to a regional warehouse (carried by a van driver) for fulfilment, along with a delivery note to go in with the goods. Replenishment orders for stock are also carried by the van drivers back to HQ.

Contracts for laundering for an organisation are negotiated by the General Manager or her deputy. Drallab-O-Mat supply and launder, to an agreed standard, bed and table linen and towels. Some organisations like to supply their own linen with logos, etc. Agreed collections take place from the client's premises by the area van driver. The replacement of dirty roller towels in, for example, a pub, is left to the discretion of the van driver, who will do the necessary change-over. The quality of the roller towel service is very much at the discretion of the van driver.

- Staffing – head office, Basingstoke: General Manager (GM) and deputy GM; secretary to GM and DGM; storekeeper; 2 people dealing with laundry and materials – visit current customers and try to move into new areas; Accounts Manager – supervises accounts staff; invoicing clerk – bills customers; purchasing clerk – orders from suppliers, settles debts; wages clerk – calculates salaries and wages; van drivers – 6 – based at Basingstoke. (All van drivers at Basingstoke have to be trained in the maintenance and installation of hand driers and roller towels and be prepared to travel the whole of the South East to install driers.)
- Staffing – regional warehouses: storekeeper at regional warehouse, loads and unloads laundry, loads materials, keeps stock records; van drivers – 5 – associated with each warehouse, but will move into other areas if needed.
- Company profile – all services:

Sales (increasing at 25% p.a.)	£9.4 m
Net profits (increasing at 20% p.a.)	£0.75m
Number of employees	43
Number of customer accounts	1,750
Terms of credit	60 days net
Accounts receivable balance	£1.6 m
Invoices per month	950

Invoices are posted to the client approximately ten days after the delivery date of the order. Customer statements are prepared every other month. Customers settle their bills on average 55 days after receipt of the invoice.

1   Use general systems theory to identify the constituent system components at the central warehouse and at a regional warehouse.

2   Identify any feedback that currently occurs. What additional feedback could be used to improve the performance of the business?

References for this text

1 Churchman C.W., *The Systems Approach*, (Chapter 3) Delacorte Press, 1968

Further reading

Anderson R., *Management, Information Systems and Computers* (Chapter 6) MacMillan, 1986

Curtis G., *Business Information Systems,*(Section 6.1) Addison Wesley, 1989

Lucey T., *Management Information Systems, 6th Edition* (Chapters 3, 4 and 12) DPP, 1991

Schoderbek *et al., Management Systems, 3rd Edition* (Chapter 1) Business Publications, 1991

Senn J.A., *Information Systems in Management, 4th Edition* (Chapter 3) Wadsworth, 1990

Part 2
Hardware

4 The microcomputer

Objectives

By the end of this chapter, you should be able to:

- understand the main components of a micro-computer system
- specify and compare a range of input and output devices for use in particular applications
- describe a range of storage media and understand the advantages and disadvantages of each method
- understand and compare basic descriptions of microcomputer configurations and select hardware appropriate for specific business applications.

Introduction

In recent years the microcomputer has become extremely powerful, even exceeding earlier larger (main-frame) systems (see Chapter 5). It would be difficult to find a business of today that does not have a number of microcomputers used for a variety of tasks. Microcomputers have become easy to use, they are convenient, do not take up much space, and can easily be accommodated in the office. The range of potential applications is immense, and the microcomputer's accessibility to the business user has resulted in enormous growth over the past years.

Most people regard a microcomputer as a system sitting on a desk with a keyboard and screen. However, microcomputers are available in a number of formats. For instance, in addition to the desktop variety, microcomputers are available as laptop computers and (hand-held) pocket computers. All these varieties use the same technology and are built around the microchip (semiconductor chip).

Basic building blocks

The essential components of a microcomputer are shown in Figure 4.1. Each of the components will be explored in more detail in the following sections.

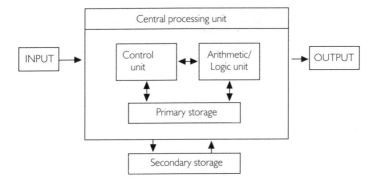

Figure 4.1   Components of a computer system

The central processing unit

The central processing unit (CPU) is essentially the heart of a computer system. Most of the activities involved in any task will take place and be managed from within the CPU. It consists of three main components:

- the control unit
- the arithmetic/logic unit (ALU)
- the primary storage.

The control unit

The control unit primarily directs operations taking place within the CPU. For example, the control unit will read instructions input by the user, and will supervise the flow of data between the other elements in the CPU. The control unit can also read program instructions and interpret these instructions. Any program or application package is read into the Primary Storage – the so-called random access memory (RAM). A program can consist of thousands of instructions. Each of these instructions is decoded in the control unit and interpreted, and the instruction is then carried out, invariably resulting in the transfer of data or the use of the arithmetic/logic unit.

The arithmetic/logic unit (ALU)

The ALU carries out all the calculations required in specific instructions. Numbers can be added, subtracted, multiplied and divided. Furthermore, logical operations such as the comparison of two numbers or two sequences of text can be performed.

Primary storage

Data that has been input to the central processing unit will be stored in this area. The primary storage, or random access memory (RAM), usually uses microchip technology to store data. This is a so-called volatile method of storage and requires a continuous electrical current to preserve the data. If the electric power is turned off, then data in the RAM is lost. The advantage of this type of storage medium is speed of access. Data can be located and transmitted to and from the RAM very quickly. This is vital, as data is frequently being moved between the RAM and control unit or ALU. This speed of access is critical for the efficient operation of the whole system.

Another type of storage is called read-only memory (ROM). As with the RAM this storage is usually contained within a microchip. In contrast to the RAM, data on the ROM cannot be altered by the user. The information contained on the ROM is fixed and cannot be added to or deleted nor can it be destroyed when the power fails. Most microcomputers incorporate some ROM containing basic operational functions used, for example, when switching the systems on.

Describing the CPU

The power and performance of the central processing unit can be described in a number of different ways. One way is to specify the amount of primary storage (or RAM) available. This is stated in terms of the number of **bytes** that can be stored. A byte can be considered equivalent to a single character or key press on the keyboard. For example, A, B, C, 1, 2, 3, (,) all take up one byte of storage space. So, for instance, the word COMPUTER will take 8 bytes of RAM. Usually the amount of RAM available is specified in kilobytes (Kb) or megabytes (Mb). A kilobyte is roughly 1000 bytes and a megabyte is about 1 000 000 bytes. Standard microcomputers will have 1, 2, 4, or 8 megabyte of RAM available, though more recent microcomputers can have significantly more than this. For example, the DEC 3000 model 600, launched in 1994 has 64 MByte of RAM as standard, upgradable to 256 MByte.

A second measure of performance is the processor speed. A clock is used in the control unit to determine precisely the timing of computer operations. The **processor speed** is measured in terms of the **clock speed** and can be interpreted as how many instructions can be performed within a given amount of time. This speed is measured in terms of Megahertz (MHz). A standard microcomputer would have a clock speed between 25 and 66 MHz. The higher number represents a faster processor. For example, a 50 MHz processor is twice as fast as a 25 MHz processor (all other elements being equal!). Higher clock speeds will become available for microcomputers. For example, already the R4000 processor offers a clock speed of 100 MHz. The Alpha processor by Digital (DEC) performs at 200 MHz, although the initial version available for PCs will run at 120 MHz.

Processing speed can also be measured in terms of the number of instructions that can be processed in a given amount of time. This speed is often expressed in terms of the number of **MIPS** (millions of instructions per second). The development of processor speed has been a critical factor in the increasing range of business applications currently available. Speeds of between 100–400 MIPS are not uncommon in the new microprocessors. For example, the Alpha processor operates at 400 MIPS, whereas Hewlett-Packard's PA-4 processor runs at 132 MIPS.

Another way of measuring performance is to state the **word length** used. In computer jargon, a word is a number of bits that form a unit of data. This unit of data (word) can then be transmitted in one chunk, between elements in the computer system. Commonly, microcomputers use eight bits to a byte, i.e. eight bits are required to represent a single character. So, if a computer system has a word length of 16 bits, then this means that 16 bits can be transmitted at a time and therefore 2 characters can be transmitted at the same time. Consequently, the higher word lengths can provide a more efficient, faster system. For instance, a 32-bit word length is twice as fast as a 16-bit word length. The word length is normally stated simply as part of the processor description. For instance, we would talk about a 16 bit processor, or 32-bit processor. The 16 bit and 32 bit processors are standard in most microcomputers of today. 64 bit processors are available on some microcomputers, such as the Alpha processor developed by DEC or the R4000 processor by the MIPS company.

Finally, the actual microprocessors (microchips) used will be important in considering the computer's performance. Intel and Motorola have been major producers of microchips over the past decade. The early IBM PC used the Intel 8088 microprocessor, whilst Apple used the Motorola 68000 chip in the Macintosh. Further developments in the late 1980s saw the use of the Intel 80286, followed by the 80386 and then the 80486 chips, with increasing performance in terms of speed. Motorola achieved comparable advances with the 68020, 68030 and 68040 chips. The Pentium 586 chip is now available for the latest machines. The DEC Alpha AXP processor is one of the most powerful microprocessors currently available.

Self-assessment questions

1   Consider an analogy to how a microcomputer system works. How do you work at your desk? Consider the main components: input, output, central processor and secondary storage. Are there analogies to these with the way that you work? How about the elements contained within the CPU? Can you find analogies here also?

2   Look at advertisements in local press and journals for computer systems. How is the computer described in these advertisements? Can you discover the processor speed, or amount of RAM or the type of processor used in these systems? Compare the prices of these computers.

Methods of input

There is an enormous array of input methods available for microcomputers. An input device can be regarded as any mechanism that will enable data to be read into the computer processor. Such devices are many and varied, and this section will summarise the main methods currently used.

Keyboard

The keyboard is by far the most common form of input. Characters are typed in using a keyboard similar to a standard typewriter layout. These characters are sent to the CPU for further processing. There is, however, a variety of keyboards currently on the market. Designs range from the standard typewriter layout, the enhanced keyboard which includes extra keys such as the function keys and arrow keys, down to simple numeric keypads or restricted keypads more often used with hand-held pocket computers.

Many potential computer users are inhibited by the need to use a keyboard for data entry. For this reason many of the latest advances in microcomputer applications have involved the use of alternative input methods.

Mouse

The mouse is the primary alternative to the keyboard enabling speedy entry of commands. The mouse usually contains a small roller-ball which moves when the user slides the mouse across a flat surface. A mouse movement is then translated into a pointer movement on the screen. The pointer can then be moved to a particular option on the screen and the option is chosen by clicking a button on top of the mouse.

Many of the latest applications require the use of a mouse. The screen displays small pictures (or icons) representing a variety of options. Using the mouse to point and click on the icon will enable the user to choose a specific option or command. The Apple Macintosh was a forerunner using this type of input method. Microsoft's Windows provides a similar environment for IBM-compatible computers where many of the basic procedures can be selected by using the mouse. This type of interface has become standard for many of today's applications. For most users, the mouse combines the advantages of speed, flexibility, ease of learning and comprehension over the keyboard.

A variation of the mouse is the **track-ball**. This looks like an upside-down mouse, so that the roller-ball is revealed. The user then just rolls the ball with their hand providing the same effect as moving the mouse around. This type of input is often embedded into laptop microcomputers for easy carrying.

Scanner

The digital scanner (or optical scanner) works in a similar way to a photocopier. The scanner can 'capture' images from a document and, unlike the standard photocopier, translate them into digital signals suitable for input to the computer. In this way a scanner can be used to input documents containing text, diagrams and even photographs. Scanners can be used to recognise individual characters on a printed page. Thus a scanner together with some **optical character recognition (OCR)** software can input text available on hard copy directly into the computer. This text can then be edited using a text editing or word-processing package, saved and reprinted when required.

A range of scanners is commercially available. The more expensive ones are the larger **flat-bed scanners** incorporating OCR. Hand-held scanners are also available. To utilise these the user has to roll the scanner across the required page area. Hand-held scanners are less precise than the flat-bed scanners and are usually not appropriate for OCR applications.

Optical recognition

Optical recognition input systems can read text, numbers or just marks on a page. A scanning device is used as described in the previous section. Optical character recognition (OCR) software is used for converting text and numbers into an appropriate format for direct input. Simplified software and basic scanners can be used for optical mark recognition (OMR). This has many applications including simplifying form filling. For example, standard stock reports or questionnaire responses can be input using marks placed on a pre-defined form. There are also applications for this type of device in training and education, such as the use in marking assessment tests and examinations and in self-profiling such as psychometric testing or career planning assessment.

Another type of optical recognition system involves the use of bar codes. This is used extensively in the retail industry. Most items in a supermarket will have a **bar-code** attached. A sample is shown Figure 4.2. The bar-code will uniquely define the product. A simple scanning device can then be used at the point of sale to read the bar-code. The product is thus identified and the corresponding price appears on the cash till. Furthermore, this information will enable the store's computer system to update the stock record for this particular item. Such a system enables the stock control process to be managed more efficiently.

9 780719 026126

Figure 4.2   Typical bar-code

In addition to retailing, there are many other applications of bar-code systems. For example, the tracking of parcels through the postal system can be achieved efficiently. Each parcel has a bar code attached when entering the postal system, enabling the progress of this parcel to be closely monitored. Bar-codes provide a simple and reliable method of keeping track of items through any system. The management of goods through an assembly or production line, or traffic management, are also potential applications.

Tablet and pen

The digitising tablet and pen provide an easy way of inputting a particular type of data. This device consists of a tablet – a flat area usually marked with horizontal and vertical lines for easy positioning of the pen. This tablet is pressure-sensitive and when touched with the pen sends a signal to the processor giving the appropriate position coordinates. In this way a user can draw a line or shape on the tablet and this will be converted to the same design on the screen. This type of input device can be very useful for graphics and computer aided design (CAD) applications.

Light pen

The user touches the surface of the screen with a light pen to indicate which option or icon is required. The computer detects a change in the electrical current and interprets this as a specified command. Similar systems are available using a special pen or stylus in the same way as the light pen.

Alternatively, **touch-sensitive screens** are available, allowing the user to touch the screen on the required option. Again, the user's touch is detected, accurately positioned, and interpreted by the processor as a specific command.

Such input devices are often used in highly mobile situations. For example, staff performing stock checks in supermarkets can walk around the store and use a small portable touch-sensitive screen to input information on the quantity of stock items available.

Digital camera

Using a digital camera will enable the input of photographs into the computer. The camera is simple to use, and operates in the same way as a standard compact camera. The user takes a photograph which is then stored in digital form within the camera's memory. A number of photographs can be stored within the camera just like on a roll of film. When required, the camera is linked to a computer by a cable, and the pictures are transferred electronically over to secondary storage. The photographs can then be erased from the camera's memory and more pictures taken. With appropriate software, the user can even edit the photographic image, for instance clarifying blurred edges, changing colour and altering background.

This technique enables high quality images to be input into a computer at relatively low cost. The applications of such a device are only just evolving. Simple examples would include the provision of ID cards incorporating photographs for all employees, or inclusion of photographs on an employee database or product range database. Other applications include those in training and development.

Video camera

Video images can also be stored and processed by a computer. The important elements of each frame in a video sequence can be stored digitally. This requires a massive amount of storage space and fast processing times to provide a high quality full motion video. Many systems can currently only provide full motion video on a part – typically $1/6$ – of the screen. The remainder of the screen can then be used to display text, options and standard icons. However, current developments in data compression and hardware and software enhancements indicate that video will be an increasingly important medium in computer systems.

Voice

Recent developments in voice recognition systems mean that this input method has become a practical proposition for use in computer systems. The user simply speaks into a microphone, and the sound is converted into electrical signals which are sent to the processor. Using sophisticated software the processor converts these signals into recognisable words and these are stored as standard text. In this way it is feasible for a user to speak into a microphone in order to create a text document. There are still problems with this type of input. Many current systems have been set up for specific voices and as such the system would not be able to interpret a new user on the system. One can imagine the range of voices and accents that a fully versatile system would need to handle. Some systems have been developed to recognise a wide range of voices but these tend to be able to handle a limited vocabulary. Despite the limitations, this is an important method of input and improvements in software and hardware performance will undoubtedly lead to more comprehensive voice recognition systems in the near future.

Those of us who struggle with the keyboard will realise the advantages and potential of voice input! There are many applications of this method. In most circumstances, having to write down details or type in data at a keyboard is limiting. It is often an advantage to be able to speak into a portable microphone whilst carrying on with a task. Current applications include luggage handling at airport terminals, where the handler of each suitcase or bag can talk into a microphone and very quickly give details of flight number and destination. Other applications include the use by quality inspectors to report faults on a production or assembly line, sales persons to input an order or query from a customer, postal workers sorting letters and parcels and surgeons obtaining information on patients during an operation. All of these systems may only require a limited vocabulary to operate effectively.

Magnetic recognition

Many magnetic recognition techniques are used primarily in mini or mainframe computer systems, but they do also have important uses in some microcomputer applications: simple versions of magnetic recognition systems are found in the use of bank and credit cards. The magnetic strip on the back of these cards provides details on the user's unique password and account number. The cards can be used at cash points or **automatic telling machines (ATMs)**. The card is inserted into a machine which reads the information from the magnetic strip and then allows the user to conduct certain transactions, such as withdrawing cash or obtaining a statement of balance.

Magnetic ink character recognition (MICR) has been used since the early 1950s. It is used today almost exclusively in banking. Magnetic ink characters are placed on cheques and deposit slips. MICR readers can then speedily process these transactions.

Self-assessment questions

1   List the types of input methods currently available. How many of these media are in use, either in your workplace or a company or department with which you are familiar?

2   What are the advantages of a mouse interface over the standard keyboard? In what type of applications would you consider a mouse to be essential?

Methods of output

As with input media, there are many varied ways of outputting data from computer systems. An output device can be regarded as any method of transmitting information out from the central processing unit (CPU) to the user. This section will summarise the most important of these methods.

Video display unit (VDU)

The video display unit (VDU) is by far the most common form of output from a microcomputer. It looks like a portable television screen and provides an immediate form of output for the user. The immediacy of this method is vital for many inputting procedures and enables full interactivity between user and computer system. When a user types in data the computer displays this directly onto the screen, and provides direct feedback to ensure accurate entry of data.

VDUs are produced in various shapes and sizes. Colour monitors are most common, though monochrome screens are still available for many computer systems. Most screens use **cathode ray tube (CRT)** technology similar to standard televisions: images are displayed by means of a beam of electrons aimed at the screen. This beam emits light from the screen in single points. These points are called pixels (standing for Picture Elements). Colour monitors function using three beams of electrons (one for each of the primary colours red, green and blue).

The resolution of the VDU is measured in terms of the number of pixels that can be displayed on the screen. A higher number of pixels means a better quality picture. Earlier microcomputer systems used **CGA (colour graphics adaptor)** screens with a relatively poor resolution. CGA has a resolution of 320 x 200 pixels, i.e. 320 pixels across the screen and 200 from top to bottom. These CGA screens were superceded by **EGA** screens with a resolution of 640 x 350 and an increased selection of colours. Now most computers are supplied with **VGA** (video graphics adaptor – resolution 640 x 480 and up to 256 colours) or **SuperVGA** (resolution varies up to 1280 x 1024) monitors. Additional add-on graphics boards and monitors can provide even higher resolution. Such enhanced systems are useful in situations requiring the reproduction of top-quality images such as in graphics design and media production.

Flat-panel displays

One of the disadvantages of a visual display unit using the CRT technology described in the previous section is that the screen takes up a large amount of space. A flat-panel display overcomes this problem and is ideal for use with portable, laptop computers. Flat-panel systems work on either liquid crystals or plasma (electro-luminescent) displays. They can provide a very high-quality, high-resolution, full-colour image. Another advantage is that the flat-panel display can run using significantly less power than a CRT screen; a small battery pack is sufficient for a number of hours' use, which is ideal for improving portability.

A disadvantage of this type of display is that when viewed at an angle the screens tend to display a faded, inconsistent image.

Printers

There is a range of printers available providing a choice between cheap, low-quality printing and more expensive, top-quality output. Printers are usually classified as either character printers, line printers or page printers. Character printers print individual characters at a time, while page printers produce the whole page at a time. Most of the common printers available are character or page printers. Character printers can be classified as dot matrix, daisywheel, inkjet and thermal printers. Most page printers use laser technology.

Dot matrix printers

Dot matrix printers produce individual characters on the printed page by means of a series of dots. These printers provide a low quality (often referred to as draft quality) print. However, they can be used to produce graphical output, unlike some of the more expensive printers.

Daisywheel printer

The daisywheel printer produces characters in much the same way as a typewriter. All the available characters are imprinted onto a daisywheel. The wheel spins around and when the appropriate character is in position, a hammer strikes the wheel, leaving an impression on the paper. A variety of characters can be produced in this system by interchanging the daisywheel used. However, such printers cannot be used for printing graphics, and have largely been superseded by higher quality dot matrix printers.

Inkjet printers

Inkjet printers are available in monochrome or colour. They work by squirting drops of ink onto the page. The ink droplets immediately dry and form the required characters. Inkjet printers produce very high quality output of text and/or graphics and are usually preferred to daisywheel and dot matrix printers.

Thermal printers

Thermal printers work by producing dots of heat onto heat-sensitive paper to produce the required image. Thermal printers can produce monochrome or colour images of high quality. These printers cost less than inkjet printers. However, running costs tend to be higher because special heat-sensitive paper is required.

Laser printers

Laser printers produce top quality output in both monochrome or colour. They tend to be more expensive than the other printer types, but their speed, lack of noise, and quality have ensured their popularity and general use in many businesses.

The performance of printers is usually specified in terms of the quality of their output and speed. Quality is usually defined as:

- draft quality
- near-letter quality
- letter quality
- typeset quality.

This quality is measured in terms of the resolution achieved, and is given in dots per inch (dpi). A typical laster printer produces 300dpi. Near typeset quality will give over 1000dpi.

The speed of printers is measured in terms of the number of characters per second (cps) or the number of pages per minute (ppm). A typical dot matrix printer would operate at 360cps printing draft quality and down to 50cps for letter quality. Draft quality printing at 720cps and letter quality printing at 150cps would not be unusual. Inkjet printers would be relatively fast, operating at around 2ppm. Laser printing would usually be much faster and a normal range of print speeds would be between 4ppm and 16ppm.

Graphics plotters

Graphics plotters have the ability to produce high-quality, precise drawings in one or more colours. These plotters operate by moving pens over the page under the computer control. Different pens can be used to vary the width and colour of the output.

This type of plotter is often seen in drawing offices and design departments and is being increasingly used by designers and architects. The plotters produce high-quality, colour output at a relatively low cost.

Speech synthesis

In an earlier section, speech was listed as an input medium. The natural extension of this is to develop systems whereby the computer can also talk back! A speech synthesizer is a device that converts electronic signals into sound output in the form of a natural sounding voice. Speech synthesis has developed fast in recent years and there are now many systems that provide reasonable quality voice output. (Speech synthesis must be distinguished from voice reproduction systems. In voice reproduction, a computer simply selects pre-recorded elements – for example words or numbers – and transmits them. This type of system is used in the automated directory enquiries systems operated by a number of telecommunications companies both in Europe and North America.)

There are many potential applications of speech synthesis. It can be used in training and education, for example training an operator while using a machine or using voice output in multimedia systems. Speech synthesis would be ideal for users who are physically impaired. Alternatively, business users might find it useful in order to access data files such as sales documents, stock details or client information, in situations where only a telephone link is available to the office .

Self-assessment questions

1 List the range of output devices currently available for microcomputer systems.

2 Investigate the use of output devices in an organisation with which you are familiar. What type of printers are available? If there is a selection, are they used for different applications?

Secondary storage

Secondary storage is a vital component in the efficient operation of a modern computer system. In many business applications of today a vast amount of information needs to be processed and stored permanently. Such information is kept in secondary storage and is retrieved into the primary storage area (RAM) within the CPU only when required for processing.

There are some distinctions that should be made between primary and secondary storage:

- secondary storage is permanent: whatever medium is used to store the data, this must remain unless deleted or overwritten with fresh data. In primary storage (RAM) this need not be the case. Data is said to be volatile in primary storage, i.e. if the power is switched off the data in the RAM will be lost
- speed of access: data in primary storage is there to be processed and transferred to and from other elements in the central processing unit as quickly as possible and access time for data in primary storage must be very quick. This is not as important for data in secondary storage. Information is transferred in large chunks into the CPU from secondary storage and the speed of access is not as critical. **Access time** for any storage device is of course important, but invariably the access times for primary storage will need to be much faster than for secondary storage
- the capacity for storage of data is significantly different: modern computer systems have large primary storage devices. For example, 8 Mbyte or 16 Mbyte of RAM is not uncommon (see *Describing the CPU* earlier in this chapter). However, secondary storage devices must have a much greater capacity to handle the range of business tasks that can be performed by the microcomputer.

There are a number of secondary storage media currently used in microcomputer systems and these are described in this section.

Magnetic disks

This type of secondary storage is by far the most common medium used with today's microcomputers. Magnetic disks are referred to as direct access (or random access) storage devices since information can be read directly from any part of the disk surface. There are two main types of magnetic disks: floppy and hard.

Floppy disks

Floppy disks (diskettes) are made from a flexible magnetisable material and are usually encased in a more rigid plastic cover for protection. Their size can vary, though the most common diskette is $3^1/_2''$ diameter and is used by both IBM compatible and Apple systems. Diskettes are designed to be portable. They can be inserted into a disk drive in order to read data from, or to write data to the floppy disk. Once this operation is complete, the diskette can be removed and stored separately from the computer or used on a different computer system. Thus a single user can have many diskettes enabling the storage of an almost unlimited amount of data. One of the problems with floppy disks is the low storage capacity (a standard 3.5″ disk stores 1.44 Mbyte of data) as compared with hard disks. However, more recent developments in floppy disks have improved their capacity: a new floppy disk (called a **floptical disk**) uses optical tracking for higher precision giving much higher capacities – up to 20–30 MByte for the 3.5″ version.

Hard disks

A hard disk is permanently housed into a sealed unit together with the disk drive. Most hard disk systems are installed permanently into modern microcomputers and cannot be removed. However, there are some removable hard disk systems now available. For example, cartridge hard disks are available and operate in a similar way to floppy disks. The cartridge can be inserted and removed from the disk drive if required. Portability presents some problems and means that these disks do not have the same capacity as fixed disks and also have slower access times. However, these disks are improving, and capacities and access times are increasing with new developments. For instance, 3.5″ hard disk cartridges with 200–300 MByte capacity are available. Bernoulli disks provide an alternative form of removable hard disk with slightly better performance in terms of capacity.

There are a number of advantages of using hard disks over floppy disks. The main advantage is speed of access. Hard disks spin continuously and at a much faster rate. Consequently, the time taken to read from or write to a hard disk is much less than for a floppy disk. Also, hard disks are much more reliable because they are contained within an airtight dust-free environment. Floppy disks are much more likely to develop errors and become unreadable because of the wear and tear they undergo. A hard disk will also have a much larger capacity for storage than a floppy disk. The capacity of standard microcomputer hard disk systems range from 20Mbyte up to 800Mbyte of storage. This contrasts with floppy disks with less than 2Mbyte of storage per disk.

Another recent development is the introduction of **magneto-optical disks**. These disks are removable, and store data magnetically, like the standard magnetic disks. However the way that the data is stored and retrieved differs from the standard media. A laser is used which actually heats up the disk in order to store the data efficiently. The laser is also used to read this 'magnetic' data at a later stage. These disks offer high capacity (for example 150 MByte on a 3.5″ version) with good access times, though slightly slower than the hard disk systems.

Table 4.1 summarises the main differences between floppy and hard disks for microcomputer systems. However, it should be noted that as previously described, recent developments have improved the performance of both these media.

Table 4.1 Comparison of disk systems

	Hard disk	**Floppy disk**
Storage capacity	800+ Mbyte	1.4 Mbyte standard
Access time	Fast	Slow
Portability	Usually fixed	Portable
Reliability	Excellent	Good

Most microcomputer systems are now sold with a hard disk system and one slot for inserting diskettes. This enables the user to transfer data between the floppy disk and hard disk to make back-up copies of data.

Magnetic tape

Magnetic tape systems for microcomputers usually involve the use of **cassette tapes** and **tape streamers**. Data is stored magnetically onto the tape in much the same way as on an audio cassette tape. This type of storage device involves sequential access of data – data must be read sequentially from the tape. In other words, to read a piece of information located at the end of the tape, the whole tape must be run through. Understandably, this involves a significant amount of time, and access times for magnetic tape are much slower than for magnetic disks described in the previous section.

High capacity magnetic tape provides a much cheaper method of secondary storage than disks and is used largely for keeping back-ups (so-called 'archiving') of existing data. The creation of back-ups is essential in most business applications, to ensure that if the computer system goes down or is even destroyed, important data is stored elsewhere and can be easily retrieved onto a replacement computer system. In such circumstances, the access time for data is much less important than the reliability of the medium used. The storage capacity of magnetic tape is much larger than comparable disk systems. For example, 2 Giga Bytes (2000 MBytes) or 4 Giga Bytes (4000 MBytes) tapes are fairly common.

Optical disks

Optical disks (or laser disks) provide a high-quality, reliable method of secondary storage. Like magnetic disks, an optical disk is a direct access method of storage. Laser beams are used to read from, and write to the optical disk. Optical disks can store much more data than a magnetic disk of the same size. Also, the time taken to read or write data is significantly less than for floppy disk magnetic media, although optical disks are currently slower than fixed hard disk magnetic media. Another advantage of this medium is that laser disks do not need to be fixed in place. They can be interchangeable and thus provide an extremely versatile storage medium.

Compact disks using this technology are becoming increasingly popular for microcomputer applications. They have a massive storage capacity (250–1000 Mbytes). As such they are ideal for storing high-quality video images and sound. The **CD-ROM** (Compact Disk–Read Only Memory) is being used widely. This form of CD can only be read. The information is placed on the disk during manufacture and cannot be altered or deleted. The CD-ROM is ideal for accessing databases such as library information, references, law abstracts and business or financial databases. There is also a wide range of multi-media applications ideally suited to this storage medium.

Other forms of CD are also available, but they are usually much more expensive. The CD-WORM (CD–Write Once, Read Many) device is commercially available. This allows the user to write to the disk permanently and then use it in the same way as a CD-ROM. Current developments in the eraseable CD will ensure that this method of storage is increasingly used in the future.

Secondary storage devices compared

The previous sections have described a range of storage devices including media using magnetic and laser technologies. The advantages and disadvantages of the different media have been discussed in the appropriate sections. This section provides an overview of the main differences between the media.

Table 4.2 Comparison of storage media

Comparison of the media is made using a scale between * and *****

*	= Poor
**	= Below average
***	= Average
****	= Good
*****	= Excellent

	Hard disk	Floppy disk	Tape	Optical disk
Storage capacity	***	**	****	*****
Type of access	Direct	Direct	Sequential	Direct
Access time (to locate the media)	****	**	*	***
Data transfer rate (time taken to transmit data between media and processor)	****	***	***	****
Portability (removing and transferring between computers)	*	*****	****	****
Reliability	****	***	***	****
Initial cost of device	***	****	**	**
Cost of media (extra disks, tape)	**	*****	***	*

Table 4.2 illustrates the relative effectiveness of each storage media in a variety of categories. However, it should be noted that the distinction between such media is becoming increasingly vague. Particular attention should be made to the difference between the performance of hard disk and floppy disk systems. There is now a range of such systems available, and the table simply compares the traditional magnetic media.

Self-assessment questions

1   List the main types of secondary storage currently available for microcomputer systems. Consider a computer with which you are familiar and determine which storage devices are used.
2   Give the advantages and disadvantages of magnetic tape and magnetic disks as methods of secondary storage.

Programming

A program is a sequence of instructions that the computer can follow, in order to perform certain tasks. A computer could do nothing without the use of a program. The program is loaded into the primary storage (RAM) and tells the computer when to read data, calculate formulae, compare values, output data or move to a different instruction or program.

An application package such as a spreadsheet, word processor or accounts package is made up of a number of programs. A program is written in a particular programming language. Many such languages exist for use with microcomputers: BASIC, Pascal, Modula 2, Fortran, Cobol, C, Ada are among the most popular. Most business users will not need to have any knowledge of these languages. There are advantages and disadvantages with each of them; they are covered in more detail in Chapter 8, Centralised Computer Software.

Operating systems

Chapter 7, Microcomputer Software, gives a comprehensive look at operating systems. However, when looking at microcomputers it is important to consider specific operating systems.

An operating system is a collection of specialised programs to supervise the overall operations of a computer. The operating system will function automatically, without interference from the user, and will organise the transfer of data, running of other specialist programs and operation of applications packages. All modern computer systems run using operating systems. Usually a microcomputer will run under a single operating system. This will manage a range of application programs that can be run at different times by a number of users, as shown in Figure 4.3.

In a microcomputer, the user has frequent contact with the operating system, though this may not be apparent. The operating system must be loaded before a computer can perform any functions such as run programs or applications. In most microcomputer systems the process of loading the operating system (**booting up**) is automatic. When the user switches the power on, the computer boots up by loading the operating system from the hard disk into the primary storage (RAM).

There are many operating systems currently available for microcomputers. Operating systems such as CP/M, MS-DOS, UNIX, OS/2 and the Macintosh OS are among the most common in use. CP/M was produced by Digital in the early 1970s and has now been replaced by the more powerful MS-DOS operating system for many microcomputer applications. The UNIX operating system is a well known, powerful OS particularly useful for multi-user systems. IBM's Operating System/2 (OS/2) is more user-friendly, and is popular for some of the more powerful microcomputers.

The Apple Macintosh uses an operating system incorporating a graphics user interface (GUI), and consequently does not require knowledge of the command language in order to use the operating system effectively. This type of approach has been developed for DOS-based systems in Microsoft's Windows. MS Windows provides an intermediate stage between the user and the operating system. Using icons and a mouse pointer, the user can communicate with the operating system without the need to learn a complicated command language.

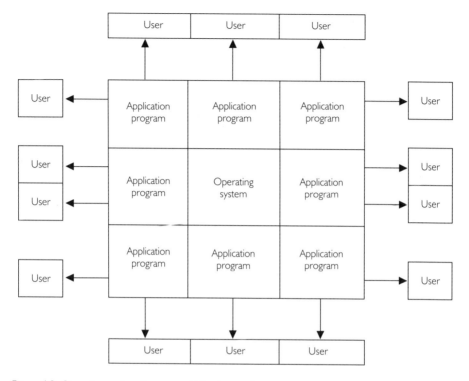

Figure 4.3 Operating system for many applications and users

As in other computing areas, operating systems are being regularly developed and improved. New developments in operating systems include DEC's new OSF/1 launched in 1994. This system has been developed in collaboration with UNIX and incorporates a 64-bit processor.

Choosing systems

A typical question is 'Which computer should I buy?' Not surprisingly, there is no straightforward answer. Any potential buyer must first answer questions such as 'What applications do I want to run on the computer?' or even more basically 'What problems do I want help with?' Consideration of these will then lead on to a more reasoned decision. It is advisable to look at software selection before considering hardware. Figure 4.4 overleaf illustrates a typical situation incorporating the following elements:

- analyse requirements: how could a computer help me in my work? What sort of jobs need doing? How can I make my business more efficient? How can I save money and become more profitable?
- information gathering: look at alternative application packages currently available.

Do they perform all the jobs that I require? Gather information on hardware for possible purchase

- consider alternatives: which computer hardware would be suitable for my applications? How much does it cost? How reliable is it? Can I expand it later if required? Is it readily available?
- choose system: select appropriate hardware subject to the constraints described above
- install system: purchase hardware and install, possibly with the help of a technical expert!
- run and maintain: use the system for the required jobs. This will often lead to the development of new ideas on potential applications of the computer system, thus leading us back to analysing new requirements.

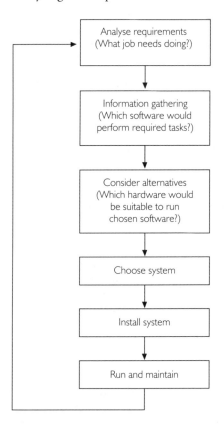

Figure 4.4 Systems lifecycle

The choice of hardware largely depends on the range of applications which the computer will be used for: the right computer for someone who intends to do basic word processing is not the same as that required for use in computer-aided design. With these considerations in mind, actually selecting a particular microcomputer involves comparing systems objectively. The following list gives the most important measures of a computer's performance and suitability for a specific task:

- **capacity of RAM:** the amount of primary storage space available in the CPU can have a major effect on the performance of a computer. A basic microcomputer of today would have at least 1Mbyte of RAM – 8 or 16 Mbytes of RAM are not unusual
- **speed:** the 'clock speed', given in Megahertz (MHz), gives an indication of how long the computer would take to perform a specific task. 25–80 MHz is a typical range for today's microcomputers
- **processor:** the type of processor used is almost always specified in any description of a microcomputer. The Intel range of microprocessor chips is used extensively on IBM-compatible computers with the Intel 80286, 80386 and 80486 being most common. These are usually referred to simply as 286, 386 or 486 processors. The higher number indicates a better performance. The 486 processor is now standard on many computers; 586 computers are becoming more readily available
- **word length:** a computer using an 8-bit word length will be slower than one using 16-bit. Most current microcomputers range between 16- and 64-bit processors. This word length will again have a major effect on the speed of processing
- **hard disk:** microcomputers without hard disks are rare nowadays. Anything between 20 Mbyte and 2000 Mbyte (2 Gigabyte) of hard disk is likely in today's microcomputer
- **graphics:** a full colour Super VGA screen is near the top of the likely range available with most microcomputers. A VGA screen is next best, with EGA a poor third
- **expandability:** can I expand the system later if required, i.e. are there extra ports to enable me to link my computer with other devices, such as printers, scanners, mouse, light pen, extra disk drive or tape streamer? Can I insert extra RAM if needed?
- **operating system:** which operating system does the computer run on? Is it DOS or UNIX, Macintosh OS or OS/2? Are there other operating systems that it uses?

Essentially, a computer's performance is price-sensitive. If you wish to improve on any one of the criteria shown above then it is likely to increase the cost. Usually the choice of a computer becomes a balancing act between conflicting requirements. You will have a budget and you will need to make a choice between some of the following: extra RAM, more hard disk space, improved speed or high-quality graphics. The choice depends on your specific requirements. Table 4.3 gives some indication of the sort of configuration required for particular applications.

Table 4.3 Minimum requirements for specified applications

Application	RAM	Clock speed	Word length	Hard disk	Screen
Word processing	0.5 Mbyte	25 MHz	8/16 bit	20 MB	Any
Spreadsheet and accounting	2 Mbyte	25 MHz	16 bit	40 MB	Any
Database	4 Mbyte	33 MHz	16 bit	80 MB	Any
Graphics	8 Mbyte	33 MHz	16/32 bit	100 MB	VGA
Design	8 Mbyte	50 MHz	16/32 bit	120 MB	Super VGA

It should be stressed that the specifications given are minimum values; and in many cases the actual applications will demand higher requirements. For example, basic word processing applications do not require large amounts of RAM or fast processing speeds. However, this depends on the type of word processing package used. Some of the latest word processing systems with mouse and icon interface require additional RAM and run more efficiently using 16-bit processors. Indeed there are few 8-bit computers around today. Such packages also require a significant amount of hard disk space – up to 16 Mbyte just for a single word-processing package. Thus a 20 Mbyte hard disk would not be sufficient for such a package, bearing in mind that other files and documents will also be saved.

Such limitations are valid for all applications. Actual hardware specifications need to be linked to the requirements of particular packages that you may need to run. Remember to allow plenty of room for growth. You can be sure that this time next year your requirements will have increased, so you need to ensure that your hardware can expand as well.

Illustration 4.1: Hardware selection example
The following are brief descriptions of microcomputers given in a local newspaper advertisement. Discuss the important element in each of the descriptions and give a comparison of the computers described in terms of performance.

- **Computer A**   High-performance fully upgradable PC, powered by a 486SX 33 processor, fast 170 MB hard disk drive with 94 KB buffer, 14" SVGA colour monitor.
- **Computer B**   Motorola 68030 processor running at 25 MHz speed, 4MB RAM expandible to 36 MB, 120 MB internal hard disk drive, 1.44 MB floppy disk drive.
- **Computer C**   25 MHz upgradable to a DX2/50, 4 MB RAM expandable to 20 MB, 170 MB hard disk drive, 14" SVGA monitor.

Descriptions similar to these are typical of promotional/advertising literature produced for today's microcomputer market. Some of the information given in these details may not be familiar; however, the majority of details should make sense to you after reading through this chapter. The terminology used in each description may look slightly different, but there are certain important elements that you should look for. If the details required are not specified in the literature then you must make sure that you clarify them before considering buying. Let us summarise the details given in these advertisements.

- **Speed:**   Computer A: 33 MHz (this is given in the description 486SX 33)
                 Computer B: 25 MHz
                 Computer C: 25 MHz
  Comments: Computer A is fastest!

- **Processor:**   A: Intel 486 (The SX means that this is the basic 486 processor. The alternative is the DX which is an enhanced 486 processsor, or DX2 which is even better.)
                 B: Motorola 68030 (this is probably an Apple computer)
                 C: not specified, though probably 386 or 486 since it can be expanded to DX2 running at 50 MHz.

Comments: A and C are likely to be IBM-compatible machines. There seems to be little difference between the three processors, though the specification for Computer C is unclear.

- **RAM:** A: not specified
  B: 4 MByte
  C: 4 MByte (expandable to 20 MByte)

Comments: Although computer A is not specified, it is unlikely to be less than 4 MByte; all the computers have similar specifications.

- **Hard disk:** A: 170 MByte
  B: 120 MByte
  C: 170 MByte

Comments: Computers A and C look better.

- **Screen:** A: 14" SVGA
  B: not specified
  C: 14" SVGA

Comments: It is likely that computer B also has an SVGA monitor.

Overall comment: Computer A looks slightly better than the other computers, particularly because it runs at 33 MHz. However, the final decision on choosing one of these computers will depend on the sort of applications you may wish to run. An analysis of your requirements before choosing specific hardware is vital.

Summary

This chapter has introduced the microcomputer and how it works. This has included a brief description of the main components within a microcomputer and an overview of many of the input and ouput methods currently used in modern microcomputing applications. The microcomputer is made up of a number of elements such as the central processor (CPU), input, output, and secondary storage. The CPU itself consists of a number of interrelated components: the control unit, arithmetic/logic unit, and primary storage (RAM). The CPU housed on a microprocessor chip is of primary importance in considering the performance of the whole system. Important guides to the CPU's performance include the following elements:

- speed: measured in MHz
- size of RAM: measured in MBytes
- processor type: for example Intel 486, Pentium or Motorola 68040.

A description has been given of input devices such as the keyboard, mouse, scanner, tablet and pen, cameras, voice recognition, magnetic and optical recognition. Methods of output have been considered including Visual Display Unit (VDU), flat panel displays, printers, graphics plotters and speech synthesis. A range of secondary storage media has been described including hard and floppy magnetic disks, magnetic tape and optical disks.

Other performance measures of the overall computer system incorporating these additional devices have also been considered, including:

- the type of secondary storage available, for example floppy disk, hard disk, optical disk
- the size of secondary storage, measured in MBytes
- the type of monitor used, for example SVGA
- the type of printing device available, for example laser printers, plotters.

Computer programming languages and a brief overview of operating systems have been included and these elements have been combined in considering how to choose a particular microcomputer for a given application.

Questions for discussion

I   What is the difference between primary and secondary storage media? Group the following methods of storage into primary or secondary:

a)   optical disk

b)   RAM

c)   magnetic tape

d)   CD-ROM

e)   magnetic fixed disk

f)   floppy disk.

2   Compare the storage methods listed in Question I in terms of the following categories:

a)   speed

b)   capacity

c)   cost.

3   List the main input and output methods available for microcomputers; what are their advantages and drawbacks?

4   Some devices can be considered as being both input and output media. Can you describe any such device?

5   The most common method of secondary storage on microcomputers is still the fixed hard disk. Discuss why this is the case, even when there are more powerful flexible alternatives available.

6   A microcomputer can only have one screen attached. Is this true? Discuss the types of screens currently available for use with micros.

7   Indicate the minimum configurations that you would advise for anyone purchasing a microcomputer to perform each of the following tasks. Your configuration specification should include:
- processor type
- speed

- amount of RAM
- hard disk space
- any other element that you think is appropriate.

8 Look in advertising literature for help in specifying the likely cost of these systems:
   a) 'I just want something to use to produce the odd letter and report. I don't want anything special but I will need to be able to obtain print-outs at home.'
   b) 'I want to be able to produce reasonable-looking reports and include some accounts and even some basic graphs in the documents.'
   c) 'I need something for some desktop publishing. I am starting my own business and I want to demonstrate to clients how professional my documents can look.'

Problems

1 The performance of a microcomputer can be expressed in a variety of ways, including speed, primary and secondary storage capacity. Explain how each of these elements is measured and expressed. Give examples of typical computer systems with which you are familiar, stating appropriate values for these three categories.

2 OCR and MICR are two similar ways of inputting data into a computer system. What are differences between them? What type of business applications would be appropriate for each of these methods? What other ways can be used to input data quickly?

3 A computer system used by the ZYX supermarket chain uses voice input to assist in stock control. Explain how such an input method could be used. What other applications would be appropriate for this method?

4 The finance manager in your company has heard that there is a 32-bit microcomputer commercially available with some accounting software that he would like to acquire for his department. Discuss the meaning of the term 32-bit . Does this necessarily mean that it will perform better than the existing 16-bit micro currently used? Give reasons for your answer.

5 A colleague from your company approaches you because he has learned that you are supposed to 'know something about computers'. He wishes to buy a computer for use at home and has about £1000 to spend. How would you go about advising him on the right choice?

Case-study 4.1: Selecting a PC from an advertisement
The following advertisement for two computer systems was shown recently in a national monthly computer magazine:

When you buy a personal computer system designed by BCG Inc. you are sure to get value for money. You can rely on our systems using the latest Intel 386 and 486 microprocessors. We support a range of operating systems such as MS-DOS, OS/2 and UNIX. Try to beat this for value:

- BCG Mk 1 Intel 80386 SX/25 MHz processor
- 4MB Ram, expandable to 12 MB
- 120 MB hard drives
- $3^{1}/_{2}$" – 1.44 MB floppy drive
- VGA screen including DOS 5.0

OR for something else:
- BCG Mk 2* Intel 80486 DX/50 MHz processor
- 8MB Ram
- 85/200 MB Hard Drives
- SVGA monitor including DOS 6.0.

For more details contact us on 111 2121 or fax 111 2001.

The details given in this advert are typical of the jargon associated with microcomputers. Most of this jargon you should now recognise.

1   Compare the two systems advertised. Describe, in plain English, what each system actually offers the user.

2   Discuss which system you would buy and why.

Case-study 4.2: Specifying your own PC requirement
The finance manager in your company has made a decision to purchase microcomputers for his department, which currently contains 14 employees. She is planning to purchase 6 computers now and expand later, subject to requirements. She is trying to be very systematic about the choice of system, and has designed a form that incorporates all the important aspects of her requirements. She has circulated this form but has not had any useful comments from the department.

The manager has come to you for comments on the form she is using, and wants to know whether there is anything else to consider before trying to obtain a short list of computers for possible purchase. This is the form she has produced:

Finance department microcomputers

Requirements

Hard disk capacity: _____

Processor type (e.g. 386, 486): _____

Primary storage (RAM): _____

Input devices: Keyboard: _____

Mouse: _____

Disk drives: 5.25": _____

3.5": _____

Hard disk: _____

Monitor: Colour:: _____

VGA: _____

SVGA: _____

Other requirements: _____

_____

1   What sort of answers would you expect the finance manager to be looking for in each of the items indicated in the form? Give examples in each case.

2   Advise the manager on other hardware aspects that should be considered.

3   Are there other comments you would make to the finance manager on how to make the best decision on hardware purchase?

Further reading

Athey, T.H., Day, J.C. and Zmud, R.W., *Computers and End-User Software* (Chapters 3–5), HarperCollins, 1991

Capron, H.L. and Perron, J.D., *Computers and Information Systems* (Chapters 9–12), Benjamin/Cummings Publishing Company, 1993

Long, L., *Managment Information Systems* (pp 490–510), Prentice-Hall International, 1989

Long, L. and Long, N., *Computers: 3rd Edition* (Chapters 4–6), Prentice-Hall International, 1993

Mandell, S.L., *Computers and Information Processing: Concepts and Applications: 6th Edition* (Chapters 4, 5, 6 and 8), West Publishing Company, 1992

5 Central computer systems

Objectives

By the end of this chapter, you should be able to:

- distinguish between a micro, mini and mainframe computer
- assess the relative merits of mini and mainframe computers
- identify the different configurations that are available for a centralised computer system
- identify how appropriate a system is to a given situation
- answer the case-studies at the end of the chapter.

Introduction

The last chapter discussed the microcomputer or PC (personal computer), the kind of computer you are most likely to be familiar with on the office desk or at home. Many of the components of and peripherals for a **minicomputer** are the same as for the PC and, as we shall see, minicomputers can, in some cases, be less powerful than some PCs. In this chapter, we will discuss the implications of these differences and the choice between using minis and **mainframes.**

Traditionally, microcomputers were less powerful than the more versatile mini and mainframe computer. Now the more powerful microcomputers (supermicros) can be more powerful than some minicomputers, and networks of microcomputers can have more processing power than many models of minicomputer. Indeed, there is some debate that, in due course, microcomputers will subsume minicomputers, leaving only micros and mainframes.

The most important difference between microcomputers and minicomputers or mainframes is one of function. The latter are able to provide common resources for use by a number of PCs, particularly the receipt, storage, manipulation and communication of common information within the business. Obvious examples are the receipt and processing of sales transactions, the recording, updating and presentation of sales information, and the preparation of standard accounts or payroll. As a result, minicomputers and mainframes will have more than one central processing unit to handle the volume of data and range of processing activities. In addition, the operating system needs to handle input from and output to a large number of devices. All of the input devices mentioned in the previous chapter can be employed, but a major means of input is the 'dumb terminal'. These have no processing power and therefore do not have the ability of graphical representation, but they are cheap.

Often they are geographically remote from the computer. The computer might be based in London, whilst the terminals are in all corners of the country linked to London via wide area networks (see Chapter 6). Personal computers may be used to interrogate the mainframe, but it will need a 'terminal emulator' resident in its memory. This is so that it behaves like a normal terminal for that particular mainframe.

Mainframe computers generally use the same means of output as found on a personal computer. The difference is the means by which the signal reaches the output device. With many simultaneous users, and perhaps a number of different printers available for use, users' print jobs are 'spooled' before printing, i.e. they join a queue which is fed to the printer in the sequence in which they arrived. The computer stores the file to be printed in a temporary store on disk until the printer is free to start the next job.

Mainframe computers

Mainframe computers are the original business computer which became standard equipment in large businesses in the 1960s. IBM was, and still is, the market leader in the field. Unlike PCs, where the central processor is manufactured either by INTEL (IBM-compatible) or MOTOROLA (Apple), mainframe manufacturers produce their own central processing units. One exception is DEC, which allows the use of its Alpha processor in mainframes, minis and PCs.

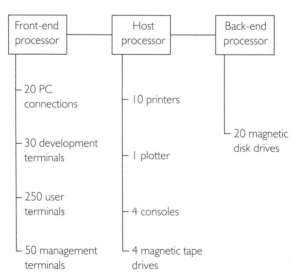

Figure 5.1   Typical mainframe computer configuration

An example of a mainframe computer configuration is given in Figure 5.1. As the diagram illustrates, to handle the volume of transactions (many thousands per minute), the **host processor** is aided, in this example, by two minicomputers, comprising a front-end and a back-end processor which specialise in particular tasks. The front-end processor is dedicated to handling all of the terminals attached to the system, whilst the back-end processor handles the movement of data to and from the disk drives. The host processor is devoted to doing the calculations necessary for each transaction and controlling printers and the plotter. This type of configuration is popular for situations where a large number of transactions must be processed quickly.

Mainframes require a secure environment and a relatively large number of staff to maintain the system, monitor and adjust it for maximum performance. However, many mainframe operating systems now have built-in expert systems which are able to do this for themselves, resulting in a decline in recent mainframe operating costs.

The strength of mainframes is their capacity to process a huge number of transactions from a large range of terminals. A particularly good example is the use of cashpoint machines by banks. The mainframe can receive, process and transmit to each cashpoint machine with the minimum delay. On the other hand, as we shall see when comparing it with alternatives, the mainframe's single, central system can be less flexible and responsive to the needs of individual users. It is particularly well suited to large-scale, relatively predictable tasks such as transaction processing where volume and speed are more important than adaptability to changing requirements.

Self-assessment questions _____

1   Which parts of a business may be best suited to the use of mainframe computers?

2   Why?

Minicomputers

As mainframes developed to meet the needs of larger businesses, minicomputers emerged to cope with more small-scale requirements. The main difference between the two is the number of remote terminals that can make use of the system. Although the two systems might have the same type of processor and main memory, they operate at different speeds. As we have seen, mainframes cope especially well with large volumes of relatively standard activities coming from a large number of terminals, for example transaction processing. Minicomputers are more likely to be employed where interactive or real-time access is required, e.g. stock control. It is used to keep a record of what has been purchased and sold.

The configuration of any particular system is dependent upon the requirements of that particular company. It is quite possible that no two systems have the same configuration. In one example, terminals are utilised by the three user departments, Sales, Credit Control and Purchasing, and each has a printer available to them, probably in their office. Management have five terminals available to them for the production of reports and to aid decision-making. There are eight terminals for the use of the systems development staff. The transactions are stored on five magnetic disk drives and their is a magnetic tape drive for archiving at the end of the day.

An obvious advantage of minicomputers is cost, where the scale of operation does not warrant a mainframe solution. In addition to the cost of the hardware, basic maintenance costs are much lower, though, as we shall see, much depends on how minicomputers may be used within a network. Minicomputers are also more flexible than mainframes in allowing more immediate access and interactivity. Users can program a minicomputer to fit their own requirements much more easily than a large company-wide mainframe.

Self-assessment questions

I   What scale of business might be best suited to the use of minicomputers over a company-wide mainframe?

2   Why?

RISC and parallel processing

At one time, the limiting factor on the speed of the computer was how quickly the inputting of data or the removal of output could take place. In recent years, the pressure on the speed of operations has moved from the capacity of the peripherals, e.g. printers, to process quickly to that of the processor. This limitation is caused by the necessity to convert programs that we understand into something that the computer will understand. Currently, all instructions that we give to the computer go through the **CPU** (Central Processing Unit) so that each instruction can be carried out.

The Reduced Instruction Set Computer (RISC) is an attempt to speed up the translation of instructions by reducing the number that the CPU has to understand. This has the advantage of speeding things up, but the disadvantage that the flexibility of the computer to do certain things is reduced. This is because the programmer has to find a way of getting the computer to do something for which there is no direct instruction. There is a great deal of debate in the industry and in academic circles about the value of RISC processors. They are extremely useful for some dedicated applications whilst, in others, they are only a stop gap measure until they, too, will become too slow. The limiting factor of the speed of electricity must at some time be reached. Some authorities say that this is already occurring.

Parallel processing approaches the problem of increasing the speed of operation from a different direction. Instead of trying to push the instructions through the bottleneck – the processor – an array of processors operating in parallel can be employed. The concept is simple to understand, but very difficult to organise. The processors can be wired together satisfactorily, but the problem lies with the software needed to control them. In theory, an instruction can be sent to any CPU that is not occupied and therefore the processor is no longer the bottleneck. If it does start to become critical, we add more processors. The larger computer firms such as IBM and DEC have commercially available parallel systems, but they only make use of a small number of processors. Large parallel systems are available commercially, but are used for particular applications, usually technical in nature. Currently, there seems to be a ceiling to the increase in performance provided as parallel systems get larger. The business systems that use parallel processing do not obtain an increase in performance in proportion to the extra processors that have been added. An overhead has to be carried by the system to allow for the routing of instructions to the different processors.

Different network configurations

Previous sections have pointed to some of the advantages and disadvantages of mainframes and minicomputers. For most businesses, the options they face are:

- a large centralised mainframe computer
- a small network of small mainframes
- a larger network of minicomputers
- a PC network.

If the network of mini or mainframe computers is geographically spread, possibly to different sites owned by a company, it is known as a **decentralised system.** This is distinct from a centralised system, in that is places processing power away from a central location and control. It allows local management to use the computer on their site to supply them with the information that they need to run their part of the business. In this section, we will look at some of the configurations possible within this range of options.

As we have seen, most PCs are not appropriate to a central computer role, but it is possible to create a centralised system linking PCs. A personal computer network consists of a number of small computers linked by a communication medium and is described more fully in Chapter 6. The network is controlled by a **file server** or server terminal which oversees the messages that the individual computers want to put onto the cable. Networks vary in complexity, but it is normal for information that is to be shared by all of the personal computers to be on the file server. This type of network is used where documents need to be shared and security of software is required. It is not possible to copy networked software.

Figure 5.2 illustrates a personal computer network. The network might be geographically spread through the company, but the file server will need to be in a secure location under someone who has the necessary fault finding and support knowledge readily available. The personal computers attached to the network can vary in number, but it is not uncommon to have up to 250 using the system at any one time.

Printing on personal computer networks is handled in a similar manner to the mainframe, i.e. the print jobs are spooled in a queue to await a turn to be printed. However, the **print server (spooler)** is in its turn a personal computer dedicated to that one job, i.e. spooling print jobs for one printer that is attached to it. It is possible to attach printers to other machines on the network and for them to act as part-time print servers whilst being used as a normal PC. Such a network has the advantage of creating some commonality between PCs allowing, for example, documents to be called up from one PC by another.

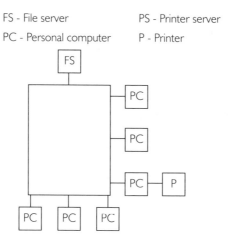

Figure 5.2   *Typical personal computer network*

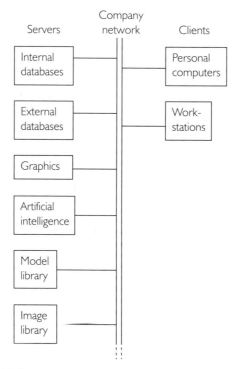

Figure 5.3   *A client/server system*

A more advanced network linking PCs, minicomputers and, perhaps, small main-frames, is a **client/server system.** Figure 5.3 provides a schematic illustration. In this network, individual PCs (clients) have access to a group of server minicomputers, each specialising in a particular field. As an example, a manager might, through her PC, wish to access the company's internal database to call up sales figures, then obtain broader market trends from a Government or commercial database outside the company, analyse the data using a decision-support system and compile a report using the image library and graphics system.

Self-assessment questions

1   How might a PC network help a business?

2   What are the advantages of using client-server technology in comparison with mainframe computing?

Minis versus mainframe

During the last 14 years, the number of large mainframe sites in the United States has declined from 1600 to 1000. This has been as a result of 'downsizing' or 'rightsizing' or the moving of applications off a mainframe onto a smaller system, whether a PC network or client/server system using small mainframes or minicomputers. There are a number of reasons for this shift towards **distributed computing**. In part, there has been an attempt to cut down the staffing and overhead costs needed to maintain the large, centralised, mainframe. Client/server systems shift power away from the centre and allow local managers to exploit and adapt the system more easily in running their part of the business. In addition, smaller systems can be more rapidly and easily adapted, for example, by the addition of more **network software**. There is a wider variety of standard software available and tailor-made software can be more easily written and implemented by a single user department. Finally, as the last remark suggests, networks give clients greater involvement, range and flexibility, both inside and outside the system. Whilst the more rigid mainframe imposes boundaries which it is difficult, slow and costly to change, a client/server environment can be more easily grown and adapted by end-users.

In reality, more recent research has suggested that choice is less clearcut, especially on cost. Networks are not as secure or reliable as mainframes and successful management of the system is much more demanding given its diversity. Traditional activities such as archiving past sales information may be less easy and less well developed as they are on mainframes. Xephon, a UK market research company identified the relative costs of operating different configurations of system within a large organisation.

PC Network   £9,400 – £15,500 per user

Minicomputer   £7,200 – £7,900 per user

Mainframe   £5,282 – £5,973 per user

The Swedish-based Compass group studied the costs of mainframe and client/server systems being used in information centres in a number of large companies.[1-3] The 300 organisations surveyed reported that mainframe costs were falling rapidly, whilst there were many hidden costs associated with client/server systems. Running costs were £1,750 per user on a mainframe compared with £6,400 for client/server.

In the US, decentralisation to local networks has been seen as a way of reducing country-wide communication costs, though this problem is less acute in the UK.

Whilst these comparisons may be extreme (both companies supply services to mainframe users), most experts in the industry would agree that PC networks and client/server systems should not be implemented solely to make cost savings.

Summary

In this chapter, centralised systems have been reviewed from current practice to developments that are just becoming commercially viable. The development of the PC network has affected both the market for mainframe and minicomputer systems and the use to which they are now put. The development of client/server systems is having a major impact on the computing world as computer developments are tending to be user-driven. It has brought together mainframes, minis, workstations and PCs to give the user far greater access to information than would have been possible by any other means. This growth is occurring despite the financial premium that must be paid to install such systems. The speed of processing is becoming the limiting factor in some applications and developments in parallel processing are, again, just starting to enter the commercial market.

Questions for discussion _____

1　Mainframe computers are the backbone of British business computing. Why is this?

2　Why are PC networks playing an increasing role in the supply of a company's information needs?

3　Discuss the differences between a mainframe and a minicomputer. What makes them distinctive from each other?

4　List the differences between a mainframe or minicomputer system and a network of personal computers.

5　Discuss the difference between a network of personal computers and a client/server system.

6　There are at least two ways in which the computer industry is trying to speed up the processing ability of computers. What are they and why are they necessary?

7　Given the relative costs of PC network, client/server, mini and mainframe computer systems, why is there such a rise in the popularity of the network solutions?

Problems

1 A company has decided to use WordPerfect as the word processing package in its typing pool. The typing pool produces letters from a bank of standard paragraphs as well as letters that have been dictated by managers and supervisors in the company. It is possible to buy WordPerfect to run on mini or small mainframe computers, such as a VAX or AS400, or on a network of personal computers. Discuss the advantages and disadvantages of each option and the implications for the staff using the system.

2 With the current developments going on in the computer industry in mind, the Systems Director of ESAC Limited has suggested disposing of the IBM mainframe that has been in place for three years. ESAC Limited is a chain of retail clothes shops with a good turnover and plans for expanding into other clothing markets. The director is proposing to spend £9 million over the next three years for a distributed client/server system with minicomputers in each shop and a network of PCs linked to another minicomputer at head office. This proposal was not a surprise to the Board of Directors, as discussion groups had been working on different suggestions for some weeks. Discuss the pros and cons of this proposal in the context of EXAC Limited.

3 CODAL is an independent financial advice company. The agents employed by the company give independent advice about an individual's financial situation. The company and its agents rely on commission given by insurance companies and other financial institutions when a client invests with them. The Management Board of CODAL hope to supply each agent with a lap-top personal computer and modem so that they can have access to current information while at a client's house. Discuss the infrastructure necessary to provide such a service to agents.

4 Swift Dynamics have grown rapidly from a small manufacturing firm to a conglomerate owning over 15 operating companies. This has occurred since Jonathan Swift became the chief executive and main shareholder. Each organisation had its own information system when taken over. Some were manual and some made use of small mainframe or minicomputers. Swift now wants to consolidate the group and establish an integrated information system that will provide each operating company with the information that they need, as well as supplying Jonathan with the information he needs to manage the conglomerate. Describe the alternatives open to the group. What are the risks and benefits that centralised and decentralised systems have in this situation?

5 John Venning is the chief executive of a chain of food stores. As the company has expanded and increased its number of outlets, so it has been necessary to develop a better means of recording transactions. This has been done using a centralised mainframe from one of the world's leading suppliers. However, this machine is now four years old and the response time is such that the EPOS tills are experiencing a considerable delay at peak times. Discuss the options open to John Venning to remedy this situation.

Case-study 6

David Waterman has just taken over as principal partner at Sproggins & Wilkes (S&W) a firm of management consultants. They are amongst one of the largest consulting firms in the UK and also have offices in the main capitals of Europe. The company offers consultancy to many different types of businesses including manufacturing, transport and logistics, various types of engineering, as well as the financial sector. Currently the organisation is entering the local authority and health services sector.

There are over 600 consultants and senior consultants working from offices in different parts of the country. Each office is managed by a partner, and a consultant is based at an office which is in one of the larger conurbations. If a client produces a project that an office does not have immediate expertise in, then a consultant might be involved with three or four different projects depending upon his area of expertise.

Any particular office has expertise available to consult in anything from financial planning to marketing and market research, production planning and control, to communication networks and computer systems, sales force establishment to industrial relations and training. A proud boast of the company is that they have available to them expertise in every aspect of planning, organising and controlling all the resources in a business.

Many of S&W's clients have establishments in more than one of the company's office areas. This means that the consultants from the different areas will need to communicate regularly with each other about the client's problems to ensure a reasonable level of continuity. At the present time, consultants telephone each other, keep notes in diaries or leave messages with a secretary or a colleague from the office. Several important communications have gone astray recently which resulted in, for example, consultants not turning up for meetings with clients or the same research and analysis being undertaken at two different offices. Waterman is very aware that these types of mix-up give a bad image to the company and can cost a considerable amount of money.

The consultants also need a great deal of informational support from their own office as well as Head Office in Milton Keynes. Some assignments need the use of external databases and information about third-party products or services. Consultants are finding increasingly that the information they want from the client is computer-based. Sometimes on a mainframe or minicomputer or, increasingly, on a PC.

David Waterman has called a meeting of his own consultants on computer systems to discuss how to improve the service to clients and aid the communications between staff.

I Write a report suitable for this meeting outlining the options available and discussing their pros and cons.

References for this text

1 *Computer Weekly* 2nd June, 1994
2 *Computer Weekly* 30th June, 1994
3 *Computer Weekly* 19th May, 1994

Further reading

Long, L. and N., *Computers* (Ed. 3), Prentice-Hall 1993

Tanenbaum, A., *Structured Computer Organisation* (Ed. 3), Prentice-Hall 1990

6 Communications

Objectives

At the end of this chapter you should be able to:

- understand the main elements in a data communication system
- describe the hardware and methods used in data transmission
- describe different types of local area network systems and how they can be linked together
- specify the business applications of networking and data communications
- understand the main attributes of a networking system and how to decide on the most appropriate system in a given business context
- answer the problems and case-study questions at the end of the chapter.

Introduction

The use of computers in business and industry has changed dramatically over the last ten years. Information is becoming increasingly important for the modern company, and speedy access to such information can make the difference between success and failure in the business world. Until recently the telephone was the primary source of communicating information quickly between and within businesses. It is now equally essential to link computer systems in order to transmit data and share information.

This chapter considers the ways in which computers are linked to each other to provide efficient **data communication.** It is important to understand the variety of methods for linking computers including the procedures for links between microcomputers and microcomputers with mainframes. There is an increasing range of business applications for such **communication links.** Indeed, computer links are in many cases essential for the effective operation of businesses, providing a competitive advantage that is difficult to ignore.

Data communication

Data communication involves the movement of data or information between electronic devices. This should be distinguished from the more general term **telecommunications** involving the transmission of any signals between remote systems. Such signals could be data, or television, or simply telephone (voice) messages. Data communication can occur over any distance. For example, this term could be used for transmitting data between two computers sited in the same office, or between many computer systems located in different continents across the world. Data can be transmitted via a variety of methods including cables, telephone lines or satellite, which will be considered later in this chapter.

Efficient data communication is critical for today's businesses. Within a particular site, employees need to 'talk' to each other, send messages, receive replies, disseminate information, and circulate updates. Traditional methods of performing these tasks such as telephoning, writing memos and circulating reports can be inefficient and time-consuming. The modern office provides computer links with key personnel, enabling communication to be improved. Similarly, a business located on several sites, or in many buildings in a specific area, will require such channels for speedy communication. Indeed it is important in many circumstances that different companies or businesses have similar efficient intercommunication methods available. For example, a company may require immediate feedback from a variety of suppliers, and/or prime clients. Such a company could obtain immediate feedback on availability of goods, estimated delivery dates, and updated prices, and re-direct selected information to the client.

In all these cases, whether within a company, or between companies, data communication can play an important role in making the business more efficient. The ability for diverse computer systems to be linked together in order to send and transmit data is called **connectivity**. Without connectivity, computers would not be able to communicate with each other. The following sections introduce the ways in which connectivity between systems can be achieved.

Data communications hardware

Data communications hardware enables computers to be linked together in order to send and receive data between systems. The range of hardware required includes a device for sending data, a device for receiving, and the appropriate communication link. For example, for a typical mainframe system, a **work station** can be used to send information, data can be transmitted via a **coaxial cable**, and the **central processing unit** can receive the details. Similarly, data can then be transmitted from the CPU to any other work station. For the transmission of data between two remote computers, a telephone line can be used as the communication link. In such a case, a **modem** is required to connect the computers at each end into the communication link.

It should be stressed that modems are not required when linking two or more local computers. Simple cables can be used in such a case, and communications software is installed in each computer to enable the link to be achieved. (Refer to Chapter 7 on Microcomputer Software for more details of Communications software)

Modems

A modem is used to enable computers to be linked into the telephone system. The computer is connected to the modem which is in turn connected into the telephone system. A modem is required for use with some telephone systems since the signals used are incompatible. Computers work on digital (on/off) signals, whereas some of the telephone systems use signals in a wave form (so-called analogue signals). The modem converts digital signals from the computer into analogue signals carried over the telephone system. The signal is received into a second computer via another modem which converts the signals back into digital format.

Figure 6.1 illustrates two computers linked using modems at each end. It should be noted that with the use of digital telephone systems, modems are unnecessary. However some method of 'packaging' the signals to send via telephone lines is necessary. This will be discussed later in this chapter.

Figure 6.1   Computers linked via modems

The procedure whereby signals are converted from digital to analogue is called **modulation,** and the conversion back from analogue to digital is called **demodulation.** Hence, the modem is used to perform the tasks of **mod**ulation and **dem**odulation. The performance of modems is measured in terms of the speed of transfer of data between systems. This is usually measured in terms of the number of bits per second (bps). For example, a modem operating at 10,000 bps (10 Kbps) will be able to send or receive 10,000 bits every second. Speeds for modern modems range from 2,400 to 57,600 bps. A typical speed would be 9,600 or 14,400 bps. Such speeds are sometimes referred to as **Baud rate.** Thus, a typical modem can be described as having a 14,400 Baud rate.

There are a variety of modems available. Internal modems are sited on a board and housed inside the computer system with the central processing unit. External modems are located in a separate box and are more useful if portability is required. For instance, the same modem can then be used for a number of different computers when required. Acoustic coupler modems are also useful in certain circumstances. These modems connect by attaching to the telephone receiver rather than direct into the telephone line. Such a system would be ideal for those users who are very mobile, and may need to connect into a computer system from a variety of sites, including using public telephones.

Usually modems will include a number of features to assist the user in the communication process. The following features are common to many of the latest modems, and are often referred to as 'Hayes-compatible' modems, named after an early modem produced by the Hayes Company:

● **Auto-dial** enabling the user to dial another number automatically. This would usually involve the user selecting from a screen menu of pre-defined numbers to link to other computer systems

- **Auto-answer** would mean that the modem would automatically answer any incoming calls
- **Auto-disconnect** will disconnect the line when the other computer has been disconnected. Without this facility the line would look as though it was 'busy' even when data transmission has been finished.

Front-end processor

A front-end processor is often a separate microcomputer and is used as a communications control system. The front-end processor simply relieves the main computer (the host computer) from the basic tasks involved in communicating with a variety of sites. The front-end processor will establish links between the required computers in a process called **handshaking**. The front-end processor will perform tasks such as checking messages to ensure that they are error-free before sending them to the host computer. Also it will perform functions such as labelling messages. Figure 6.2 illustrates the front-end processor as a component in the communications system lying between the host computer and a number of other computers/workstations.

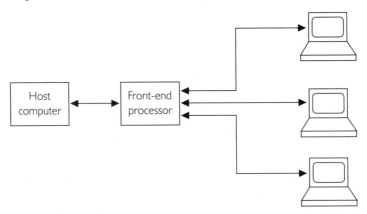

Figure 6.2   Using the front-end processor

Down-line processor

The down-line processor is useful when a host computer is linked to a number of other workstations or devices at a remote site. The down-line processor is sited at the remote site and is linked into all the required workstations. This can then transmit and receive messages to/from the host computer over a single line. This line could then operate at a much faster speed than would be possible using the slower workstations/devices. Figure 6.3 illustrates a down-line processor linked to devices at a particular site with a single high speed link to the host computer. The down-line processor performs the function of a **multiplexor** combining together signals from a variety of devices in order to send along a single line.

The down-line processor also acts as a **concentrator** sending the data down a line to the host computer in 'bundles' when enough data has been collected, rather than sending data bit by bit, in order to make more efficient use of the fast communication channel.

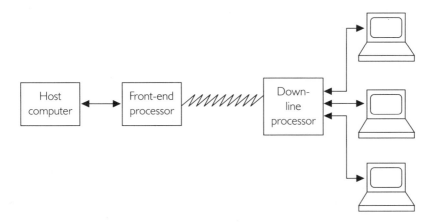

Figure 6.3 Using the down-line processor

Self-assessment questions

1 Discuss the use of modems in linking computer systems together. Are modems used in your own Organisation/Company? If so, describe where they are used.

2 Describe the range of hardware required to obtain communications links between computers.

Data transmission rules

If two computers are linked by a permanent line, then there is usually no problem in sending data between them. For example, if two microcomputers are sited in the same office and connected by a cable, then provided appropriate **communications software** is used there can be little problem in sending data between the two computers. However, even in a simple situation like this, problems can occur such as the remote possibility that both computers try to send data to each other at the same instant! Clearly, when more than two computers are involved, possibly sited at remote locations, the problems of data transmission are increased significantly. Data transmission rules must be established in order that efficient, reliable communication takes place. Such rules are often defined by the use of communications **support software**. This section outlines a number of basic transmission rules and techniques that are often adopted.

Polling

If a number of computers or devices are linked using a single communications channel then the channel is called a **multidrop line** (or **multipoint line**). In such a case the devices need to share a single channel, and a procedure called polling can be used to ensure that messages from all the devices can be sent. Using this method, the computer or front-end processor checks (or polls) each device in turn to discover whether a message is ready to be transmitted. If the line is clear then the message is sent, and the next device is polled. If the line is busy then the front-end processor waits before checking the line again.

Contention

Using this procedure any device/workstation that has a message to send, automatically contacts the host computer (or front-end processor) to send the message. If the line is busy then the device waits before attempting to contact the host computer. This is repeated until the line is free and then the message is sent.

Protocols

Protocols are rules that dictate how devices can communicate with each other. Unless the devices use the same protocols then data cannot be transmitted between them. Communication without protocols would be like two people communicating over the telephone using different languages. In fact, it would be worse than that; it would be similar to trying to communicate in different languages, one using the telephone, and the other a Fax! Communications protocols are defined for various levels (so-called **protocol layers**). For example, the **OSI (Open System Interconnection)** model contains seven levels. Each level in the OSI model defines a specific function. The seven levels define the Physical, Data Link, Network, Transport, Session, Presentation, and Application protocols.

Many such protocols exist including an early protocol called XON/XOFF, and others such as X.12 and X.75. Two standards in common use are **X.25** and **ISDN (Integrated Services Digital Network)** providing standardised methods of linking computer systems via communications networks. More recent developments in protocols such as **X.400** and **DCA–DIA** (Document Content Architecture and Document Interchange Architecture) have improved the transmission of data between systems on the network. Other protocols of increasing importance are the Transmission Control Protocol (TCP) and the Internet Protocol (IP), known as **TCP/IP.** Providing two connected devices use the same protocol then they will be able to communicate with each other without any particular problems. In fact, there are ways of connecting systems working under different protocols such as the use of bridges and routers (refer to section on Linking Networks later in this chapter).

Asynchronous transmission

There are two standard ways of transmitting data one of which is known as asynchronous transmission. Using this approach, data is sent character by character whenever required. Thus, the transmission of data is irregular. A good analogy of this would be two people talking on the telephone. As soon as one person talks, this message is sent down the line and is received by the other. However little is spoken, whether one word or 1,000, the message is sent word by word straight away. This type of data transmission is wasteful for high speed (expensive) lines since there will be large random gaps between the data being sent. Such transmission is normally used only for low speed lines such as those connecting microcomputers with printers.

Synchronous transmission

Using synchronous transmission the devices at each end of the communication channel work in a synchronised manner. Using this approach, data is sent down a line in blocks, rather than as single characters. This method is much more efficient and is invariably used for high speed lines such as those connecting two remote computers together.

Transmission modes

Data is transmitted down a line in one of three ways: simplex, half-duplex or duplex shown in Figure 6.4. In the simplex method, data can only be transmitted down the line in one direction. Information cannot be received back. Half-duplex transmission occurs when data can be transmitted either way in a communications channel, but not simultaneously. **Duplex** enables the sending and receiving of information down a line simultaneously. Thus, devices at both ends of the line can send and receive data at the same time. This requires the use of two channels to enable this to take place.

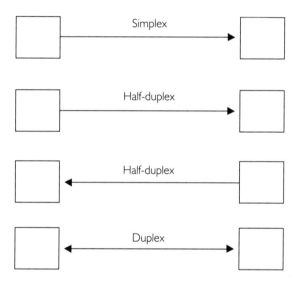

Figure 6.4   Modes of transmission

Packet switching

Packet switching is used when data is being transmitted between remote nodes on a network. Figure 6.5 illustrates data being transmitted from node A to node B by various routes. Instead of the data being sent via a fixed route between the two nodes, it is first split into 'packets' of information. Each packet together with the appropriate identifiers (e.g. information on where the data is being sent to, identification of the data and packet number) is sent via the most appropriate route to the required destination. The packets are then reassembled at the point of destination so that the message is received correctly.

This method of transmission is managed by a packet switching system (PSS) or packet switching exchange (PSE). This method ensures that the data is sent in the most efficient way, and means that busy routes on the communications network can be avoided whenever necessary. Computers are needed at each node on the PSS in order to receive messages and transmit them via the best route.

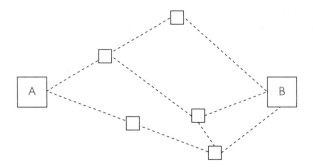

Figure 6.5   Packet switching system

Self-assessment questions

1   What problems can occur when two or more microcomputers are linked together and data is transmitted between them? How can such problems be overcome?

2   Define what a protocol is and why it is necessary in data communication.

Transmission media

A range of media can be used to transmit signals between computers/workstations at remote sites. In practice, when computers are linked over long distances, it is likely that several different methods of transmission will be adopted at different parts of the data journey. This section summarises the main methods used in data transmission.

Telephone lines
Standard telephone lines can be used to carry signals/data between computers. This is a useful medium since telephone connections are available to virtually all businesses, and indeed a comprehensive network (**Public Switched Telephone Network – PSTN**) is established throughout the world. The standard telephone network is not ideal since it cannot handle high speed rates of transmission. This means that the telephone network is not appropriate for sending large quantities of data. However for many applications such as private individuals communicating by using modems, this form of data transmission is perfectly adequate.

Coaxial cable
Coaxial cable is made up of groups of copper or aluminium wires. Insulation helps to reduce distortion in the electrical signals transmitted using this medium. This medium allows data to be transmitted at high speeds, and is often used in connecting computers in close proximity. Remote computers are usually not connected in this way.

Twisted pair

This medium, referred to as the **unshielded twisted pair** (UTP) provides a reliable way of connecting individual computers or other devices.

Fibre-optic links

Fibre-optic cable uses laser beams to send data along tiny fibre tubes. This medium is significantly smaller than a corresponding wire cable, is much less expensive and is extremely reliable. The use of light to send data results in an almost error-free transmission. Fibre-optic cables allow data to be transmitted in a digital form, and therefore the use of modems to convert analogue to digital and digital to analogue are not necessary. Transmission via this medium is very fast.

Microwave links

Microwave transmission is similar to the sending and receiving of television and radio signals. Microwave signals are sent through the air often via satellites or between ground stations. This method provides an extremely fast, reliable way of communication. Such a method is ideal for linking computer systems over long distances and is often used for international computer networks.

Data transmission services

As stated at the beginning of the Transmission Media section, in general it may be useful to incorporate a mixture of the media described into one communications channel. For example, a company with offices in a number of countries may wish to have computer links between the major sites in each area. Figure 6.6 illustrates such a situation where three main offices located in London, New York and Sydney are all linked via communications channels.

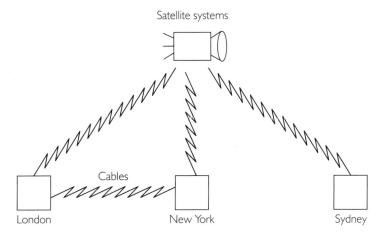

Figure 6.6   Communications links between remote sites

Clearly, the company requiring links between offices, however large, will not have the capability of independently establishing communications links between these three sites. The Company will need to call upon the services of specialised organisations (so-called **common carriers**) involved in this area. Companies such as AT&T in the US, and BT or Mercury in the UK offer this type of service. Common carriers are then able to utilize the range of communications media available. Services offered by these Common Carriers include the provision of the following links:

- **Private lines** provide dedicated communications links between two remote devices. The user company is charged a rental for such lines based on the speed capability and distances involved.
- **Switched lines** provide flexible links with computers at many points. Users at a particular site can dial up computers at remote sites, and link up with the assistance of modems located at each end of the communication channel. This is a much more flexible method of communication than the private lines, though is generally slower, and is therefore less useful for bulk data traffic.

Self-assessment questions

1   Describe how standard telephone lines can be used to carry data signals between computer systems. What additional hardware is required in order to be able to use such a link?

2   Describe the functions of common carriers. How can they assist business communication?

Networks

Networking involves the linking of a number of computer systems in order to share data and resources. A computer network contained within a restricted area (such as a single office or within a few miles) is called a **local area network (LAN)**. A system connecting computers and other devices spread over long distances (such as linking systems in different countries) is called a **wide area network (WAN)**. Wide area networks involve the linking of computer systems over communications channels such as the telephone network, as previously described. These will often involve host computers linked to remote devices such as microcomputers. The micros will have access to data stored at the host end and will be able to **down-load** (bring data in from the host) and **upload** (send data to the host) using the WAN. Wide area networks may contain links between a selection of local area networks at remote locations. In this section we will concentrate on the elements of a local area network and the various configurations used for today's business applications.

Local area networks

A local area network (LAN) consists of a group of computers and other devices linked together in a restricted area, in order to communicate with each other and share a variety of resources such as data, software, and hardware. Figure 6.7 shows a typical LAN of computers contained within a single office. The network consists of a number of microcomputers, linked together sharing resources such as printers and data files.

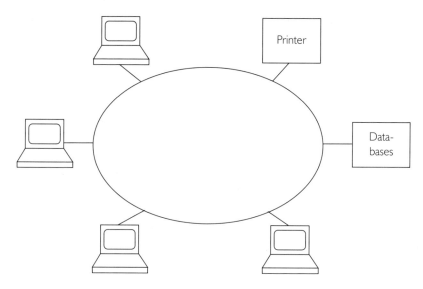

Figure 6.7   Local area network

The primary advantages of installing a LAN over using stand-alone computers can easily be seen. The following are the main reasons for the introduction of a LAN:

- **Sharing hardware.**   The sharing of peripheral devices such as printers is very beneficial. A printer is an expensive component that is often standing idle. Stand-alone computers would require their own individual supporting printers which can be prohibitively expensive. One printer shared between a number of computers on a LAN can be a cost-effective solution.
- **Sharing data.**   If users on stand-alone systems wish to use the same data files, then copies of these files need to be stored on each system. This then soon leads to anomalies between supposedly identical files. A user on one system will update a file, without informing other users possessing the same file. Unless regular manual updating of all the shared files is performed then problems sooner or later will arise. The ability to save a data file on a central system, with access available from a number of other users, solves such problems.
- **Communications.**   Users of computers on a LAN will be able to send data to each other via the network. The alternative for stand-alone system users is to copy data onto secondary storage media (e.g. magnetic or optical disks) and physically send this to the appropriate destination. Clearly this type of 'physical' data transmission is inefficient, time-consuming and cumbersome. Other basic advantages of a LAN include the ability to send and receive messages between users such as in the use of electronic mail.

Many different types of local area networks are currently available. The layout of Networks can be arranged in a variety of ways, and the following sections give a number of the standard configurations (or topologies) currently used. Figure 6.8 shows the main topologies described. Most of the current network configurations involve the use of a **file server** in order to manage the system. The file server (or simply referred to as the **server**) can be a more powerful microcomputer, and is used to supervise dialogue between other components on the network. The server will often contain additional data and software for access by users on the network.

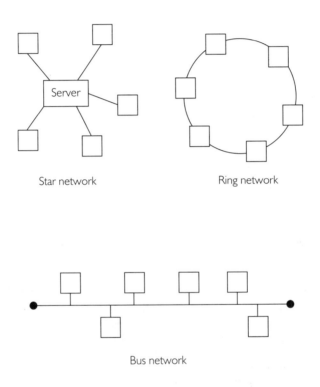

Star network   Ring network

Bus network

Figure 6.8   Network topologies

In most practical business networks a combination of the following layouts may be used.

Star network
A star network topology consists of a server linked to all other components on the network. All the microcomputers are linked into the server and all data files and other devices such as printers are also connected. Any data or message sent between components on the system will be transmitted via the server.

Ring network
This type of network links all the computers and other devices in a circular manner. Any message or data sent from a user will be transmitted around the ring until arrival

at the appropriate destination. In this layout there is not necessarily a particular server managing the communications.

Bus network

Using the bus topology all computers and other devices are connected via a central communication channel. This enables new components to be added to the system and existing ones to be removed very easily. Many of the current networks use a bus type of topology.

Hierarchical network

This type of configuration consists of one central computer managing the whole network, with a number of other smaller devices themselves managing a particular element of the communication system. This enables smaller clusters of devices to share information specifically required by them without everything being located in a single server. However each cluster can have access to other users when necessary via the central computer.

Fully distributed networks

It this type of layout, every element on the network can communicate directly with every other element. This requires each device to have the necessary communication software in order to carry out these connections successfully rather than the use of a central server.

Client/server arrangements

Current network systems use the client/server arrangement for organising communications. As previously described, the server is used to manage the total system. This removes much of the responsibility from the other elements on the system and therefore the system operates in a much more efficient way. Clients consist of all the other elements (such as microcomputers) on the system. Clients require some software to be stored locally in order to gain access to the server. The server will have direct access to any shared data and software required by the clients.

Self-assessment questions

1   What are the main reasons for linking devices by using networks?

2   What sort of devices would you expect to be linked on a local area network?

3   Describe the most common topologies (layouts) used in local area networks. What are the layouts of networks at your company or organisation?

Network types

A range of network types are available for the business user. This section describes some of the more common types of network in current use and discusses differences between them.

Ethernet

This type of network has been available for many years and is extremely popular for business applications. Ethernet uses a bus configuration for the network. Essentially, one cable links all of the devices (so-called **nodes**) on the network. Problems can occur if two devices attempt to send messages (data) at the same time. Consequently, a system must be devised to ensure that this does not occur. In Ethernet, a device that wishes to send a message, first checks that the line is free. If so, then the device takes control of the line and the message is sent. If the line is busy then the device waits for a fraction of a second and tries again. The device will keep trying in this way until the line is free. If two devices send messages at exactly the same time then a 'collision' will occur, and the transmission is cancelled from both nodes. Each device will wait a different amount of time before trying to send the messages again. This type of procedure is called **carrier sense multiple access with collision detection (CSMA/CD)**.

Many of the current networks use the Ethernet system of communication. It remains the most popular networking system available. Ethernet allows data to be transmitted at speeds of around 10 Mbps (10 megabytes per second). A variety of media can be used in the Ethernet system depending on the physical distances involved. For example, Thick Ethernet (standard coaxial cable) can be used for distances up to 500 metres. Thin Ethernet can be used up to 185 metres, and UTP (Unshielded Twisted Pair) for a maximum of 100 metres.

Token ring
The Token Ring system, developed by IBM, uses a ring network configuration. Using this method, a 'token' is continuously travelling around the network. If the token is 'free', then any node on the network can catch hold of it in order to send a message to another node. When this occurs the token then becomes 'busy' and will stay so until the message is delivered at the correct destination. The destination node then places a 'message received' label with the token and sends it on round the network, back to the original sender. The token then becomes free again and can be used by any other node on the network to send messages. Figure 6.9 illustrates how the Token Ring system operates.

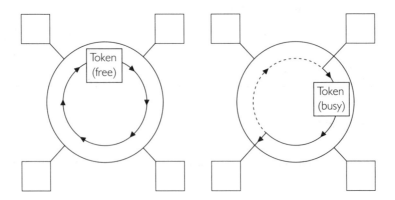

Figure 6.9   Using the Token Ring system

This type of network management has proved to be very efficient running at speeds of up to 16 Mbps. The Token Ring system has been adopted almost exclusively by IBM users. A similar idea of 'token passing' using the bus network topology is also available but not widely used.

FDDI

The Fibre Distributed Data Interface (FDDI) provides a fast method of communication. This type of network is based on ring topology using fibre-optic cable. FDDI consists of two rings with information travelling around each ring in opposite directions. One ring can act as a back-up if the other link fails. This type of network is most commonly used to connect a number of networks or servers together, rather than to connect individual nodes. FDDI provides a fast, reliable link between systems, though it is rather expensive compared to most Ethernet systems. Current speeds for this medium are around 100 Mbps.

Arcnet

Arcnet (attached resource computing network) is a common system used for local area networks. It uses a token passing system on either a bus or a star network. Speeds of up to 20 Mbps over standard coaxial cable are now possible with Arcnet Plus. This low cost system allows computers to be linked together over distances up to 300 metres on a bus network, and 600 metres on a star network configuration.

ATM

Asynchronous Transfer Mode (ATM) defines a framework for linking various systems together. It is extremely fast, running at up to 650 Mbps. As such it is a powerful medium for the transmission of video signals, where a large amount of data needs to be transmitted very quickly. Furthermore, such a fast link would be useful for linking networks together, where a significant amount of data needs to be transmitted between the various nodes.

Wireless LANs

Current developments in LAN technology include the use of wireless LANs. As the name suggests, this type of network does not require the use of cabling to link nodes to the server. A link can be made between the components of a network using various technologies including radio waves or infra-red systems. Currently, a number of radio systems have been developed using two different methods: **spread spectrum** and a system operating under the standards defined by Digital European Cordless Telecommunications (**DECT**).

Linking networks

In many of today's business applications there is a need to connect a range of computers, possibly already connected into distinct local area networks, into a larger communications system. For example, two offices with their own LANs may require to be linked together. Such a linking would result in a larger, more complex, local area network. Alternatively, a Head Office, with its own central computer system and network, requires links with regional offices, some of which has networks. This would result in a wide area network (WAN) being formed. The range of permutations of possible network layouts is almost endless.

Figure 6.10 illustrates the type of complex networks that may be in use in today's companies. In reality, the type of networking decision a business person may be required to make could be more complex than whether to go for an Ethernet or Token Ring system. It is more likely to be a decision concerning the best way of linking such existing systems together.

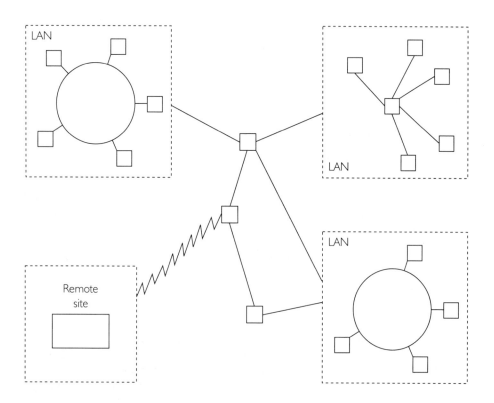

Figure 6.10   Links between local area networks

Local area networks can be connected to each other using a range of methods. The three main approaches are the use of **bridges, repeaters,** or **routers.** This section summarises these three types of connections.

Repeater
A repeater is used to link two LANs of the same type. The repeater simply receives a message from one source, enhances it by removing any 'noise' in the signal, and passes it on without any changes to its destination. Figure 6.11 shows a repeater used to link two simple networks.

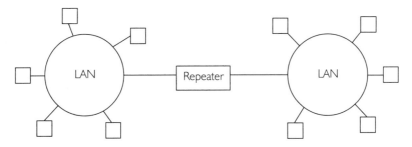

Figure 6.11   Using a repeater

The repeater can be used simply to enlarge an existing LAN. For example, an Ethernet system using a coaxial cable to link the nodes can only operate over a short distance – approximately 200 m (or 500 m using a thick Ethernet).

At this distance a repeater can be used to enhance the signal and thus extend the range of the network. A repeater cannot be used for linking networks of different types.

Bridge
A bridge is slightly more complicated than a repeater and requires extra processing in order to operate. The bridge only sends a message across when necessary. If the message is sent to a 'local' node then the bridge will not send this message across. This is in contrast to a repeater which will send the message across regardless of its destination. Figure 6.12 shows a bridge linking two networks A and B.

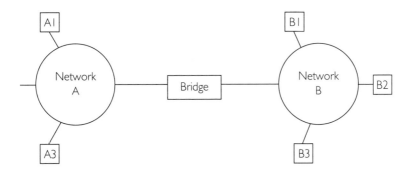

Figure 6.12   Using a bridge to link networks

A message sent by node A1 to node B2 will be passed across the bridge. Conversely, a message sent from node A1 to node A3 will be checked by the bridge and will not be sent across. This makes the bridge much more effective in reducing the amount of data being sent around the networks. Unlike the repeater, a bridge can be used to connect different types of network together. For example, an Ethernet network can be connected to a Token Ring network via a bridge.

Router

A router performs in a similar way to a bridge. However, a router is slightly more sophisticated. In addition to checking a message before sending across between networks, the router will determine the best route to send the message on to its destination. The best route could involve factors such as distance, speed and cost. This type of additional facility can be useful especially when linking networks over long distances. Figure 6.13 shows the complex linking of a number of networks, where the router can determine the best (or most appropriate) paths between source and destination.

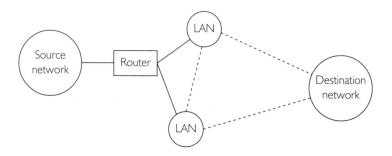

Figure 6.13   Using a router to determine the best path between networks

Routers tend to be more expensive to purchase than bridges. However the extra cost can be repaid very quickly when considering the cost of data transmission over distances. Some systems provide a combination of bridge and router (referred to as a **Brouter**) in order to link networks.

Gateways

Gateways perform in a similar way to bridges except that they can be used to connect two different networks. Data from one network can be sent across a gateway and converted into the correct format for receiving into the destination network. Thus gateways can be used to connect networks running under different protocols, perhaps produced by different manufacturers.

Complex networks

The links introduced in the previous sections can be incorporated in an overall network providing a complex information and communication system. The bridges, routers, and repeaters can be used where appropriate to provide a total system. Figure 6.14 illustrates such a complex network enabling the linking of different computer systems, and various networks.

Such a communication network would be regarded as a wide area network, and could involve the use of a variety of different communications channels such as X.25 and ISDN.

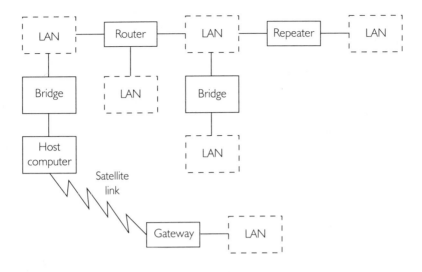

Figure 6.14   Using a variety of links in a complex network

Self-assessment questions

1   What is the difference between an Ethernet and a Token Ring network?

2   Many businesses currently use a number of different networks linked together. Describe how these separate networks can be linked.

3   Consider the type of networks used at your work-place or at your college. Describe these networks and how they link together.

Network software

In order to make the local area network operate effectively the **network operating system** is used. This comprises a range of programs to supervise the various networking functions. Some of these programs are located at each node on the network i.e. each microcomputer has a part of the LAN operating system stored locally in its RAM. This enables a link to be set up with the server, where most of the remaining LAN programs are located. The LAN operating system then enables communication between the various nodes and server, and supervises the sharing of resources such as printers, data files, and application packages. A number of LAN operating systems are currently available including *LAN Manager* produced by Microsoft, and *Netware* from Novell. Other packages such as **SNMP** (Simple Network Management Protocol) enable such networks to be managed efficiently. For example, SNMP provides a graphic view of all the current nodes on the network, and enables the network manager to isolate problems such as breaks in the lines, or workstations not functioning.

As has already been stated, one of the applications of a network is the ability to share application packages. The software can be stored on the server, and accessed by individuals at any node on the network when required. For example, a database package could be stored on the server, and loaded by an individual when necessary. If the database is updated by a user, then other users can automatically see the updated files. The alternative to this would be the necessity for storing this software on each separate workstation, which would involve significant increases in the secondary storage capacities required on each node. Also problems of duplication of files can then occur. The popular term for such software is **groupware** implying that it is shared by a group of users. Thus, when a user connects up to the network, it is likely that a screen menu will be displayed containing a list of groupware available. The user can then simply choose from the menu in order to access the required groupware package for use.

Applications

The advantages of linking computer systems, whether locally or more widespread, are self-evident, and have been introduced in the previous sections in the chapter. The ability to link computer users on different sites enhances communication, allows sharing of resources, and reduces the possibility of duplicating work. There are numerous applications in business of such links, whether using WANs or LANs. A brief description of some of these applications are given in the following items.

Electronic mail enabling users to send and receive messages and files between nodes on the network. Clearly this could replace the need for sending memos, and using the telephone. It is sometimes more effective than the traditional methods of communication since messages can be sent even when the user is absent from the office, and the sender knows if and when the message has been read.

Electronic diary enabling users to check whether others are available at specific times, thus simplifying the organisation of meetings. A meeting can be arranged and the appropriate times automatically inserted into the diaries of the members of the meeting.

Electronic bulletin boards allow users to set up messages (notices) that can be accessed by other users on the system. This is really a simplified version of electronic mail allowing less interaction between users. However, this process does allow a simple method of displaying information to be read by all users on the system. For example, management in a company could distribute notices to all employees which will be displayed as soon as the users connect up to the network.

Tele-conferencing enables the linking of a group of users at remote sites using the telecommunications network. Thus managers at different offices around the world can meet in 'conference' over the network. In its simplest form this would involve voice communication. However, with the development of faster, more efficient communications channels, the application of sound and video images in linking remote users in a conference (**video-conferencing**) is becoming more frequent.

Voice mail. The use of voice mail is an extension of the electronic mail application. Audio messages can be transmitted to an individual or group without the necessity of the receivers being present. Consequently this method has many advantages over the standard telephone system where problems can arise because either the call is not answered or the receiver is absent and a message is left with no confirmation of whether the message has been received.

Tele-working or **tele-commuting** allows many employees to work from home without the necessity of attending the office. The worker uses a computer with modem link to communicate with the main office. In many occupations the need for actually attending a central workplace is unnecessary. The tele-worker can communicate with other colleagues via electronic mail, files can be created and transmitted between users. Occupations such as journalists, accountants, typists and sales persons, could all be satisfactorily performed using the tele-working approach. Current predictions estimate that 2,500,000 people in the UK will be involved in tele-working in 1995 from around 300,000 in 1993.

Electronic banking means that customers can access their bank to perform transactions such as requests for statement of account, or requesting or cancelling standing orders and direct debits. The customer uses a modem link to access the bank's computer system, and would enter the appropriate account name, account number and password in order to gain access. Similarly, banks are able to communicate with each other, facilitating the transfer of funds between accounts.

Home shopping allows home users to access details of available products from a range of suppliers. Such details could include photographic images of some of the items for sale. Users can order the goods via the communications system, and even pay for the items required.

Travel reservations The travel industry use the telecommunications links to provide an effective method of checking holiday and flight availabilities, and booking places when desired. Thus seats on airlines can be reserved from remote points around the world, linked to central computer systems storing data on prices, flight times, destinations, and availability. Other similar services are available on a national level for leisure activities such as sports and theatre bookings.

Information services
A range of information services are available in diverse subject areas. The use of commercial databases to obtain information is widespread. Many such databases are available in the UK enabling users with a computer and modem link to access a wealth of information. This type of service would be called an **on-line database.**

Alternative methods of obtaining current business information include the use of **CD-ROM** to provide regular updates on specified subject areas. Whether by communications link or the use of CD-ROM, the majority of these databases involve subscription charges. Paying a subscription would provide the user with the relevant passwords allowing access into the database. Thus users can obtain access to a range of information services available. The use of such information services has increased dramatically in recent years. This is due to a number of factors including improvements in technology and communications systems, availability of required hardware and software in the business environment, and an increased awareness by the business user of benefits from using such systems. The type of information available on such systems is extremely varied including databases containing information on business news, legislation, mergers, share prices, market research, economics and finance, as well as international trade. (Refer to the *Online/CD-ROM Business Sourcebook,* published by Headland Press)

Current information services in the UK include:

- **Financial information.**   This is an important area in database usage. The financial sector makes extensive use of databases to access information on Stock Market prices. For example, the ICC Sharewatch provides an on-line database for subscribers to obtain information for shareholders in UK companies. The Stock Exchange's TOPIC is another popular database providing up-to-date information on current prices. Other databases are available in this area such as Datastream, Citiservice, Citiwatch, and ICC Direct.
- **Business news.**   This provides details on all current news items in given business categories. Many databases exist in this area including DIALOG, FT-PROFILE, NewsFile II and Planex. Many national newspapers provide the contents of their publications on database. For example, *The Guardian, The Daily Telegraph* and *Sunday Telegraph,* and *The Times* provide this service.
- **Market research.**   This type of database contains information such as market reports, including details such as market trends, recent developments, and company profiles. Databases in this category include ICC Key Notes, MEAL (Media Expenditure Analysis Ltd), Mintel, and Marketing available on FT-PROFILE.
- **Industrial databases.**   These databases contain details of production outputs, new product launches, company details in specific sectors, business conditions, commodities, and relevant research and development news. Such databases include Chem-Intel (Chemical Intelligence Services), IMSworld, API Energy Business, Electronic Markets and Information Systems.

Self-assessment questions

1   What would you regard as the most important reason for networking computer systems together?

2   Describe the term 'tele-working'. Give examples of where this could be in operation.

3   Consider your own workplace (or a company/organisation with which you are familiar). Find out whether any external information services are used by this company. If so, what are they, and what type of information do they provide?

Choosing networks

The choice of a suitable network system is an important task in developing good communications within an organisation. A number of requirements should be considered when choosing an appropriate network to install in a business situation. Such a choice could follow the pattern of the development life-cycle described in Chapter 11 of this text. This would involve firstly analysing the requirements, then designing a solution, followed by developing and implementing the design. The development stage would involve the acquisition of appropriate hardware and software prior to implementation. The choice of such systems will depend on the analysis stage where a range of requirements will be defined. The following conditions will need to be considered:

- **Traffic density.** The volume of traffic (i.e. amount of data) that will be transmitted over the network will determine the type of system required. For instance the Ethernet system would not be appropriate for heavy traffic, but is ideal for the transmission of less data. If video signals are required to be sent then a network suitable for heavy traffic is essential such as FDDI or ATM. Also the number of users and number of nodes on the network will affect the choice of system. Future growth should also be considered here.

- **Transmission speed.** The speed of transmission of data over the lines is important. Again, if it is likely that there will be large amounts of data to send at any one time then a faster system such as ATM will be necessary. For example, Ethernet speeds of 10 MBytes per second are common, compared with FDDI running at 100 Mbps, and ATM at 650 Mbps.

- **Distance.** The distances between nodes on the system will determine the media that is appropriate. For example, **Thicknet** is used for larger distances (up to 500m), whereas **Thin-net** and **UTP** are used for shorter distances (185 and 100m respectively).

- **Security.** The sensitivity of data to be transmitted may be a factor. For instance, those in the banking sector may require higher security than those in other industries to ensure that data transmitted over the lines cannot be tampered with. The use of fibre-optic cable (e.g. FDDI) would be ideal in such circumstances as it is much harder to intercept signals sent on this medium. Other factors such as virus checking, backup and recovery of files would be considered in this category.

- **Reliability.** There is always a chance of breaks occurring in the system, and the degree of reliability required should be taken into consideration. For instance some systems used primarily for internal communication by electronic mail may be affected less by any interruptions in the networks than other applications such as financial or banking systems. FDDI would be much more reliable than an Ethernet system. Systems using Thin-net are less reliable than UTP links. For instance, a break in Thin-net will result in a whole segment of the network being lost.

- **Cost.** Clearly the price of alternative network systems is an important factor. Ethernet provides an inexpensive method of networking which in part accounts for its widespread use. Alternatively, FDDI is a relatively expensive networking method. ATM is also expensive, in particular requiring expensive communication cards to be fitted to each workstation on the network. The overall costs of networking would not only include hardware, software and cabling, but also maintenance, training, and network administration and management expenses.

The decision on which network system to adopt is largely a matter for the technical experts in collaboration with users. As has been stated in previous sections, no single networking method will be appropriate throughout the organisation. Often a combination of solutions will be used to make effective use of the available networking systems.

Summary

This chapter has dealt with the linking of computer systems and the transmission of data between them. Such links often occur via standard telecommunications networks, and would be referred to as wide area networks (WANs). A range of data communications hardware is required such as modems for linking computers into the telephone system and translating signals into the appropriate format for transmission. Other hardware such as front-end processors, and down-line processors are used when a computer is linked into a number of other devices. Various rules for the transmission of data have been described such as polling, contention and protocols. The media by which data is transmitted has been briefly described including coaxial cables, fibre-optics, and microwaves.

The use of local area networks (LANs) to link devices in a relatively confined area has been considered. Local Area Networks are arranged in a variety of ways including star, ring, and bus topologies. The main types of network currently available include Ethernet, Token Ring, wireless LANs, and FDDI. Many networks in current business use are complex, involving the linking of a range of 'separate' networks. Such links between networks have been described and include the use of bridges and routers. The management of such networks is performed by means of a range of software referred to as the network operating system.

This chapter has included a range of potential applications for networks including electronic mail, voice mail, bulletin boards, tele-conferencing, electronic banking, and travel. A number of remote information services specifically for business applications have been introduced. Such information services, called external databases, include those providing details in finance, market research, and legislation.

Finally, when selecting network systems for business applications the alternatives will be compared using a range of factors such as traffic density, speed of transmission, distances, security required, reliability, as well as cost.

Questions for discussion _____

1 Would you agree that data communications is equivalent to telecommunications? If not, give your reasons.

2 A modem is used to convert computer signals into signals to be carried over telephone lines. Is this an accurate description? Give details of what a modem actually does.

3 Describe the range of facilities normally available on modern modems.

4 What is the difference between a front-end processor and a down-line processor?

5 Describe the functions of a multiplexor. In what circumstances would a multiplexor not be required?

6 Discuss the terms simplex, half-duplex, and duplex.

7 Describe the differences between synchronous and asynchronous data transmission. Would you agree that asynchronous transmission is better? If so, why?

8 A packet switching system can provide an efficient way of transmitting data between remote computers. How does such a system operate?

9 Fibre-optic cables provide the fastest method of transmitting data. Discuss this statement. Is it true? If not, what is the fastest method?

10 What is the difference between a LAN and a WAN?

11 What are the advantages of linking computers in a single office by using a local area network over running stand-alone computers?

12 Describe the different network configurations in current use.

13 Discuss the advantages and disadvantages of star and ring networks.

14 Discuss the main factors that should be considered when choosing a networking system.

Problems

1 Ethernet is one of the most popular types of network currently used in business. Describe how Ethernet works, and compare it with any other network type with which you are familiar.

2 'The problem with networks is that they are very restricting. Computers have to be connected using bulky cables, and so they are not easy to move around.' Discuss whether or not you agree with these comments.

3 Networks can be linked together using a variety of techniques such as repeaters, bridges, and routers. Briefly describe each of these methods, and comment on the advantages and disadvantages of each process.

4 An operating system is generally required to manage the operations on a network. Give examples of some current operating systems available, and describe their function.

5 Would you agree that electronic mail is one of the most important applications of using a network? What other applications of networks would you consider to be more important?

6 Examine in which of the following situations you would expect a network to be required. Describe, where appropriate, the type of network required, and the ways in which such a network could be used.

(i) An office containing six secretaries, each with a micro-computer only used for word-processing.

(ii) A design company located in an office block on four separate floors. Twenty-five employees have their own computers used for graphics and desk-top publishing applications.

(iii) A large retail establishment containing thirty management and administrative staff, together with retail space incorporating over twenty cash tills spread throughout the store.

(iv) An estate agency with ten offices spread over the north of the UK.

7 In a recent conversation with your manager, she has stated, 'A really useful application of our LAN is tele-conferencing. If we had this facility I am sure that we could often use this in our office.' Comment on this statement with reference to how LANs can be applied in a business environment. Would you agree with your manager's comments?

8 Describe how networks can be used in the following business areas:

(i)   banking

(ii) stock-broking

(iii) journalism

(iv   travel and tourism

(v)   production.

Case-study 6.1:   The Ball & Chain Estate Agency

The Manager Director of a large estate agency company (Ball & Chain Co.) has been considering the possibility of linking all the computer systems in local offices together. There are currently thirty offices located throughout England and Wales. The Ball & Chain company has expansion plans and wishes to add another twenty offices in the UK over the next three years.

Currently the Ball & Chain offices are independently run. Microcomputers are used in all the offices to keep details on current and past properties for sale. The company also has a Property Management branch which takes care of rental of houses and flats. Such information is also recorded on the computers.

Purchase of computers has in the past been left up to individual managers, or more recently, Regional Managers. Thus, a range of different microcomputers are in use in the local offices. Weekly reports are produced on all available properties and hard copies are circulated to other offices within regions. Monthly reports are also produced and sent to Head Office including information on the number and value of sales, record of each sales person, fees collected and advertising expenditure.

Problems have arisen because:

● the details sent between local offices have not been up to date;
● information quickly becomes inaccurate due to sales taking place and new clients registering business.

The Managing Director has appointed a consultant to advise on the viability of linking all the computer systems together. Describe the main points that the consultant is likely to present to the Managing Director on each of the following areas:

I Describe the type of networks that could be used to aid communications between and within the offices.

2 What sort of additional hardware would be required in order to implement such a system?

3 Would there be any problems concerning the different computer systems in current use? If any, how could these problems be resolved?

4 In addition to improving the existing communications system in Ball & Chain Co. what other applications could such a system be used for? List the types of problems that the company could deal with using such a system that would not be possible with the existing systems. How can such a network system improve the service to Ball & Chain's customers?

Case-study 6.2: Wafer & Dough plc, food distribution

A large food distribution company (Wafer & Dough plc) incorporates eight production factories and a headquarters. The factories are dispersed throughout France, with the headquarters located 30 miles outside of Paris. The headquarters contains all the main administrative and managerial staff. A large warehouse is located on the same site to store all the items produced from the eight factories prior to distribution to customers.

The products that are produced and distributed by Wafer & Dough are largely perishable items, including bread, pastries, biscuits and cakes. The shelf-life of many of these items is less than a week, and therefore it is imperative that items are distributed to customers as quickly as possible. More than 95% of Wafer & Dough's turnover comes from large supermarket chains. Currently the company caters for six main retail chains, delivering to a total of 200 separate superstores and hypermarkets.

- Each supermarket generates its own requirements and this information must be sent to Wafer & Dough's headquarters on a daily basis.
- This information is then collated and total requirements for each item in the product range is communicated to the appropriate production site.
- Items are then produced and transported to the headquarters, prior to distribution to the individual retail outlets.
- Each factory produces a unique range of the required products.
- None of the individual items sold by Wafer & Dough is produced in more than one site.

Consider this situation in relation to the network systems required at both the customer end (at individual retail outlets) and the distribution end at the headquarters. In relation to the Wafer & Dough company consider the following points:

1 Where could local area networks be used in improving these systems?

2 Are wide area networks required in the efficient operation of this business? If so, how can they be used?

3 What problems can you foresee in using such systems?

4 In addition to the customer and the headquarters are there other areas of this business that would benefit from better communications? Give details of possible applications.

Case-study 6.3:   UMRC, a market research organisation

The United Market Research Company (UMRC) is involved in a range of studies involving home shopping. In particular, one current long-term project involves the investigation of shopping trends in food, drink and household goods. This survey project has been in operation for the past five years. Information obtained from this survey is collated on a weekly basis and is then sold to a range of clients in the advertising, marketing and retailing areas.

UMRC keeps track on a selected sample of the general public. 4,000 households are currently involved in the survey. Each household must record every purchase made in the required range of goods. This is achieved by the use of a simple computer terminal located in each house. The microcomputer has a simple restricted keypad allowing the entry of prices of goods. Each computer also has a bar code reader to enable the speedy identification of each item. Thus at the end of a shopping trip, the householder enters information on purchases in the following way: The bar code reader is used to identify each item, and then the corresponding price of each item is typed in. Information on all the purchases is then stored in the computer's memory in each household.

Each household microcomputer is permanently linked into the standard telephone network via the use of a simple telephone plug and socket. A central computer system at the UMRC headquarters can then dial into each home-based computer to up-load all the shopping details recorded. This is generally automatically performed at night without the need for any intervention by a member of the household.

The details are thus collected from all participants, and collated into statistical data on shopping patterns and trends.

1   Describe how such information could be collected without using a computer system. How effective would this manual system be?

2   Discuss the advantages of the computer-based method of data collection over a manual system of collection.

3   What are the problems of collecting information in this way? How can such difficulties be overcome?

Further reading

Athey T.H, Day J.C. and Zmud R.W, *Computers and End-User Software,* Harper-Collins, 1991

French C.S, *Data Processing and Information Technology,* (pp 155 – 168). DPP, 1993

Hicks J.O, *Information Systems in Business: An Introduction* 2nd ed, (Chapter 14) West Publishing Co, 1990

Long L. and Long N., *Computers* 3rd ed, (Chapters 7 & 8) Prentice-Hall, 1993

O'Brien J.A., *Management Information Systems: A Managerial End-User Perspective,* (Chapter 6) Irwin Publishers, 1993

Senn J.A., *Information Systems in Management,* 4th ed (Chapter 9) Wadsworth Publishing Co, 1990

Part 3
Software

7 Microcomputer software

Objectives

At the end of this chapter you should be able to:

- identify and describe a range of current applications software for microcomputers
- specify particular examples where such software could be used to assist management decision-making
- recommend the use of appropriate software in business and management situations
- understand the differences between applications and systems software and the role of operating systems.

Introduction

In this chapter we will consider the range of **application software** currently available for microcomputer systems. In some cases the software will have been designed for a specific type of user, e.g. accountants or production managers. However, most of the software described here is suitable for use in a wide range of applications and for users in a variety of disciplines.

Software can be split into two main categories, namely applications and systems software. Some systems software is essential for the operation of a computer. Usually, application software is purchased as part of a package. The application package consists of the software together with appropriate documentation such as user guides and manuals. The software (a suite of programs) is often supplied on a number of floppy disks. These disks can then be copied over to the required microcomputer for immediate use.

The following sections in the chapter include a description of many types of application software. Some specific uses are explored, though a more detailed look at applications in a range of functional areas is covered in Chapter 9.

Available software

A range of application packages are available to assist the manager in specific problem areas. Such packages can be acquired 'off-the-shelf' and are often relatively easy to use.

Application packages that could be of assistance to the manager include those in the following categories:

- Databases
- Document presentation
  - word processing
  - graphics
  - desktop publishing
  - design
- Data manipulation
  - spreadsheets
  - accounting
  - data analysis
  - mathematical software
- Management aids
  - project management
  - stock control
  - training
  - expert systems
  - simulation
- Integrated packages
  - database/spreadsheet/word processing
  - desktop publishing/graphics
- Systems software
  - operating systems
  - desktop accessories
  - communications

This is by no means a complete list of the software available today. However this list does include the most popular types of packages in addition to the most common systems software. Some of the packages listed (such as spreadsheets and databases) are of particular value to the majority of managers and consequently they will be described in greater detail in the following sections. Other packages that are applicable in specific functional areas (such as stock control and design) will be described more briefly.

Databases

Database packages provide an important information source for today's managers. This section describes the essential elements contained within a database and considers some basic applications to illustrate the salient points covered.

Information storage

A database package enables the user to create computer files in order to store and handle large amounts of data. Such files can help to improve an organisations' record-keeping processes and are vital in many areas of management decision-making. Database systems can be enormous, requiring large amounts of storage facilities. In such cases, it is likely that a minicomputer or mainframe system would be more appropriate as described in Chapter 8. However, many powerful microcomputer systems are available as described in this section.

A database consists of a number of files linked together. For example, consider a company that uses a suppliers file and stock file. The stock file would contain information on each item of stock, including where the item was supplied from. More details on the supplier could then be obtained from the suppliers file. These two connected files will form part of the company's database.

Each file contains a number of **records.** A record contains all the details on an item in the file. For example, a single record in the suppliers file will contain all the details on one supplier. Each specific detail is kept in a separate **field** within the record. For example, the suppliers file may contain details such as supplier's name, address, telephone number, account number, etc. all contained within separate fields of each record. Figure 7.1 illustrates such a file containing details of each supplier on a separate record. In this example each record contains only four fields. The actual content, size and range of fields contained will describe the **file structure** described in the following section.

Record 1	Adams & Co.	12 New Road, Swindon	0249-38276	A2698Y
Record 2	Kopfler plc	2816 Cancun Way	01783-46291	B1017S
Record 3	Kimber & Robertson	The Lodge, Richmond	017-384-2961	A2118Z
Record 4	Herbert, Lally & Partners	318 Bridge Avenue	0269-41825	C0126Y

Fig. 7.1   Example of suppliers file

File structures

The file structure must be designed with reference to the ways in which the information may be used at a later stage. Careful consideration of the potential applications in the early stages of database design is therefore essential. If the file structure created is inappropriate, then problems are bound to occur when accessing information. Typical complaints that managers have concerning information systems are that the system:

- does not contain the required details
- contains unnecessary details

- produces output in an inappropriate format
- does not produce the required information.

Many of these problems can be prevented by good **file design** and the use of suitable file structures. The file design can then be developed by using an appropriate database package. The design of a file is determined by an analysis of requirements described more fully in Chapter 11 on the information systems life-cycle. To show this progression a specific application is considered in the following section.

Application

A wide range of applications for databases and other packages are described in Chapter 9 on business and management applications. However in order to illustrate how an analysis of requirements will lead on to database design let us consider a simple marketing problem. A Marketing Manager requires information on the company's current clients in order to determine how best to use a limited advertising budget. The manager needs to be able to catagorise the clients into industrial segments such as manufacturing, services, finance, and media. Thus a field in the client database must be created to provide this information. The database may then provide details on the customer mix, and lead on to determining a marketing strategy. For example, a report produced from the database could give details such as '60% of existing clients are from the manufacturing sector'. This information may lead on to the Marketing Manager making a decision to concentrate the limited advertising resources in that sector in order to increase market share, or conversely concentrate on improving the market share in other industrial sectors.

In addition, the Sales Director needs to know whether the company is increasing its client base by achieving orders from new customers. Consequently, information on when the customer placed the first order must be available. The client database would need to include a field giving the date of the first order received from each client. Then an analysis on the number of new customers over a period could be obtained. In a basic client database such information may not be readily available. Thus a careful consideration of the requirements before developing the system would affect the content and structure of the database.

Functionality

Database packages can be used to perform all the standard file handling operations such as adding, deleting and editing records. Other applications include the ability to search for records quickly and list records satisfying given conditions (e.g. obtaining a list of all the suppliers of a particular item of stock). A database package can also be used to sort records in a required order and produce reports of selected data in a specified format. Such facilities will enable a manager to make decisions based on accurate and reliable information. Figure 7.2 illustrates how a detailed analysis of requirements leads on to a practical database design and development. Such a database ultimately provides information for the manager enabling more informed and rational decisions to be made.

Some business and management applications are often linked to databases such as stock control, project management and elements of accounting. These application packages take the required data from computer files and manipulate them to suit specific requirements. Such applications will be discussed in the following sections in this Chapter. Some of the well known database packages include *dBase, Paradox, Access, FoxPro* and *DataEase*.

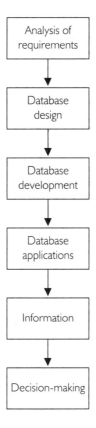

Figure 7.2   Database development and use

Self-assessment questions _____

1   Consider any organisation with which you are familiar. List the types of files that are likely to be kept by such an organisation.

2   An insurance company keeps a file on all its customers. List the various fields you consider should be included on each record in such a file.

Document presentation

The following packages in this section summarise a range of software involved with the production and enhancement of documents together with some graphics applications. The packages described here include Word Processing, Desktop Publishing, Graphics and Design.

Word processing

A word processing package enables the user to create documents such as letters, forms and reports. The documents created can then be edited, modified and printed very quickly and easily, and can be saved onto a disk for later use. Word processing can significantly improve the presentation of documents by highlighting text (e.g. underline, bold and italics), using different font types and sizes, and of course eliminating many of the typing errors before printing.

Most of the popular word processing packages have **spell checkers** with dictionaries and thesaurus available. Another important facility available in many word processors called **mail-merge**, is the ability to link text to data files in order to create customised documents. For example, a **standard letter** could be produced, names could then be taken from a database and transferred into the standard letter in order to produce personalised letters. A number of word processing packages have graphics capabilities enabling graphs, diagrams and tables to be incorporated into any document.

Some well-known word processing packages include *WordPerfect, Word, WordStar* and *Ami Pro.*

Self-assessment questions

1   Word processors have a variety of facilities to assist in the creation of documents. Describe each of the following common facilities and list their advantages:

   (i)   moving and deleting blocks of text
   (ii)   changing margins and tabs
   (iii) using a thesaurus
   (iv) mail merging.

   Are there any disadvantages and potential problems in using any of these facilities?

2   Word processing packages are not very useful when dealing with documents containing complex graphics or pictures. Would you agree with this statement with reference to the latest word processing packages?

Graphics

Graphics packages can be used to create **images** – graphs, symbols, diagrams and logos. Such packages will have drawing facilities enabling the user to draw lines, circles, rectangles and simple shapes as well as freehand drawing. Colours and shading can be used to enhance the images created. Text can usually be added in a variety of fonts and sizes. The editing facilities in most graphics packages would normally allow images to be moved, rotated and re-sized. Many graphics packages include libraries of sample graphics and page designs (e.g. backgrounds, borders and colours).

Such packages can be used to produce professional graphics for use in screen shows or the production of presentation slides. Graphics packages can be extremely useful for those involved in training, marketing, sales, or any area where high quality presentations are desirable. Figure 7.3 shows a sample screen taken from a popular graphics package.

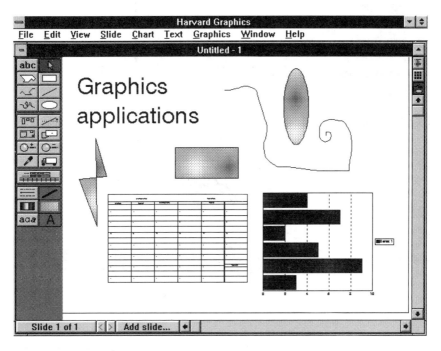

Figure 7.3   Graphics – sample screen

Packages such as *Freelance, Harvard Graphics, PC Paintbrush, CorelDraw* and *Adobe Illustrator* are well-known packages in this area.

Desktop publishing

Desktop publishing (DTP) packages enable the user to combine text and graphics into a professional layout for possible publication. Page design and formats are chosen such as the use of newspaper-type columns for text. Text and simple graphics can be created in these packages or more often imported from other packages. Basic creation and editing of a large amount of text is best achieved using a word processing package. Blocks of text can then be brought into the DTP package for further manipulation and enhancement. It should be noted that many word processing packages have DTP facilities already incorporated.

DTP packages are excellent for producing publishing-quality material and can be used for creating a range of documents such as news sheets, communications material, promotional literature and sales leaflets. Figure 7.4 shows a sample screen from a well-known DTP package. This screen shows the preview of a full page using a newspaper layout. The screen includes a standard Windows-based display with a main menu, scroll bars and a tools bar displaying some icons for the creation of text and basic graphics.

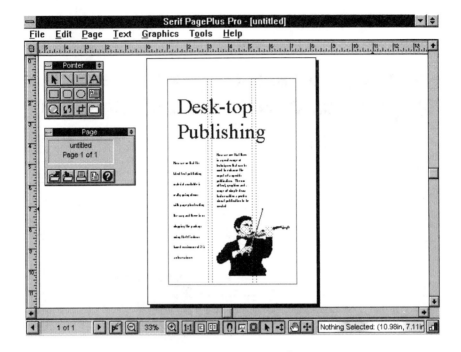

Figure 7.4   Desktop publishing – sample screen

Some well-known DTP packages include *Pagemaker, Ventura, Timeworks* and *Gem* DTP.

Design

Computer-aided design (CAD) packages enable the user to produce designs much quicker and easier than traditional pen and paper systems. Using a **CAD package,** the designer can produce drawings on the screen. Three-dimensional images can be produced, rotated, and viewed from any angle. The overall design can be split into any number of components and can be amended and redrawn when necessary. Finally, the CAD package will produce top quality prints of the designs when required.

Such packages are used in various design environments such as engineering (e.g. designing cars), architecture and interior design. A recent development is the combination of CAD software to manufacturing (computer-aided manufacturing – CAM). **CAD/CAM systems** enable direct links between the actual design process and the tools used for production. For example, a change in the design of a particular item or component may require certain machine settings to be modified. The CAD/CAM system will enable this process to be automated.

Some examples of CAD packages include *AutoCAD, Elektra, Claris CAD* and *IBM CAD.*

Self-assessment questions

1 Discuss the differences between graphics and desktop publishing packages.

2 You have been asked to produce an internal information bulletin for your company. Your manager tells you that in order to produce it you will need DTP and graphics packages. Is that correct? Are there other packages that you may need? If so, why?

Data manipulation

The following packages illustrate how data can be used and manipulated to provide information for the manager. In this category packages such as spreadsheets, accounting packages, data analysis, and mathematical software will be considered.

Spreadsheets

A spreadsheet package enables the user to create a table of data on the computer screen. A table produced using a spreadsheet package consists of a number of rows and columns. The rows and columns are usually labelled as shown in Figure 7.5. Each cell can be identified by its row and column as illustrated. Data such as numbers, text or formulae can be inserted into any cell within the table.

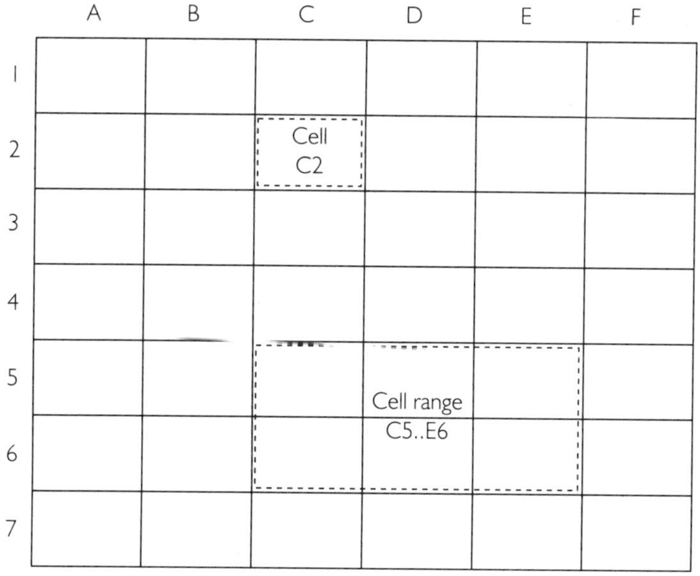

Figure 7.5   Spreadsheet – rows, columns and labels

Spreadsheets are one of the most popular microcomputer packages. They can be used for a wide range of applications. The spreadsheet package will enable the user to add columns of figures, calculate percentages and perform a range of complex calculations on any of the cells contained within the table. Such spreadsheets can be used to produce a variety of information such as budgets, cash flow, stock lists and sales forecasts. The spreadsheet could be used for controlling and monitoring performance, as well as planning and forecasting based on the available information. Figure 7.6 shows a sample screen containing a cash flow example produced using a spreadsheet package.

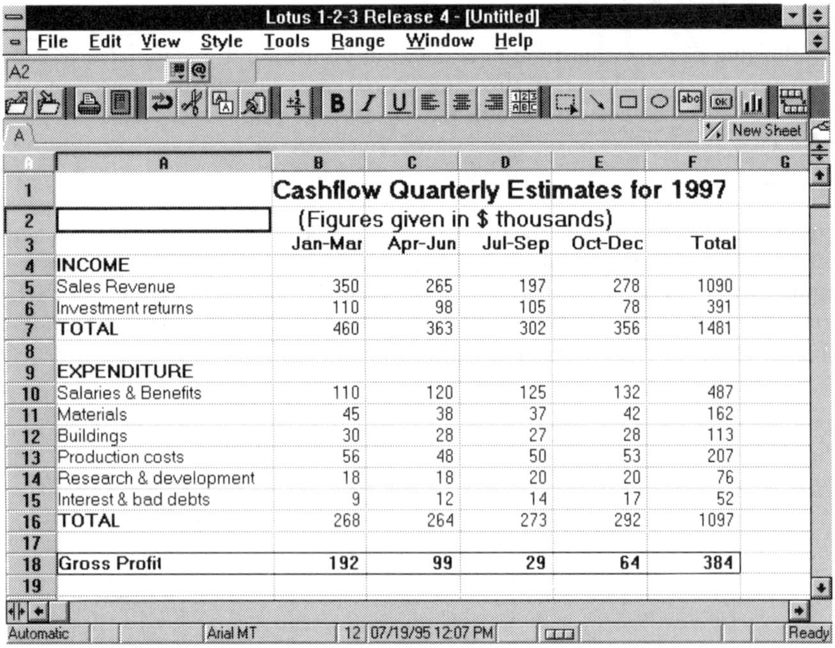

		Lotus 1-2-3 Release 4 - [Untitled]					

Cashflow Quarterly Estimates for 1997
(Figures given in $ thousands)

	A	B	C	D	E	F	G
		Jan-Mar	Apr-Jun	Jul-Sep	Oct-Dec	Total	
4	INCOME						
5	Sales Revenue	350	265	197	278	1090	
6	Investment returns	110	98	105	78	391	
7	TOTAL	460	363	302	356	1481	
8							
9	EXPENDITURE						
10	Salaries & Benefits	110	120	125	132	487	
11	Materials	45	38	37	42	162	
12	Buildings	30	28	27	28	113	
13	Production costs	56	48	50	53	207	
14	Research & development	18	18	20	20	76	
15	Interest & bad debts	9	12	14	17	52	
16	TOTAL	268	264	273	292	1097	
17							
18	Gross Profit	192	99	29	64	384	
19							

Figure 7.6   Spreadsheet – sample screen

Spreadsheets can also help solve the 'What If?' problems. For example, what if we increase advertising expenditure by 10% how will it affect sales? What if salaries are increased by 4% how will it affect our profitability? If the spreadsheet has been set up correctly such questions can be considered simply by changing values in appropriate cells in the table.

Most spreadsheet packages have graphics facilities enabling the user to produce graphs (e.g. **pie charts** or **bar graphs**) of data entered into the table. Some spreadsheet packages also have simple database facilities enabling lists of items in cells to be sorted, or specified items located quickly.

Some of the well-known spreadsheet packages include *Lotus 123, Excel, Quattro Pro* and *Supercalc.*

Self-assessment questions

1 Consider the variety of data and information you handle at work. Give examples of the data that could be set up on a spreadsheet. How would the spreadsheet package help?

2 Are spreadsheets being used in your department/company or organisation? If so, obtain a list of the spreadsheet packages available.

Accounting packages

Accounting packages enable the user to produce a range of accounts such as sales ledgers, purchase ledgers, balance sheets and profit and loss accounts. This is one type of application package that is clearly aimed at a specific user, and it is assumed that such users will have a working knowledge of the processes involved in the creation of such accounts. A user with no financial/accounting background would find such packages very difficult to use. However, the latest packages provide on-screen help facilities including help in context, and a novice user who is familiar with the use of other packages, should be able to use the basic processes without too many problems.

Accounting packages can often be linked to other systems such as databases as well as more specific software such as stock control. Packages such as *Sage, Pegasus, Sterling* and *Axis* are available in this area.

Data analysis

Data analysis packages (so-called **statistical packages**) enable data obtained from surveys to be collated and results produced in a meaningful way. Raw data obtained from questionnaires or interviews are fed into the package and can be analysed in a variety of ways. Simple counts of responses to questions can be obtained. Relationships between responses to different questions can also be obtained using cross-tabulation. Figure 7.7 shows such a cross-tabulation giving the responses of employees to a question on working conditions compared with their current grades.

Further statistical analyses can be performed on such data. For example, to investigate the relationship between the two sets of responses shown in Figure 7.7 a variety of **significance tests** can be used such as those involving correlation, chi squared, and analysis of variance. Such tests can generally be performed using most of the available data analysis packages.

Many data analysis packages will enable the user to produce graphical output from the information collected and more sophisticated analyses such as correlation and regression can be obtained. Such packages can be used to analyse market research data and information obtained from surveys of customers, clients and employees.

Some well-known data analysis packages include *SPSS, Workbench, Plan* and *Statgraphics*.

		Number of responses				Total
		Excellent	Good	Average	Poor	
	A	15	42	50	9	116
	B	20	24	48	15	107
Departments	C	30	20	27	8	85
	D	6	54	17	5	82
	E	3	28	62	11	104
Total		74	168	204	48	494

Figure 7.7   Cross tabulation – responses to survey of employee attitudes to working conditions

Mathematical software

This type of package can be used to perform a variety of mathematical processes. For example, there are packages to perform algebraic manipulations e.g. equations can be entered and the package used to transform and solve for different variables. Such packages would also allow for equation editing at each stage. Mathematical or **numerical packages** would be useful for engineering and scientific calculations.

More complex mathematical processes can be incorporated such as analytical algebra including vectors, matrices, differential and integral calculus. Other facilities such as nonlinear simulation, optimisation, recursion and iteration are also available. Non-mathematicians would be well advised to avoid this type of package! However, there are simpler facilities available that can be very useful, and can benefit the less mathematically able such as two-dimensional and three-dimensional plotting, and curve fitting. Such facilities will display the plots or curves on the screen. Using the screen display, changes in specific values can then be made and the corresponding changes in the plots visually produced. Finally hard copies of such plots can usually be obtained.

A selection of the mathematical or numerical packages currently available are *Derive, Axiom, Maple V, Math CAD* and *Sciconic*.

Management aids

The packages in this section provide a range of tools to assist the manager in specific diverse applications. Some of these packages such as Stock Control can be used to link in to database packages but can be used as standalone systems. In this category we have packages such as stock control, project management, training, expert systems and simulation.

Project management

Such packages enable the manager to plan, monitor and control projects involving a number of interrelated activities. Details on these activities are fed into the package such as expected durations and relationships with other activities. The package then produces an analysis of the overall project such as graphical outputs, networks and Gantt charts. A simple example of this is shown below, though a detailed look at project planning is outside the scope of this book.

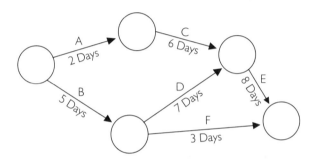

Figure 7.8   Network – illustrating the links between activities

Consider a project consisting of six activities A, B, C, D, E and F. The duration of these activities and the relationship between them can be illustrated on a network as shown in Figure 7.8. For example, the network shows that activity C comes after activity A. Also activity E follows both C and D. The Gantt chart of this project given in Figure 7.9 shows the durations of the activities and the possible start and finish times. The dotted lines indicate flexibility for some activities. For example, activity A should finish after day 2 though could actually go on until day 6 if necessary.

Such diagrams could be produced by a project management package. The manager can use this information to consider when activities should be commenced, how much flexibility there is, and which activities are critical in terms of completing the project on time. Activities that have fallen behind schedule can also be highlighted. Such packages can be invaluable for the management of large projects involving hundreds of activities.

Project, Project Manager Workbench, CA Superproject, TimeLine and *Pertmaster* are examples of project management packages.

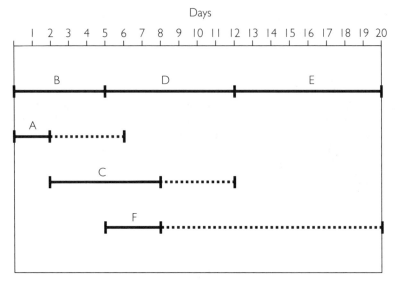

Figure 7.9 Gantt chart – illustrating activity start and finish times

Self-assessment questions

1 Consider possible applications of a project management package in your own organisation. Can you think of large projects, involving many activities, currently being undertaken? How are staff scheduled on such projects?

2 You have been asked to conduct a survey into employees' attitudes to current working conditions. Your survey should include questionnaires, interviews and observation of employees to discover which company facilities are used. List the activities that you consider would be required in such a project. How would you estimate the timescale for the completion of this survey?

Stock control

Stock control (or **inventory control**) packages assist in the managing of stock levels in commercial or industrial situations. Such systems are often linked to a database where details of each stock item would be stored. The stock control package will contain details such as re-order levels for items order quantities, delivery times, alternative items, and suppliers' information.

The package can produce reports on current stock, items out of stock and usage details. The stock control package may be able to automatically re-order items when stock levels have reached a minimum level, and can be linked to the Accounts systems for keeping track of expenditure. These packages are sometimes linked to point-of-sale systems. For example, when an item is purchased, this is registered at the pay till, and automatically the stock level record is adjusted.

There are a number of off-the-shelf stock control packages available, though companies often require modifications to these packages or develop tailor-made packages in order to satisfy their own specific requirements.

Training programs

Computer-based training (**CBT**) packages are available in a variety of subject areas. Such packages enable the user to study a particular topic by using a standard computer system. The training tends to be **interactive** – the user follows information and details on the screen, responds to questions, and can be tested at regular intervals to reinforce learning points. Business simulations, case-studies, and self-testing can all form part of a CBT package. Popular areas of application for CBT are, not surprisingly, computing and the use of computer packages (computer-based tutorials). Other disciplines are also catered for by a range of CBT materials, including training in accounting, finance, management, communications, languages and industrial-based applications.

Developments in laser disk technologies (see Chapter 4) have enhanced the potential of CBT. For example, **interactive video** has been used in management training for many years. CD-ROM, CD-I and DV-I are potential tools for improving CBT by incorporating high quality graphics and video sequences into a learning programme. The development of new Authoring tools has made the production of such CBT a realistic proposition.

Many **authoring systems** enable users to generate training material, often without the need for programming skills. Such systems range from those requiring an in-depth knowledge of a programming language to those where a mouse interface is all that is required. Many of the authoring systems are menu-driven, and enable the 'author' to produce training packages by creating individual screens and then specifying the links between these screens. A number of the most popular authoring packages are Windows-based, allowing easy manipulation of graphics and text, and providing straightforward methods of setting up complex routings between screens.

Figure 7.10 shows a typical screen in an authoring package enabling the user to choose the next screen (or page) to view by clicking the mouse whilst pointing to an appropriate button or area on the screen. The types of packages that can be produced using such authoring tools range from purely presentation systems, where a sequence of screens is continuously displayed, to fully interactive systems enabling the users to determine their own unique paths through the material.

A range of authoring tools are currently available including *Authorware, IconAuthor, MM-Box* and *Top-Class.*

Expert systems

Expert systems are computer packages designed to mimic the decision-making processes of experts in a given field. Such systems should enable the non-expert to perform as effectively as the expert. An expert system contains knowledge and rules on the given topic and has the ability to learn new rules as it is being used. In order to solve problems the system can interrogate the user. The user responds to questions presented, and the system will make inferences from these responses. The system will then make the best decision, or offer alternatives, based on the information available.

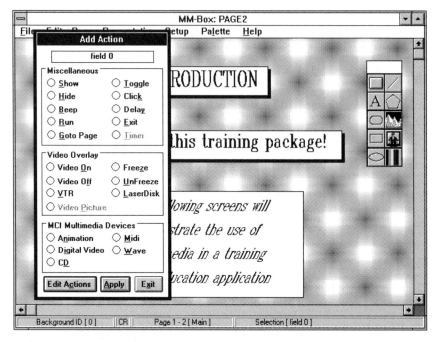

Figure 7.10   Typical authoring package screen display

Early expert systems were developed for medical diagnosis. A doctor would be asked questions about the patient's symptoms. This would prompt the doctor to perform certain tasks e.g. take the patient's temperature or measure pulse rate. Finally the system would be able to give a diagnosis and recommend certain treatments e.g. drug prescriptions.

A range of expert systems are available including those in the following areas: investment analysis, advice on pension rights and tax liabilities, company marketing and strategy, dismissal procedures and credit ratings. Not surprisingly, there is even an expert system to help select the best computer system available, subject to a user's requirements.

A number of so-called expert system shells are commercially available. A 'shell' provides a framework for the creation of expert systems in a variety of applications. The knowledge expert, working with a computer specialist, can use such a shell to generate systems in specific areas. The shell will often be menu-driven, and converts the users' choices into complex commands to be used later when the expert system is operated.

Some current expert system shells include *Leonardo, Poplog-Flex* and *XpertRule.*

Simulation

Many of the basic simulation packages could be included in the mathematical package section. Such packages, sometimes referred to as Modelling packages, include the ability to simulate (or model) specific situations in order to consider possible or optimum solutions. Applications for such packages would include the consideration of many financial and economic problems. Other applications include those in stock control, queueing, pricing and employment areas. Discrete event or continuous simulation systems are available for manufacturing and business modelling. Often such simulations include graphics and animation to provide a visual display of the simulation in progress. A range of such graphical displays are available from the use of simple pictorial models using pictures, text and graphs, to dynamic models of populations and complex mathematical models.

Other simulation packages include those usually referred to as **business simulations** (or business games). Business simulation provides a useful training and development vehicle for understanding a range of areas such as finance, marketing, decision-making processes, team work, team building, business planning, production and scheduling. Often using such a package, users are split into groups, and encouraged to compete against each other. Each group would often represent a different company/organisation and as such the groups compete for market share, market penetration and turnover. The winning group will inevitably need to work together as a coordinated team, and would be judged on their final profitability, market share, or other element appropriate to the learning situation.

Other more focused simulations are available such as a package specifically designed for the Building Industry. This package provides simulations for the design of heating and ventilation systems. The user can input a variety of variables and evaluate the resulting outcomes such as heat loss and condensation limits. Other simulations on refrigeration, fire and smoke containment processes are also provided.

This category of software contains a wide variety of packages including *BossCat, Flair, Model Builder* and *Siman*.

Integrated packages

As indicated from the previous descriptions, applications packages available for microcomputers are many and diverse. It should be noted that the distinction between some of these packages is extremely blurred. For example, some spreadsheet packages include database facilities, word processors may contain database or graphics options, and database systems could have word processing capabilities. Integrated packages have been produced incorporating the main applications. For example, a number of software producers offer database, spreadsheet and word processing facilities incorporated into a single integrated package. Such packages enable easy transfer of data from one application to another. Consequently a spreadsheet can be produced and added into a word-processed document, or a list of records can be transferred from a database into a spreadsheet. Figure 7.11 illustrates a screen from an integrated package where three different applications (wordprocessing, spreadsheet and database) are running simultaneously.

Examples of integrated packages include *Microsoft Works, Microsoft Office, Lotus Works* and *Smartware*.

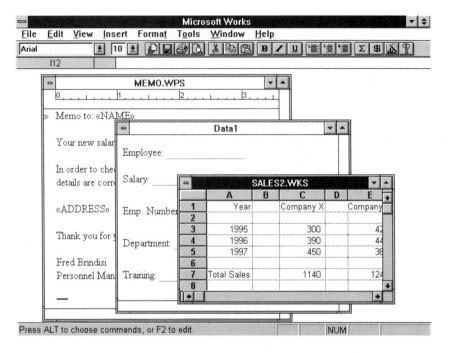

Figure 7.11   Integrating three applications on one screen

Systems software

This section contains descriptions of a range of computer software that assists the user in many technical ways. Such software would aid the user in file handling, copying and converting files, transferring data between computers, and provide useful add-ons to the range of packages already described. Without doubt, the most important software in this category is the **operating system.** Operating systems have been introduced in Chapter 4 and further details will be given in the following sections. In addition, packages such as desktop accessories, communications, and utilities are considered as part of the systems category of software.

Operating systems

An operating system consists of a suite of programs and is vital to the running of any application packages. The operating system acts as a buffer between the user, application packages, and the hardware. Figure 7.12 illustrates the relationship between the hardware, operating system, applications and end users. The operating system (OS) will perform a supervisory role for the running of all software.

Much of the operating systems will be stored ready for automatic loading when required. In microcomputers the OS is likely to be stored on a **ROM** (read-only memory) microchip with the remaining sections on **hard disk.** When the computer is switched on, the OS will automatically be loaded. This process is referred to as

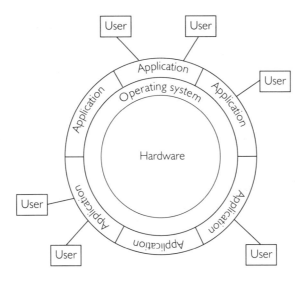

Figure 7.12   The role of an operating system

'booting up'. Examples of microcomputer operating systems include MS-DOS (usually abbreviated to DOS), UNIX, OS/2 and the Apple Macintosh system. An operating system has a variety of functions including the following:

User interface
The OS provides an interface between the user and hardware. Users can interact with the operating system by a variety of means depending on the system in use. For instance, users can type in commands at the keyboard using operating systems such as MS-DOS or UNIX. Alternatively, a mouse interface is provided on some operating systems enabling users to choose from menus or click on icons. The Macintosh OS is a primary example of this interface method, though other operating systems are now adopting the same approach such as later versions of DOS and UNIX. Popular icon-based interfaces such as Microsoft Windows provide a 'shell' for DOS users giving a standardised operating method used in a range of application packages. Whichever system is running, users can use the OS interface for a range of tasks such as to access files, execute programs, move and copy files, and carry out other file management tasks.

Input/output
The OS provides communication between the central processing unit and the input and output devices. Input/output commands are supervised within the OS which controls the flow of data to and from appropriate devices. For example, if data is printed out within an application package, the OS will control the transfer of data to the correct device and ensure that different documents sent to the printer do not get mixed together.

Memory management
The OS controls the programs and data that are stored in the computer's main memory. Modern systems enable the operation of a number of applications simulta-

neously. Since the main memory is often unable to store all the programs together, memory management will often involve the relocation of parts of programs and/or data when required. Thus, modules of the application packages required are transferred into the memory, whilst other unwanted sections are removed. From the users' point of view it looks as though all the packages and data are located together in the main memory.

Backing storage

The continual reading and writing or transfer of files between the backing stores (such as hard or floppy disks) and main memory requires management of these processes. The OS locates required files contained on the backing stores and ensures that such files are not accidently over-written.

Job scheduling

The OS enables a range of tasks to be run in parallel. Thus data can be sent for printing at the same time as other functions (such as keyboard entry) are taking place. This involves the scheduling of tasks, and giving priority to important functions so that a number of applications can be run together. The OS will prioritise the tasks required from the different programs so that the applications run in the most efficient way. This is sometimes referred to as **multi-tasking.**

Compatibility

Application packages would not be able to run without the use of a compatible operating system. The choice of specific package depends on the required operating system. Thus a user with a computer running with DOS is restricted to a choice between the DOS-based application packages. Many software manufacturers produce several versions of popular application packages to run on different operating systems. For instance there are different versions of *Microsoft Excel* (a spreadsheet package) to run on the Macintosh OS and Windows.

Desktop accessories

A range of accessories are available to provide additional facilities for the user. Such desktop accessories are often obtained as separate modules and may provide add-ons to existing packages or standalone elements. Packages in this category include those providing facilities such as Personal Organisers. In this group of software there would be the following:

- **Appointment scheduler.**   This provides a calendar into which details of meetings and appointments could be entered. The package then reminds the user when a specific meeting is due.
- **Calculator.**   Provides the standard facilities available on normal calculators such as the basic arithmetic operations, together with simple functions such as square root and memory. Some calculator accessories also include the more complex facilities such as trigonometric functions, logarithmic and exponential expressions. A number of such accessories actually display the calculator on the screen and enable the user to use the mouse to click on buttons, thus mimicking the actual key presses on a hand-held calculator.
- **Notepad.**   A simple text editing facility often linked to the appointment scheduler for easy creation and editing of simple documents or memos.
- **Data file.**   This facility would enable the creation and manipulation of simple files

and would be ideal for small personal files on names and addresses or telephone numbers. Such accessories are not intended for large applications, and a file containing more than 30-50 records would probably be better created using a database package.

- **Auto dialler.**   This small accessory enables the automatic dialling of telephone numbers from a telephone directory previously entered, i.e. using the data file of telephone numbers described in the previous paragraph.
- **Clock.**   This enables the current time to be displayed on the screen, either permanently or at the users request. It is also likely to have some type of alarm facility to make the user aware of a particular pre-determined time e.g. for important meetings.
- **Fonts.**   Some accessories provide additional font types, styles and sizes for use in other packages such as word-processors, spreadsheets or desktop publishing.
- **Colour.**   This type of accessory can provide additional colours, or colour separation facilities for producing hard copies of documents produced using desktop publishing with colour graphics.

There is a vast range of these desktop accessories such as bitstream font packs, *Facelift*, *Highjack* and *Sidekick*. It should be noted that some software packages incorporate many of the accessories described in this section. For example, Microsoft Windows includes a number of these accessories including calculator, clock and a simple data file facility.

Communications

An earlier chapter on communications has dealt with this area in some detail. However, this chapter would not be complete without summarising some basic facilities provided in this category of software. Specifically, communications software will enable your standalone microcomputer to link to other computer systems. Such links can be via the standard telephone network and will require the use of a modem to provide the physical link between your computer and the telephone lines. A basic facility provided by this category of software will be the provision of initialisation instructions for the modem. The software will also handle the flow of data from the computer, and will interpret and transmit keyboard commands from the user, thus enabling the transfer of files over the telephone line to other computers and remote terminals.

Such software can also handle incoming data from remote terminals, display such data on the screen, and operate other devices such as printers and drives. It should be noted that two or more computers can be linked locally without the use of telephone systems and modems. Two computers could be linked simply with the use of a cable and an appropriate communication package housed on both machines. This would be useful for the transfer of data between standalone systems, and the file transfer between machines of a different configuration e.g. between an Apple Mac and an IBM PC.

A range of communication software exists including the following: *CrossTalk*, *DataFlex*, *Microsoft LAN Manager*, *Norton*, *Kermit*, *Teemtalk* and *Windows 95*.

Utilities

This category of software includes those programs produced to accomplish a variety of tasks common to many users. The category of software described under the desktop accessories section could be regarded as being similar. However, this section concentrates on the common utilities often involving file management problems.

Utilities can provide upgraded file management features such as speedy access to files and file details, and faster file transfer capabilities. Many utility programs are available to assist in the recovery of corrupted or damaged files. Other facilities include the ability to monitor program executions, performance monitoring and the graphical display of results. Disk maintenance, data protection, data back-up and virus checking are other important facilities included.

Other utilities perform a range of tasks including obtaining screen dumps (screen capture programs), conversion of files between a variety of file formats e.g. converting PCX files to TIF format, or ASCII files to text. Another group of utilities are involved in file security systems. For example, the generation of security levels on data files, or the creation of passwords to be used when moving from one application to another.

The following give a selection of this type of software: *Direct Access, Norton, PC Tools,* and *Symantic Anti-Virus.*

Self-assessment questions

I   Consider any microcomputers that you are familiar with. Which operating systems do they use? Is it obvious? Look at any documentation on the software or packages that you currently use. Does this give you information about the required operating systems?

Summary

A wide range of application packages for microcomputers are currently available to assist managers. Such packages include the following applications:

- Databases, used to create and edit computer files;
- Data manipulation packages, for the manipulation and analysis of numerical and financial data, such as, spreadsheets, accounting, data analysis, mathematical software;
- Document presentation, for the creation of documents containing text and graphical information which include word processing, desktop publishing, graphics, design;
- Management aids, involving a diverse range of packages that can assist the user in many ways such as: project management, stock control, training, expert systems, simulation.

Many of the listed packages can be linked together so that data from one package can be used in another. Integrated packages are also available that incorporate many of the applications into one suite of software. For example, an integrated package would often include database, spreadsheet and word processing facilities, and would allow easy transfer of data between the applications.

A range of systems software has also been explored including the operating systems without which application packages could not function. Other software of a more technical nature has also been explored such as: desktop accessories, communications and utilities. Specific examples of commercially available packages in each of these software categories have also been included in this chapter.

Questions for discussion

I   The list shown below gives a number of jobs which you may wish to complete using a microcomputer. In each case state the type of package or packages you could use:

- Produce a balance sheet and profit and loss account for your company.

- Obtain a list of stock items available in your warehouse.

- Produce a promotional leaflet for your organisation to include graphs and illustrations.

- Estimate sales figures for next year based on data from the previous five years.

- Create a company logo and then use it to design company stationery.

- Schedule work over the next six months for your staff who are involved in working on a major contract.

- Create a report on the monthly income and profit within each department in your company, and send this report to all 120 managers with a covering letter.

- Set up an Open Learning Centre in you organisation where employees can attend in their own time to acquire vocational and non-vocational skills.

- Analyse the responses from a questionnaire sent out to all employees in your company and produce a report of the results.

2   There are likely to be a number of databases that contain information on you as an individual. Discuss what details are likely to be kept on you in different databases such as those in:

- Central or Local Government

- Your own company

- Local clubs/societies

- Marketing/promotion organisations

Problems

I   Investigate the use of microcomputer applications in your organisation. Are spreadsheets, databases, word processors, etc. being used? List the names of the applications packages used. Note the version number for each product as well as the name e.g. Lotus 123 version 5.

2 List the advantages of integrated packages over standalone packages such as Lotus 123 and dBase. Are there any disadvantages of such packages?

3 You have been asked to write a report on the productivity of the twenty production teams in your company. The report is for senior management and should include monthly production figures for all twenty teams over the past year. Which application package(s) would you use in order to produce this report?

4 Some spreadsheet packages have simple database facilities incorporated. Discuss the advantages and disadvantages of using such a facility instead of a standard database package. In what situations would you use such a facility?

5 How are utility programs used to assist the user in the management of computer files?

6 How would a screen dump facility aid a user in producing high quality documents?

7 A simulation package is only useful for modelling mathematical situations. Is this true? Give reasons for your answer.

8 Why are operating systems so important? What functions do they carry out when you run application packages?

Case-study 7.1: Electrical goods wholesaler – data files and text processing

You are the Regional Sales Manager for a large electrical goods wholesaler. You have a team of six salespersons to cover the Southern England region. A computer file is available on a microcomputer system containing a list of over 500 clients in this region.

The UK Sales Manager has asked all the Area Managers to promote a new line of goods. She has commented, 'You all have your own data files containing lists of our clients, so it should not be difficult to produce personalised letters to accompany our new literature'.

Your secretary complains that the clients' details in the file are not in the right format to be of any use in this task. 'I can't even start the letter off correctly', she complains. 'Our file just doesn't have all the correct information. Some of the required details are missing, and others are displayed in the wrong way.'

1 Describe the process that will enable personalised letters to be obtained using an existing file.

2 State what information will be required in the clients' file in order to produce these personalised letters. For example, which fields will be needed e.g. the client's forename, surname, etc.

3 Describe in general what details should be kept on your clients in order to be sure that enough data is available in order to satisfy any possible future requirements.

Case-study 7.2:   Northern Comms Ltd, publishing and printing

You are Production Manager in a company called Northern Comms Ltd. This company specialises in the production of text-based material such as leaflets, promotional literature and advertising posters. The company has been involved in the production and editorial of a local monthly journal called *In The Know*. This journal provides information on a range of events and leisure activities in the region. Such information would include details of theatre programmes, musicals, concerts, demonstrations and sports events, opening times for local museums, galleries, displays, leisure centres and country parks. Also included is information on where to stay such as hotels and guest houses, and where to eat such as restaurants, cafes and fast food outlets.

Two full-time members of staff are involved in collecting information from all of these sources. Information is sent regularly from some sources. It is advantageous for any group or individual to have their information included in this journal. It provides a good way of obtaining free promotion of events and activities. The journal is free to readers, and is delivered to over 100,000 homes on a regular basis. Income is obtained from extra advertising purchased enabling larger displays of details for specific events or facilities to be displayed. The two members of staff also get involved in obtaining additional information by telephoning local centres, theatres, and Local Authority leisure departments and other suppliers.

In The Know has been published for the last 8 years and has been Northern Comms Ltd most successful single venture. Income from advertising in this journal has declined over the past two years, and during the last year the journal made a loss for the first time. The Managing Director has asked you on several occasions to provide a breakdown on the production costs and how they affect the overall profitability. This information has been difficult to provide because of existing systems in operation.

Criticisms of the Journal have been made by local readers, the most common ones being:

- information contained in *In The Know* is not always accurate, and up-to-date.
- a lot of events taking place in the region that are not included in the journal.
- many people, including some of the advertisers, have criticized the presentation and overall layout of the journal.
- some items are difficult to find in the journal
- pages are considered to be old-fashioned.

More pictures and graphics would be helpful to overcome some of these problems. However, changes are required which will benefit the whole range of text-based material.

1   Comment on the production of this journal with specific reference to the current problems.

2   Can you suggest a range of software that could be used by Northern Comms Ltd in order to improve on the present situation and which will benefit all the product ranges?

Case-study 7.3:   Body Beautiful Clothing, wholesalers, computer applications
A wholesale company based in Birmingham called Body Beautiful Company, is involved in distributing clothing goods to a range of retailers spread throughout the UK. Annual sales during last year totalled £1.2 million. The main warehouse is approximately 30,000 square feet and is currently operating at just over 60% capacity. Two further distribution centres are located in Edinburgh and Bristol with around 12,000 square feet of floor space at each site.

Currently standalone microcomputer systems are used at each site. However, Margaret Broadbent, the General Manager at Birmingham is dissatisfied with these systems. Currently the computers are used for accounting, in particular in calculating the payroll, and managing the billing procedures.

● Problems have been encountered in tracking a number of clothing lines.
● Some retailers are going elsewhere for certain products because of delivery delays, and orders being mis-directed and inaccurate.
● Some telephone orders have been lost because items required have not been available at one warehouse, although these items were available at other locations.
● Full information is not known by the staff receiving the orders.

More detailed information is required by the retailers about the complete range of goods available from Body Beautiful Co. Often, when sales staff call on existing customers, these retailers are surprised at the extent of the range of clothing offered.

As an external consultant, you have been requested to consider how computer systems can be used in the efficient operation of this company. In particular, give advice to Margaret Broadbent on the range of packages that could help her company.

1 Give specific examples of where each type of package could be of assistance.

2 Could a single package be purchased that covers the needs of this company?

Further reading

Athey, T.H., Day, J.C. and Zmud, R.W., *Computers and End-User Software,* Harper-Collins (Chapters 12–15) 1991

Capron H.L. and Perron, J.D., *Computers and Information Systems,* Benjamin Cummings Publishing Company (Chapters 7 & 9–12) 1993

Long, L., *Management Information Systems,* Prentice-Hall International (pp. 188–204) 1989

Mandell, S.L., *Computers and Information Processing – Concepts and Applications* 6th Ed, West Publishing Company (Chapter 13) 1992

Thomas, R. (ed) *Step-by-Step Guides* for a variety of application packages including *Lotus 1-2-3* (for DOS and Windows), *dBase III+, dBase IV, Microsoft Works, Pagemaker,* and *WordPerfect,* Stanley Thornes Publishers, 1991–1994

8 Centralised computer software

Objectives

After completing this chapter you should be able to:

- understand the role of a computer language in the development of software.
- distinguish between 1st, 2nd, 3rd and 4th generation computer languages.
- explain how to establish a database and its role in the operation of an information system.
- identify different types of fourth-generation tools and where they would be useful.

Introduction

Centralised systems usually operate on a mini or mainframe computer. The application software employed on these systems is often used simultaneously by hundreds if not thousands of people throughout the organisation.   In the past software had to be developed in-house using the procedures discussed in Chapter 11. There are now many alternatives to this situation. Advancements in both hardware and software have enabled such **software development** to be modified making savings in the analyst's and programmer's time and often more importantly speeding up the acquisition of such software.

Why does a manager need to know about programming languages and software?

The computer **programming language** and **applications software** that a company employs will affect the performance of the computing or information systems department as well as the staff in the sections or departments using the system. There have been major changes in the last decade with regard to how software is developed. Development and maintenance are very labour-intensive activities. However, since the introduction of a more powerful generation of computers, facilities have been developed that automate some of the programmer's and system developer's tasks. Once the language or software has been chosen it will probably not be changed for some years, therefore the efficiency and expenditure for the next few years is dependent upon today's choice. Many managers are unaware for example that about 75% of a computer department's costs are devoted to maintaining software that is currently in use. The term **software maintenance** is used here when referring to the following activities:

- correcting small faults or 'bugs' in a system
- amending the program to meet changing user requirements
- introducing new technology that will improve the service to users.

Chapter 11 illustrates the process that might be carried out in an organisation developing its own software. In this chapter we will explore how these procedures might be modified depending upon the availability of standard or off-the-shelf software. As the PC market has developed so has a profusion of standard software packages for all manner of applications. This has occurred because the software producers have been able to recoup their costs from a large market. The same in not quite so true for the mini or mainframe computer. The market is relatively small and thus the cost of the software cannot be spread over so many customers; however it is usually cheaper to buy off-the-shelf than for an organisation to do their own software development.

The software in use on a centralised system is not dissimilar to that available on a personal computer though its operation and abilities are somewhat different. All computers need an operating system to control the functioning of the machine. Application software and database management systems are comparable to their personal computer equivalents though because they are on a bigger machine they can handle larger databases. The computer languages that are available on personal computers are also obtainable for large machines but there are also others used for specialist situations. To help make the analyst and programmer more productive CASE tools are also available for mini and mainframe computers. Sections now follow which enlarge on each of these points.

Self-assessment questions

I   In what circumstances might a manager need to know something about programming languages and software?

Operating systems

Why does a computer need an operating system? A computer cannot function without an operating system, be it a personal computer or mini/mainframe computer. It supervises and monitors the component parts of the computer as well as its peripherals such as printers. An operating system must be able to:

1. Provide a friendly interface between the computer user and the system. This has not been the situation with mini/mainframes. In the past it has been necessary to employ systems programmers with a knowledge of the operating systems command language so that the computer could be operated efficiently. This is a very different situation to that on personal computers where 'Windows' or the 'Mac' interface made it very easy for non-computer experts to be effective users of the system.

2. Ensure that the computers resources are used efficiently. The modern centralised computer system is expensive to purchase and a return is required on that investment.

The operating system must allocate its resources appropriate to the activities that are demanding its services at that time, e.g. a large, high speed mainframe is used to service a bank's cash point tills during the lunch hour. Is the same facility needed in the early morning or late afternoon? Could the system be employed on other activities?

Chapter 7 gave a brief introduction to the operating systems available on personal computers. The operating system on a mini or mainframe computer does a similar job to that on a personal computer as well as many others. Generally speaking operating systems can be split into two types, those for single-user systems and those for multi-user systems. These two do have the following similar tasks to perform:

- organise internal RAM and external backing store;
- controlling input and output, i.e. keyboard and VDU actions, printing, communications through one of the other i/o ports;
- running an application program or database management system;
- operating compilers to convert computer programs into application software;
- display error messages when the system is not operating correctly.

The **multi-user operating system** will carry out the above activities simultaneously as well as the following.

- **Scheduling** users' employment of the central processing unit by allocating small time slices during which they have use of the system. Users are unaware of this and it gives the appearance of multi-processing because it is accomplished so quickly.
- Performing **accounting** functions such as keeping a record of the processing time each user has accumulated or the number of pages of paper used on the printer.
- **Safeguarding** the actions of the user by keeping a record of all keystrokes and other actions carried out so that in the event of a systems failure, or any other error, everything that has gone before is secure. The operating system should also control who has access to the system, e.g. by password.
- Printer control in the form of '**spooling**' will take place. A spool is a queue waiting to be printed. A large number of users simultaneously might send items to be printed on the same printer and a queue will be organised to process them sequentially in the order in which they arrived.

When is an operating system used? Most of the time the user is unaware that the operating system is in use. The operating system is utilised by the application program to save, retrieve, delete, merge, sort or print files. The user usually becomes aware of the operating system when it gives an **error message** that the application program has not been structured to deal with or where the programmer has decided that the user should get that particular message.

Where do operating systems come from? The personal computer operating system market is dominated by Microsoft's Disk Operating System (**MS-DOS**). There are competitor products for the IBM-compatible market but sales are limited. There is no significant competition from the Apple Macintosh. The mini/mainframe situation however is very different. It is dominated by the hardware manufacturer's own operating system written for that particular computer. Some manufacturers use the same operating system for their whole product range while others have a different one for each machine. Most hardware suppliers now supply their own version of **UNIX operating system**. This operating system is likely to become the industry standard and it will mean that application packages written for one system can be readily adapted to be run on any other. This will give an almost comparable situation as that prevailing in the personal computer market.

Programming languages

Programming languages are used in companies where they wish to develop software which is only applicable to their organisation. There have been many developments in this field over the years and this section will examine them.

A **language** is a system of communications. We communicate with each other using the English language unless the other person is from another country, in which case we might need to make use of a **translator.** The same is true of computers. We communicate with the computer using patterns of electrical impulses. I don't understand electrical impulses, do you? Do you want to? Some people do, and they find jobs as programmers. The development of programming languages has been to try to simplify this communication. Programming languages consist of symbols, characters and usage rules that permit us to communicate quickly with the computer. Sanders gives a good comparison of the different languages.

For some considerable time computer languages have been classified as either low level or high level depending upon whether English words can be used (as in the latter case) or not. Currently they tend to be classified as follows:

- **1st generation.**   These languages are known as **machine code** and each manufacturer of computers uses their own version. This variation in the code is dependent upon the design of the central processor that does all the work inside the computer. Most personal computers use a processor from Intel and so they all use the same machine code.
- **2nd generation.**   These are often known as **assembly languages** and are also processor dependent. However a small amount of symbolic representation is used, i.e. letters, numbers and other keyboard characters, which makes it somewhat easier to use than machine code.

These two language groups are only used today for real-time applications, e.g. machine and process control. They are not used for business applications.

- **3rd generation.**   These languages were developed in the late 1950s and updated versions of them are still used today, e.g. FORTRAN, COBOL, BASIC, Pascal. FORTRAN was originally designed for mathematical situations, i.e. FORmula TRANslation, whilst COBOL was developed as a COmmon Business Oriented Language which could file information and access it quickly. Each was good at what it was designed to do. Today these languages along with BASIC, Pascal, and a lot of others can all do the same things. They all make use of plain English words and other keyboard symbols to give instructions to the computer. The program is translated into machine code by use of an interpreter or compiler.

The use of third-generation languages is declining in the business world as programs can be developed far more quickly using fourth-generation languages. Languages such as COBOL and BASIC are still hanging on but the language suppliers have updated them so much that they are barely recognisable in comparison with the 3GL from a few years ago.

- **4th generation**. The last language to mention in this section is the most recent developments in **fourth-generation languages.** These are often spoken of as **4GLs.** Most of them make use of a **database management system** and one of the difficulties that the non-specialist might have in studying this area is that there are no standards as there are for example with Pascal. Each supplier of a 4GL produces what they think will sell best. Examples of these languages are query languages, report generators and very high level languages such as *'C'* and *ADA*.

Self-assessment questions

I   What has been the stimulus for the development of new generations of computer languages?

Programming language issues

There has been an explosion in the use of database management systems and 4GLs in the last few years and this has bought about a rethink of how computing departments are organised. The stimulus for this development has been three-fold. First the old method of program production is very labour intensive and hence costly. Secondly the advent of more powerful computers enabled the use of sophisticated tools that equip the computer to generate the software with less labour input. Finally there is the cost of failed systems which might range from not quite meeting a users requirements to major collapse and disposal costing millions of pounds.

A business manager should be concerned with a number of matters to do with the choice of how the computer software to be used in his department is obtained. Most of the points that follow might seem to be economic, as they should, but some need to take in to account other perspectives.

- The current computer staff have certain expertise: how will they fair with a new system that perhaps de-skills their job?
- How much will it cost to retrain staff to use the new system?
- What type of application is being developed? Is it in common use in many organisations or only in this one, i.e. are we going to be a test-bed for it? If it is a program that is in common usage then it might be better to purchase a standard package and have one of the end-user staff trained in the use of software. If the application is unique to one organisation it might still be possible to find an external supplier who has dealt with something similar and can modify their product to suit an organisation's circumstances. Often it is possible to buy a program that nearly satisfies requirements and the organisation's own staff can modify it to suit.
- How often will the application be processed? If the application is going to be run twenty times a second then the speed at which the system must do the job is some-

what different to a situation where a program might be run only once a day or weekly. In the first situation a **transaction processing system** or very **high level language program** might be suitable whilst in the other a **database management system** might be more appropriate. Therefore different software and possibly different types of computers will be needed for these situations.

- Will the program be changed frequently? If it can be foreseen that the software will have to be updated or changed regularly then the purchase of software that allows this is self-evident. The use of high level and very high level languages do not allow this to happen whilst many fourth-generation products, such as database management systems do.

- How well is the software supported? The suppliers of software are commercial companies that are open to the normal competitive pressures of the market place. If an organisation buys a software program they will want reassurance that the supplier will be able to modify the program if necessary or correct any faults or bugs discovered during use. Most suppliers bring out regular updates or improvements of their software. Each release of the software is given a version number to identify it as the latest version.

Self-assessment questions

I   What facilities are available to help automate the programming process? (Hint: you might need to refer to Chapter 11.)

Database management systems (DBMSs)

The discussion in this section applies in the main to large computer systems. One of the difficulties with writing on this topic at this time is that the PC network and its associated DBMS software is starting to compete with mini and mainframe computer systems. However this section applies to both.

The traditional way of developing computer applications was to identify what went on in a department and computerise it. This has to a great extent disappeared from situations where mini and mainframe computers are in use because the end-user cannot comprehend the complexities in a short space of time. However, many organisations are putting a PC on the desks of many employees and they are being encouraged to develop their own applications. This will mean that the end-user will develop uses for their PC and hold information on it that might possibly be shared with others and because they are inexpert their use of the software and PC will not be particularly efficient. Problems have also been encountered with end-users not having the logic training that is sometimes necessary to make best use of the software. This again leads to an inefficient situation where the outcome can lead to faulty results.

Figure 8.1 shows how end-users have their own applications with their own file and record structure. In this example User 1 might be the marketing manager. He will perhaps keep a record of all the purchasers of product A, month by month, in a data-

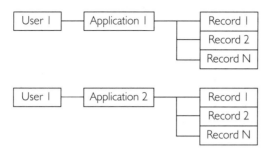

Figure 8.1   End-user file management

base (Application 1). Similarly he may keep comparable information about product B in a parallel database (Application 2). If a customer moves he will update his records with the new address. Meanwhile the accounts manager (User 2) is keeping a record of debtors, i.e. those company's that owe us money, on his own system. This will be used to chase outstanding debts to try to get what is owing to the company as quickly as possible. How will the accounts manager know that the debtor has moved? Probably when the postal service returns a bill from an empty building. In the factory the production manager (User 3) might be keeping an order file in a database so that his staff know who to dispatch the product to. Which address do they use? All three managers are making good use of their computer systems but independent systems such as this have a number of drawbacks:

- No links are developed between different departments' data. Often a department will collect data which might be useful to other departments: consider the inconvenience that might be caused in the previous example of marketing, accounts and production having different addresses for a customer.
- Data is duplicated or triplicated. This data redundancy is wasteful and can cause inconsistent updating of records so that each record is holding different versions of the same data.
- Poor security and accidental deletions. Accidents can quite easily occur with software that a person only uses occasionally. The accidental deletion of a record or field or of a whole file is not unknown, and can only be recovered by a computer expert. Similarly the casual user is often not familiar enough with the system to install adequate security.

This situation is overcome by the use of a **database management system.** A DBMS is a suite of computer programs that will create and control the data under its management. The DBMS holds each item of data only once. To be able to do this the system must be very secure and it must not be possible to accidentally delete any data. Figure 8.2 illustrates a generalised view of how a DBMS operates. Each user can have as many applications as they like and there can be a multitude of users. This system is designed to show users only the data that *they* need to see. Each user does not see all the data available and does not know from the system that other data is being held on it.

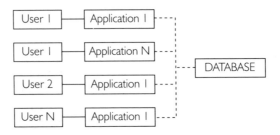

Figure 8.2   Database management

Self-assessment questions

I   List the aspects of a mainframe DBMS that are the same as a PC DBMS. What is the major differences between the two? (Hint: once again you might want to look at Chapter 7.)

The DBMS approach to managing data

The DBMS approach to data is to treat that data as a fundamental resource of the organisation that needs to be maintained correctly and kept securely. It separates the physical view and the logical view of the data, i.e. the view of the data that we get on the screen or on a printout is not how the data is stored. The data is stored in a way that suits the data and not the users or their applications. Figure 8.3 lists typical users who can prearrange to view and manipulate a subject area which will contain data associated with that subject. The changing of data within that subject area is restricted to certain people. A Database Administrator is often employed to oversee the integrity of the DBMS and authorise changes.

Each department will need to access the data they need; it is not necessary for them to have access to all of the data held. This is the reason why it is not beneficial to store the data to suit each individual user.

As the database that the DBMS controls gets larger so it becomes more difficult to keep track of data names and definitions. The Database Administrator can employ a Data Dictionary to record agreed meanings of data. In effect a data dictionary is a database that enables the standardisation of definitions or meanings and will include where the data is used and who instigated its employment.

Figure 8.3   *Typical database subjects and their possible users*

Self-assessment questions ——————————

I   What advantages or disadvantages are there to holding data definitions in a database?

Advantages and disadvantages of DBMSs

As stated earlier, DBMSs are being adopted by many organisations. This has often meant disposing of long-serving programs that the company has developed for itself over a long period of time, sometimes decades. The major advantages that these organisations have identified seem to be simplistic, and they are. The reduction of maintenance costs is a major contributor to savings, as is the ability to add applications easily. Consistent security is also of great benefit. Many of the other advantages are technical in nature but still save the organisation money.

The major disadvantage of a DBMS is the processing power necessary to create the interface between the user and 'their data' as well as allowing simultaneous access to a large number of users each with their own applications. This tends to slow the response time of the computer down and is often one of the complaints about large systems. A PC does not have this problem as its processor is dedicated to one user; in a large system it has to be shared. This speed of response is one disadvantage that has ruled DBMSs out of some applications, e.g. bank cash dispensers need to respond quickly or there will be a queue right round the block at lunch times.

Self-assessment questions _____

I   Why might the managers within a well established and profitable company not want
to dispose of software that has been developed specifically for the company by their
own staff?

Using a DBMS

The first step in employing a DBMS is to create a structure into which the data will go.
The principles involved here are no different whether a PC DBMS or a Mini or mainframe DBMS is being used.

Field name	Field length (characters)
Employee No	6
Family Name	20
name	15
Address 1	35
Address 2	35
Address 3	25
PostCode	11
Date of Birth	6

Figure 8.4   Typical database details

Decisions will need to be made about how many fields are to go into a record and how
many characters each field is to hold. Figure 8.4 illustrates the simplified structure of
part of a personnel record. Whilst most of the fields shown will contain characters it is
usually possible to specify other data types such as numbers or a date. Different staff in
the company might need to access these records but not know the employee's number.

It is possible to have a database index on any or all of the fields, however each record
must be uniquely identifiable from all or the others and this is done using the **primary
key**. In the case of personnel records it will be the employee number. If the employee
number is not known then the DBMS will search on a **secondary key**, e.g. family name
or age. This reduces the amount of searching through that must be done whilst not
having a unique **record identifier**.

Having established the structure into which data is to be placed the next stage is to
design a screen to make **data entry** as easy as possible. Continuing with the personnel
example, the data entry screen and the application form for employment would probably be designed simultaneously to facilitate ease of data entry. The ease with which
this screen can be changed is an important factor when purchasing a DBMS.

As well as entering data into each record there are other operations that it should be
possible to carry out. It is necessary to be able to:

- change the data in a field
- delete records for the database
- sort the records in different ways using indexes
- search for specific records
- carry out calculations with numeric fields.

All of these activities are carried out using a **query language** which will be discussed more fully in a later section on fourth-generation languages.

As well as record keeping and searching for individual records, a DBMS has the ability to produce regular **reports** without the need for human instruction. This is often done using the computer's clock/calender. On a particular date the system might print out a happy birthday message and send it to the employee. Well may be not. It is more likely to be a reminder from a public utility asking you to pay the bill, or a bank with a statement. The DBMS should also have the ability to produce *ad hoc* reports on things of special interest when requested. This facility starts to move the DBMS into the realm of being a part of the **management information system (MIS)** or **decision support system** and requires the use of a **report generator**. As with query languages a report generator is often referred to as a fourth-generation language and will be reviewed later in this chapter.

The last area to mention is the DBMSs ability to provide a secure environment in which to keep and manipulate data. The **security** on most DBMSs can be through the establishment of various levels of **passwords**. However with multi-user systems access can also be restricted to particular terminals or times.

Self-assessment questions _____

I   What is the difference between a primary key and a secondary key?

Types of DBMS

There are three types of DBMS available and these are mainly historical developments. Hierarchical and network database systems will not be discussed in any great depth except to illustrate their principle of operation.

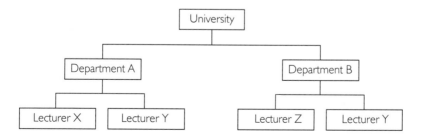

Figure 8.5   Hierarchical database management structure

Figure 8.5 shows the conceptual structure of a **hierarchical DBMS.** It has what is called a parent-child structure, where each 'child' has only one 'parent' but each 'parent' may have a number of 'children'. As the example shows lecturer Y may work in two different departments, whilst others work only in a single department.

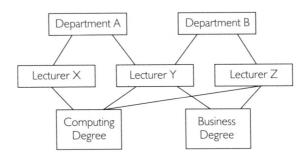

Figure 8.6   Network database management structure

Figure 8.6 illustrates a **network DBMS** which gives a much more flexible structure than a hierarchical one, as any given record can have any number of parents or any number of children. The example shows that a lecturer can work in more than one department and teach on more than one course, i.e. many-to-many relationships can be represented.

Support by the suppliers of these two types of DBMS is gradually being withdrawn as a greater emphasis is placed on **relational DBMSs.** Avison and Fitzgerald (1990) contains a concise and clear explanation of network and hierarchical DBMSs. Relational DBMSs (RDBMSs) are being widely adopted by many organisations and they offer the end-user facilities for them to develop their own applications whilst also allowing the analyst the opportunity to produce systems for more complex applications. As both of these situations can be developed on the same software, they can use each other's data.

Department records

Dept. Number	Dept. Name	Building	Head of Dept.
112			
225			
229			
365			

Lecturer records

Lecturer Number	Lecturer Name	Salary	Dept. Number
12367			
20034			
24932			
54834			

Figure 8.7   Relational structures (relations)

A RDBMS can be thought of as a simple two-dimensional table as illustrated in Figure 8.7. In the jargon of RDBMS the tables are called **relations,** and have a unique name, and depending on the books you read, the rows of the table are called **tuples** or **entities** and the columns are **domains** or **attributes.**

The process of developing a RDBMS for a complex application is much as has been described in Chapter 11. A great deal of time is devoted to the use of entity modelling techniques to ensure that data relationships are clearly defined. The use of a RDBMS is also aided by the normalising of the data. Codd (1970) developed this technique to enable the data to be structured so that it was in natural groupings and any piece of data was held uniquely whilst having the correct relationship with other data.

Normalisation

Normalisation is the process of identifying the data which is dependent upon other data for its existence. For example, Smythe Engineering might have a factory in Upper Wickham; therefore factory location is dependent on the company choosing that location.

Address

Company Number	Company Name	Address	No. of employees
22374	Smythe Eng	Upper Wickham	520
22374	Smythe Eng	Liverpool	341
22374	Smythe Eng	Manchester	133
43887	Jones Printing	Harrow	120

Figure 8.8   Relation example

Figure 8.8 illustrates a relation, called 'Address', containing details of factories and within each entity there are four attributes. The process of normalisation starts with finding a primary key for the relation. In the example of Figure 8.8 the company number might be adequate if we only want to deal with the head office but if we wish to correspond with individual factories then a unique identifier will need to be established. Subsequent stages involve splitting the relation into smaller relations so that repeating groups are removed and there is an elimination of redundant data (Howe, 1989).

Fourth-generation languages (4GLs)

The term fourth-generation language was coined to cover a variety of application languages and utilities that have been developed in recent years. They offer an increase in user friendliness and can increase the speed of program production by between 25% and 1000%. For a language to be classified as 4th generation it should have certain characteristics.

Characteristics of fourth-generation languages

With so many new products coming on the market all the time nearly all of them are promoted as being fourth-generation although they perhaps may be closer to third-generation languages. James Martin (1985) identified thirteen characteristics as identifying a computer language as 'fourth generation'. These are:

- It is user friendly.
- A non-professional programmer can obtain results with it.
- It employs a database management system directly.
- Programs for most applications can be created with one order of magnitude fewer instructions than with COBOL.
- Non-procedural code is used, where possible. (Note. A non-procedural language specifies what it is trying to achieve, not how to go about achieving it.)
- It makes intelligent default assumptions about what the user wants, where possible.
- It is designed for on-line operation.
- It enforces or encourages structured code.
- It makes it easy to understand and maintain another person's code.
- Non-DP users can learn a subset of the language in a two-day training course.
- It is designed for easy debugging.
- Prototypes can be created and modified quickly.
- Results can be obtained in one order of magnitude less time than with COBOL or PL\1 for most applications.

Martin's thirteen characteristics in themselves can be a little confusing and seem contradictory. The main message about 4GLs is that they:

- are easy to operate
- can be employed by end-users
- make use of a DBMS
- need only a short training course for the user to be productive.

So many new software tools, languages and development aids have been established in the last few years that no standards have yet been agreed. Because of these techniques interactive prototyping is/will replace the traditional systems analysis stage of user design and it is much simpler for a new analyst to modify the program or software.

Self-assessment questions _____

1   Does a spreadsheet have all or some of the above characteristics?

2   List them.

Categories of 4GLs

There are a number of ways of categorising fourth-generation languages. The one that follows seems to be the most popular.

Query languages. These are for retrieving data stored in a database or in files. They usually operate interactively in an on-line mode. They often come supplied when a DBMS is purchased though some suppliers give optional choices with their DBMSs. The defacto standard query language is **SQL** (pronounced sequel) which was developed for relational database management systems. Some DBMS suppliers still employ their own languages, e.g. *Borland* with *DBase IV* and *Paradox*.

Report generators. As the name implies a report generator can produce **customised reports** as and when people want them. They should be able to carry out complex calculations or manipulate data to go in the report. The layout of the report can be done using default settings or designed interactively by the user on the screen. IBM have marketed RPG for many years and during that time it has gone through considerable development and is used to produce reports from the files or database on a mainframe. However most DBMS suppliers provide their own report generator. So there are no standards.

Application packages. These are available for almost every business requirement that can be thought of. Application software is prewritten programs that are sold commercially to any company who wants them. Often they have a degree of tailoring available during the installation process. For example when installing an accounts package it may be possible to arrange for currency conversion to take place.

Very high level languages. *'C'* and *ADA,* with others have superseded most third generation languages. Applications produced in these languages are produced much more efficiently and in a much shorter period of time. However it is unlikely that these languages would be used in a business computing setting except for making alterations, by a programming expert, to a purchased application package which is written in it.

Application generators. These are suites of programs that enable the analyst to work interactively on the computer to specify the software requirements. The computer system then produces the program to do the job. As in so many computer areas there are no standards for application generators and the user needs to be an experienced analyst as well as have a suitable programming background to understand the logic involved. Many of the CASE tools (see Chapter 11) available to an analyst could be classed as application generators.

Decision support tools. The spreadsheet on the PC is often a major plank of decision support for managers. Following the lead of the PC market, spreadsheets are also available for mini and mainframe computers along with software which will enable access to databases or files in an entirely random way so that a manager can avail himself of data that he needs when he needs it. Other decision support tools enable information from external databases to be imported into company databases or reports.

With such a fast-moving market there is software that does not sit comfortably within these headings. The above classification is not meant to be set in stone but for use as a way of conveniently discussing what software can do.

Application software

Chapter 7 described the application software available off-the-shelf. Most of these applications are available to the mini or mainframe user but they do not have the variety in choice that the personal computer user enjoys. The only real difference between single-user and multi-user software is the ability to adjust the levels of security and file locking. DBMS's, accounting and other multi-user applications that might contain confidential data can have varying levels of password security implemented. To protect the data further and stop accidental over writing, file or record locking can be implemented. This stops two users manipulating the same file or record simultaneously.

The make or buy issue

The decision is not quite as straight forward as the title suggests. It is not just a make or buy issue as there are any number of intermediate positions between these two extremes. The following is a general rule-of-thumb that can be applied to situations.

If the software that is required will be doing a relatively simple job and is common to many organisations then buy a standard or off-the-shelf software package. Examples of this are accounting packages where there are any number of suppliers for most of the mini and mainframe computers available.

If the program is required to do a simple job but is unique to that organisation a good strategy will be to purchase **modular software** to deal with as much as possible of the requirements and have the vendors produce the 'unique' part. As the application is a simple one an alternative is to use a DBMS and train local staff to do the job.

If the application software is not simple but somewhat more complex as well as being unique to the organisation then again use modular software wherever possible but hire a competent contract programmer to produce the unique aspects that are required. Often an organisation will go to a software house that has experience of similar situations with other companies so that they can produce the package for them.

If the software is very complex and unique to the company it would probably be most economic to hire a competent programmer(s) to produce **bespoke software** for the organisation though often a software house will be asked to do this sort of job as again they may have had experiences of similar situations with other companies.

It has become common for organisations to buy all of their software from a third party supplier as it is often seen as the cheapest way of doing things. Unfortunately because an organisation is not going to go through the detailed systems analysis and design process but buy off the shelf, they also often do not do a detailed **specification of requirements**. The data structures and relationships required of the software are therefore unknown. Similarly the data structures and relationships of the standard package is also unknown which produces a double chance of incompatibility.

Self-assessment questions _____

1   What is the role of the user in the make or buy situation?

2   What will be the role of the systems staff, if there are any?

Summary

Any manager in the business situation needs to be able to discuss modern methods of obtaining software with colleagues in the systems department. The move by the computer industry away from conventional programming to other means of obtaining software has on the one hand simplified things by giving the user more power to make a choice but in doing so has hidden the need to ensure that the specification of the software is detailed enough to ensure data structure compatibility. Off-the-shelf software can make large savings for a company compared to bespoke software no matter who it is written by. The use of modern CASE tools, DBMSs and 4GLs has given a dramatic rise in the productivity of the systems department.

Questions for discussion

1 Discuss the reasons why there is so many computer languages available.

2 Why have programming languages been phased out of use for the development of business applications?

3 Discuss the reasons why database management systems have risen in popularity.

4 A software application may be developed in COBOL or using a DBMS. On screen they may look the same, but what are the main differences between them that the end user will notice?

5 What effect will using a DBMS have on the various stages of the system life-cycle?

6 For what reasons is it important to involve senior (non-computer) managers in the development of a company's information system?

7 Discuss the role of the database administrator and their possible location in the hierarchy of the organisation.

8 What are the main criteria to be considered when choosing a means of obtaining software?

Problems

1 Many end users within departments such as accountancy, marketing, personnel and general management are developing their own applications. In your own company there is a little end-user development taking place on PCs but none on the larger machines. Write a report to the General Manager explaining and giving reasons for:

a) the advantages and disadvantages of end-user development of software,

b) the type of applications end users are most likely to develop successfully.

2 The Sihe Do-It-Yourself super store has grown over the years from a small corner hardware store to its present size by moving to bigger sites around the town when expansion seemed right. The systems used within it have not progressed in quite the

same way. A batch processing computer system is used for accounts processing and payroll, and it is fairly old. The supervisor of the data processing section has been with the store since the system was installed and has not kept up with the latest developments in the computer world. At a Chamber of Commerce meeting the store owner, Fred Sihe, hears about relational databases and thinks they might be able to improve the efficiency of the company. As a newly arrived commercial graduate trainee write to Mr Sihe discussing the application of a relational database management system to the stores administration.

3   You are advising a friend on the use of computer software within his company and he is very concerned about employing a programmer or an analyst for fear of losing control of costs. He has heard about the possibility of using standard software packages. Write a report to him about the use of standard packages instead of purpose-written software. Discuss both the advantages and pitfalls.

4   You work in the administrative support section of a large insurance company. New database management software is to be introduced in the not-too-distant future and it will replace a system based on COBOL. Your manager has asked you to give a short talk to the managers and section leaders in your department. Prepare the notes for a talk to explain:

a) the difference between a database and a database management system;
b) why a DBMS might be used in preference to other forms of holding data on a computer;
c) the types of fourth-generation languages available with DBMSs and why they are necessary.

5   Your company has a data processing department which was established many years ago. All the design of new systems uses the traditional life cycle approach to systems analysis and design. The new data processing manager thinks that the use of fourth generation tools would improve the functioning of the department. Write a report to the DP manager discussing the benefits and drawbacks that could be expected if the company were to employ fourth-generation software.

6   In this day and age a company wishing to use a computer system has many alternative ways of acquiring software. This can range from writing their own programs to purchasing a standard package off-the-shelf. One such company is Aristotle Power and Heat Ltd. The billing system they have used for many years is getting very expensive to maintain and needs considerable updating. You are to make a presentation to a group of managers outlining the alternative approaches that the company could take to obtaining a new billing system, and the benefits likely to be available if redevelopment does occur. Write the notes to be issued to each person at the presentation, and indicate where any visual aids would be employed.

Case-study 8.1:   Swallow Transport Ltd, acquisition of Treacy Transport
Swallow Transport Ltd, is a transport and manufacturing company which has just taken over Treacy Transport. The takeover occurred in very amicable circumstances and it would appear that the two organisations should fit together well as they make a complementary range of products and only part of the transport networks overlap.

Treacy Transport was owned and managed by Andrew Treacy for many years and has performed well for the last five, even during the poor economic climate. Andrew's son and daughter have been active within the company during this time and are both on the board. Margaret has managed the administrative side of the business while John has looked after operations.

Mike Swallow is the chief executive of Swallow Transport and has been the driving force behind the takeover. He is attempting to gain economies of scale in a number of areas within the combined organisation and has homed in on the computer systems as one such. He wishes to standardise the systems and produce an integrated set of accounts next year. Although Mike does not know a lot about computers he does know that the information they produce can help him make decisions and stay competitive.

The Treacy computer system is quite extensive. It consists of two mini-computers one of which is used for production and inventory control while the other is used in the accounting function. There is also a network of ten PCs which are used for a variety of other activities. These have networked word processing, E-mail, spreadsheet and CAD on them. The minicomputers are connected to the network so that managers can access current data to monitor the company's activities and produce reports when required. These systems have developed over the last five years since Margaret Treacy left university and started with the firm. The systems were originally established by external consultants and now whenever computing expertise is needed Margaret is able to cope and cope well.

This is very different to Mike Swallow's company which has not made very much use of computers. They have a large rather old mainframe machine which is in the accounts department and a mini-computer dealing with stock control in manufacturing. A few (four) PCs are in use but they are not networked and each user chose the software that they favoured. The accounts system was established ten years ago and the software was specially written for the company by its own staff of programmers. The software is regularly updated by the staff in the data processing section.

Write a report to Mike Swallow on how future developments can be aided by the use of fourth generation software.

References for this text

1 Avison and Fitzgerald *Information Systems Development,* Blackwell 1990
2 Codd, E.F., A relational model of data for large shared databanks, in *Communications of the ACM,* **13** 1970
3 Howe, D.R., *Data Analysis for Database Design,* Edward Arnold, 1989
4 Martin, J., *Fourth-Generation Languages,* Vol 1, Prentice-Hall 1985
5 Sanders, D., *Computers Today,* 1988

Further reading

Curtis, G., *Business Information Systems,* Addison-Wesley, 1989

Date, C.J., *An Introduction to Database Systems,* Addison-Wesley, 1995

Laudon, K.C and Laudon J.P., *Management Information Systems* MacMillan, 1988

Lister, A. and Eager, R. *Fundamentals of Operating Systems,* MacMillan, 1993

Senn, J.A., *Information Systems in Management,* Wadsworth, 1990

Part 4
Developing an information strategy

9 IT applications

Objectives

By the end of this chapter, you should be able to:

- describe the use of IT in personal information, work-team and corporate information systems
- understand how IT assists in operational, tactical and strategic decision-making
- assess the contribution of IT to different functions in the business
- answer the questions at the end of the chapter.

Introduction

In Part 1, we looked at the decision needs of managers. Having considered some of the information technologies available, we can begin to link them up to see how the latter may be used to serve the former. We will look at IT applications from a range of perspectives. The first looks at the relationship between individual, team and corporate applications. The second looks at the use of IT in operational, tactical and strategic decision-making. Finally, we look at individual requirement variations across particular functions of the business.

Personal, team and corporate systems

Information systems can be set up in an organisation at many levels. The scope of information systems range from personal systems to global systems incorporating the whole organisation. At a basic level, individuals may use their own computer system to enhance their effectiveness, independent of other members in the organisation. Such **personal information systems** are widespread in many companies. At the other extreme are the **corporate information systems** used to integrate the business functional areas and to provide information to different levels of management. Between these extremes are the systems used by specific groups within the organisation. These **work-team information systems** may be used by individual departments, project teams, or those in specific functional areas. Such a range of information systems will necessarily involve a variety of tools and processes and these are described in the following sections. Figure 9.1 shows the relationship between Personal, Work-Team and Corporate information systems.

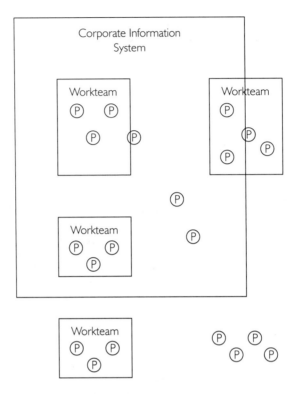

Figure 9.1   Scope of information systems

The illustration shows how a corporate-wide information system can incorporate a variety of work-team and personal information systems. Similarly, work-team information systems may utilise a number of personal systems. On the other hand, such systems can be independent of each other; some work-team information systems are not included as part of the corporate system, and some personal systems are unconnected to the work-team and corporate setups. Nevertheless, it is difficult to imagine that any information system is totally isolated from other elements. It may be that there is no physical or logical connection between systems, but that information from one system can still be utilised in some way into the other components.

Personal information systems

With the proliferation of desktop computers there has been a corresponding increase in the individual use of systems in a variety of application areas. Such individual use of computers has been inspired by, and promoted the development of, the tremendous range of business application packages now available. The utilisation of packages such as spreadsheets, word processing, databases, graphics and accounting applications is widespread in the modern business environment. The use of such packages by different employees in an organisation such as managers, technical staff, accountants, and other functional experts enable a significant improvement in the individual's effectiveness. The following illustration shows how a personal information system is used by a specific manager in an organisation. The same case will be used to illustrate other information systems later in this chapter.

Illustration 9.1:   The Euro Insurance Company

Elizabeth Gregory is the Personnel Manager at the Euro Insurance Company (EIC). EIC is a 'direct sale' company dealing in a range of insurance products including cover for car, buildings, house contents, theft and damage. In addition, other products such as personal pension schemes, redundancy insurance, and a financial advisory service are offered. The headquarters for EIC is based in Glamorgan, with subsidiary offices in the UK, France and the Netherlands. Elizabeth is responsible for the two hundred headquarter's employees and liaises with the personnel staff located in the subsidiary offices. There is a Personnel Director who controls the activities of all Personnel and Training staff including Elizabeth and her department.

One of Elizabeth's roles is to advise the Personnel Director and the EIC Board on succession plans. As such she needs to keep track of performance and development potential for all managers and professionals within the Headquarters. Elizabeth has set up a small database which she keeps on her own desktop computer to keep track of the performance of each member of staff. This information includes details of sales results, annual appraisal results, and performance on the range of assessment centres, development programs, and ad-hoc courses for each member of staff. Elizabeth has designed a small spreadsheet in which she can record scores for these measures, and rank the staff at various levels in the company as to their suitability for development and promotion. These results can be illustrated using the computer's graphics capabilities for presentation to the EIC Board at appropriate career development committee meetings.

The use of such a personal information system enables Elizabeth to keep track of the company's personnel, objectively assess each individual's potential, and present her findings in a professional manner to the senior staff in her company. There are many other small applications where Elizabeth finds that the use of her office computer results in improved efficiency and faster turn-around for many scheduled and unscheduled requests from other EIC staff. The result of this is that others in EIC consider Elizabeth to be an efficient, effective and reliable manager.

Work-team information systems

A work-team (or work-group) consists of a number of individuals who are involved in a specific task or role. A work-team could include all the members of a single department such as Finance or Marketing, or alternatively a group of employees involved in a specific task or project such as system development. Such groups would normally be located in a single site, although this is not essential. The important attribute of a work-team information system is the sharing of data and communication between team members. Thus, data may be required by several members of the group via networking.

Using a local area network, central data can be accessed by each member of the group when required. **Password systems** can be set up to restrict data so that non-members are not allowed access. Even within the work-team it may be that access to specific data is required at different levels. For instance, some members of the group may be allowed to change procedures (such as the formatting of reports), whereas others may be only allowed to change data (for instance, amending personnel details, or sales data). Furthermore, other members of the group may be restricted to simply being able to read data without changing any values. The case study given describes a work-group within an organisation and the information system being used.

Illustration 9.2:   The Euro Insurance Company work-team information system

An important work group in Elizabeth Gregory's area incorporates all the training staff at the headquarters and subsidiaries of EIC. These staff use the company's electronic mail system to communicate with each other. The electronic mail system includes the ability to create restricted areas allowing groups to set up their own 'notice board' for passing messages between the group members with no access to non-members. In this way details of forthcoming training courses with suggested delegate lists, proposed speakers, times and venues can be distributed and discussed. Furthermore, the team have set up a training database including files on staff attending courses, content of courses, training companies and consultant's details. This database has restricted access to enable staff to monitor the performance of trainers, and to assist in the choice of potential speakers at forthcoming events. The results from previous course evaluations are included on this database to ensure that unsuccessful or mediocre trainers are not used again.

This work-team information system enables the training and development staff to communicate and have access to relevant information which is not required by other staff members of the EIC. At the heart of the work-team system, the training database is accessible by the training staff at all sites of EIC by using modem links to the headquarter's central computer system.

Other independent work-team information systems are in operation at the EIC to support each of the main functional areas of Sales, Marketing, and Finance.

Corporate information systems

Corporate information systems are used to support activities throughout the organisation. As such these systems will be used to integrate a variety of users in the organisation and communicate information and data between appropriate users. Such corporate-wide information systems can consist of the integration of personal and work-group information systems as previously described, in addition to global systems linking departments. Furthermore, such corporate information systems can facilitate communication and the sharing of information resources between different organisations. The case study continued below illustrates the type of applications of such a corporate information system.

Illustration 9.3:   The Euro Insurance Company, corporate information system
The information systems catering for the main functional areas within EIC are integrated together. Thus, the corporate information system includes databases in the following areas: sales, personnel, marketing, and finance. Consequently, relevant information can be retrieved and related across these functions. For example, the sales database includes details of each sales person, their performance, the sales of items in the complete product range such as policies and investment portfolios. Much of the basic data relating to each sales person is included on the personnel database, and this is linked into the additional details provided on past performance obtained from the sales database. This information in turn can be used on the training database to, for example, highlight those personnel requiring additional sales training or product updating.

In addition to the integration of the functional areas, the corporate information system provides senior management with regular summary reports of company performance compared with the targets and objectives previously set. This information in the form of tables and graphical outputs enables the managers to monitor the company results closely and take effective early action when necessary to rectify problems if and when they occur.

Self-assessment questions

1 What is the difference between personal, work-team and corporate information systems? Describe the main elements of each type.

2 Consider an organisation such as a company or college with which you are familiar. How would the different information systems (personal, work-team and corporate) be used by the Finance Manager in such an organisation? Consider one or two simple examples of the areas of application of such systems.

Operational, tactical and strategic applications

A management information system can be defined in various ways. Clearly, the provision of reliable, accurate and appropriate information to members within an organisation lays at the core of any definition. A working definition could be that a management information system is a system to convert data into information to enable managers at all levels to make effective decisions. However, it is usually agreed that the MIS will not only be used exclusively by managers but will provide information to anyone within the organisation when required. Consideration of an MIS will inevitably lead to a study of the system development processes as well as the applications for individuals and groups within the organisation.

As introduced early in this book, the information requirements of individuals will depend on their role and level within an organisation. In this section we will consider the range of management information systems available and their applications at various levels in the organisation. A management information system will consist of a range of facilities to assist with diverse needs involving the day-to-day operations, as well as medium and long-term decision making. It is widely agreed that a corporate-wide information system will consist of a number of components including:

- Transaction processing systems
- Management information systems
- Decision support systems
- Executive information systems.

These components can be used by different levels of management.

The transaction processing systems are used at the lower levels of decision-making to assist in the day-to-day running of operations. **Decision support systems** can be used by middle or senior management in tactical and strategic decision-making. **Executive information systems** incorporate information from a variety of sources to summaries, reports, and alternatives for strategic decision-making. The scope and level of integration of these components will depend on the specific organisation being considered. Nevertheless, there are common themes in these systems which will be discussed in the following sections.

Transaction processing systems

Such systems are used to record and process the daily operations within a company. The output from such systems could be regular reports on current activities. Transaction processing systems consist of a variety of elements involved with recording current operations, updating appropriate files, and providing simple regular and *ad hoc* reports based on the data gathered. For instance, the processing of orders obtained by a company would be part of the transaction processing system. Orders arrive from customers and are entered into an orders file. The new entries are processed to validate each order, ensure that items are available, prices are correct, and to check customer's details such as credit ratings. The items are then sent to the customer, and this transaction is recorded in the system. The system can then automatically produce invoices, and send to the relevant addresses. The process is completed with the recording of payments received from the customer. Thus the following transactions are processed on the system:

- receipt of order
- checking order contents
- check customer details
- despatch order and invoice
- receive payment
- production of reminder letters for late payment etc.

Finally, the transaction processing system will produce a variety of reports such as:

- weekly sales data
- orders received
- level of stock situation
- outstanding orders.

Such a system will enable the operational manager to monitor activities on a day-to-day basis and at an early stage deal with any problems that may arise. This may involve direct action by a first line manager to monitor the effectiveness of sales staff, check problems with stock levels, or to inform the appropriate line manager of problems requiring decisions. Thus information from the transaction processing system becomes part of the management information in order to assist in the appropriate decision-making processes.

Illustration 9.4:   Transaction processing at the EIC

The Euro Insurance Company introduced in earlier illustrations in this chapter uses its information systems to process a range of transactions. For example, the sale of insurance cover occurs in one of three ways. The salesforce often respond to requests and make home visits to prospective clients. Alternatively, some policies are sold simply by telephone contact, or by clients visiting one of the EIC offices by appointment. If a sale occurs using any of these methods, then the details of client, policy, and premiums are entered directly into the computer system. During home visits this is done by entering details onto a lap-top computer and later transferring the data onto the central system for further processing. The sales process then automatically provides input which the system uses for the production of invoices, standard letters, setting up of standing orders or direct debits from clients' bank accounts, and sending renewal letters and completion forms.

Such a system is of additional benefit since it provides the salesforce with a useful tool to assist in the actual sales process. Client information can be read into the system and estimates of the cost and benefits of specific policies can be investigated during this transaction process.

Management information systems

The term 'management information system' is often used to imply the systems associated with the provision of information for middle and senior managers in an organisation. As such, the output from transaction processing systems will constitute part of this information. The actual information system required depends on many factors outlined in Chapter 11 on the system's development life-cycle. Such factors include the following:

- complexity of information to be stored
- type of decisions to be made
- scope of decisions (e.g. long-term or short-term)
- size and activities involved in organisation
- organisational structure.

An MIS is used to support the management functions of planning, organising, directing and controlling. At each stage in the management process, appropriate information is essential in order to improve decisions made. Typically, a management information system will perform the following:

- Data processing incorporating data entry and validation, and the recording and monitoring of transactions.
- Provision of information in the form of regular, exception and *ad hoc* reports to all levels of management.

- Assist in management decision making at the operational, tactical and strategic levels.
- Support the business functional areas.
- Integrate systems and facilitate the flow of information within the organisation.
- Provide necessary security for all information and levels of users.

Illustration 9.5: Management Information Systems at the EIC

A range of management information systems are in operation at the EIC. In particular, managers are able to obtain detailed reports produced by the system as a direct result of inputs performed during the sales process. Thus, the regional sales managers can obtain details of the performance of individual sales staff, and which policies and investment plans are preferred by clients. This may help the managers to reschedule client interviews and visits and to update the information available to clients with reference to the popularity of specific products. Regional managers are sent regular weekly reports on the performance statistics, and a comparison between regions.

Managers can request specific reports on detailed information such as the contracts obtained by the sales staff, success rates compared with the number of visits, and other details on the geographic location and description of clients. The regional managers are able to communicate with each other via the electronic mail system, in order to discuss issues such as problems with specific policies, performance data of pension plans and any new products to be introduced.

Self-assessment questions

1 Explain the difference between transaction processing systems and management information systems. Give an example of each type from an organisation that you are familiar with.

2 How are transaction processing systems used to produce management information?

Decision support systems

A decision support system (DSS) can be defined as a 'computer-based system that supports decision-makers'. Such a definition could have been used to define a management information system though there are important differences between an MIS and a DSS. Indeed, an MIS often will incorporate decision support tools as part of the overall system. A DSS will be distinguished by the following:

- The system will be geared towards decision-making rather than basic information processing.
- A DSS will be used primarily by middle and top level managers.
- It can provide additional information to help solve *ad hoc* problems rather than standard regular or scheduled issues.
- The system can be most effectively used to consider solutions to unstructured and semi-structured problems.
- The DSS can be used for evaluating and comparing alternative solutions prior to decision-making.

In order to satisfy these conditions the decision support systems will consist of many of the following components:

- A database with access to outline data on the main functional areas such as finance and personnel.
- A database management system to access and manipulate data.
- Modelling software for data analysis e.g. simulation, optimisation and operational research methods.
- Software for the evaluation of alternatives such as 'What If?' problems, e.g. what if all managers had a 4% salary increase this year, how would this affect the company's profits?
- Modelling software for commercial analysis and planning e.g. financial, marketing planning.
- Goal-seeking procedures, e.g. in order to achieve a particular value of a variable, what would need to be the value(s) for other variables? For instance, to obtain a 5% growth in sales next year, what would the advertising expenditure need to be?
- Graphing software for data presentation and visual modelling.
- A directory (or data dictionary) to enable managers to browse through the contents of the database.
- Expert systems/artificial intelligence systems.
- User-friendly interface enabling easy access to the various systems included.

Illustration 9.6: Decision support systems at the EIC

One decision support system in operation at the EIC is used by the sales staff in their transactions with clients. An expert system is used in order to provide assistance in the search for the most appropriate policy for a client, based on their details. The expert system contains a **knowledge base** of details of all the available policies for specific requirements. Other details including past performance, and links with specific clients are included. Thus, to summarise a simple example, a client requiring car insurance will be offered a selection of policies from different insurance companies, with the expert system giving priority for each policy in terms of criteria such as price, reliability, and exclusions. Different policies would be suggested by the system dependent on personal details such as age, sex, home address, driving experience and current job. The best policies may change, since some companies may offer discounts for a limited period for particular clients such as those over a given age, or those who drive less than a given mileage per year. Thus the system would need to be regularly updated to keep up with the latest comparisons between policies.

The expert system may also assist in the selection of the best investment plan or portfolio for a given client. This may be based on the amount to be invested, the degree of risk the client is willing to take, the duration of investment, and likelihood of withdrawal at an early stage. Other factors in making investment decisions will be past performance of specific plans, future trends, and possible added benefits such as tax-free bonuses. The system will interact with the client via the salesperson, and ask relevant questions in order to elicit the required information prior to making a decision or providing a list in order of preference for the client to consider. The system enables the salesperson to display far greater expertise as an investment analyst than would normally be the case. Thus the expert system helps the client to make decisions, and provides a significant enhancement to the service offered by the EIC.

Self-assessment questions _____

I   Consider an application package such as a spreadsheet or database system. Explain
how such a package can be used as a decision support tool.

Executive information systems

These systems are used exclusively by senior management. Executive information systems (EIS) provide support for strategic decision making. An EIS will have the following characteristics:

- The system must be user-friendly. Senior managers will not have time to learn how
  to use complex systems. Thus the systems must be quick and easy to use by the
  incorporation of menus, icons and windows-type interfaces. Minimum training
  needs to be supplied.
- Good communication with the incorporation of local and wide area networks with
  access to both internal and external databases.
- Immediate access to information including regular and *ad hoc* reports generated
  from databases.

The range of information required for strategic decision-making will include those in
the following areas:

- **Internal data.**   Key details relating to the organisation such as success factors,
  results compared with objectives or targets, and performance indicators.
- **Competition.**   Information on other companies/organisations in similar market
  segments. Useful information in this category would include knowledge of future
  plans of competitors including projected markets and products, details of competitor's sales volumes and investment plans, and competitor's organisational management structures.
- **Customers.**   Data on current and prospective customers including market segmentation and demographic changes. Changes in customer requirements and
  tastes. Customer costs such as production, distribution, administration and service
  costs.
- **Environment.**   Political and economic details. For instance, inflation forecasts,
  interest rates, currency exchange rates, commodity prices, Gross National Product,
  and economic trends. Details of new and forthcoming UK and EEC legislation and
  their possible affect on the company's business activities.

Strategic information is primarily external, requiring details on competitor's performance, political and market changes, and technology innovations. As such the executive
information system will be required to provide external data via the application of
external financial, marketing and investment databases. In practice it is likely that the
senior manager will not have direct access to such information and will rely on a sub-
ordinate to glean the required information from the various sources. However, it is
important that the decision-maker is fully aware of the range of information available
in order that the right questions can be asked and the most appropriate information
sought.

Illustration 9.7:   Executive information systems at the EIC

The directors of the EIC use the executive information systems in a variety of ways. Firstly, they receive summary reports, in both text and graphical form, from the information system on the performance of regions and policies. The directors can interrogate the system to obtain additional information required such as sales trends, forecasts, and potential of existing products. Furthermore, the senior team at EIC have access to external databases providing information on insurance policies, investment analyses and forecasts of future needs. Information from these external sources can be fed down to the middle management at EIC, and provide additional information to be used on the expert system used by the salesforce.

In particular, the senior team consider carefully the performance and products of competitors in the market, and review potential areas of expansion such as new policies or investment opportunities. Currently, the EIC board of directors are considering the acquisition of the Westchester Building Society which they foresee will complement their existing business interests. To make the final decision a significant amount of research has been carried out into the building society sector as a whole, and in the performance of the Westchester in particular. Some of this information has been accessed using external databases containing company reports, trends and forecasts of future building society performances. This together with a review of EICs existing business interests will help to determine the best way forward in the proposed acquisition.

Self-assessment questions

1 You are the Sales and Marketing Director for a large retail company. Your company is considering building a large store in a new out-of-town shopping complex. What external information would you consider to be useful making a decision on this project?

2 How could an information system be used to help you?

Relationship between levels of information systems

Figure 9.2 illustrates the relationship between information systems showing how information flows between the transaction processing systems, management information systems, and executive information systems. The illustration reiterates the ideas of the hierarchical model in management decision-making. Essentially, senior managers are concerned with strategic planning and decision-making. This role determines the type of information system required incorporating external information sources, environmental scanning and decision support systems with information obtained from the management information systems and reports generated by middle (tactical) managers. The middle manager, involved in **tactical planning** and decisions will need to respond to requests from the senior managers, as well as being pro-active in communicating appropriate information when necessary. The middle manager will also use the information systems for monitoring and controlling processes and resources, requiring information from the transaction processing systems, and using appropriate decision support and modelling tools. At an operational level, the transaction processing systems will record and monitor the basic business operations. Such systems will be linked to the management information systems to provide information, summaries and regular reports. Overall, information flows both within and between the levels of systems.

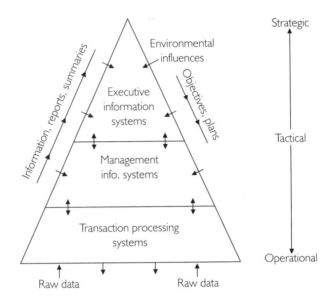

Figure 9.2   Levels of information system

Clearly, a mature and effective information system must use efficient lines of communication between the variety of systems used. Of course, there are inevitable overlaps between the variety of systems previously described. For example, elements of an MIS form part of the executive systems, and parts of the DSS may be used by middle and senior managers in the organisation. The content and relationships between such systems will be defined and developed in relation to the organisational strategy feeding into the business IT strategy.

Functional applications

The precise structure of an organisation to some extent depends on the specific activities of the business. Such business activities will also have a bearing on the importance of particular functional areas. In general terms, a business involves the use and coordination of a range of resources including people, money, and materials. This defines three of the primary functional areas within an organisation namely:

- personnel (people)
- finance/accounting (monetary control)
- manufacturing (materials).

One of the primary concerns of most businesses is to ensure **profitability.** Generating a profit will inevitably involve developing relationships with potential customers and clients, thus defining the fourth functional area:

● marketing/sales (profit/turnover).

Organisations will have a different emphasis given to each of the functions. Let us consider various types of organisation and review the primary and secondary functional areas associated with them. Examples of some business sectors are as follows:

Manufacturing organisation
In this type of organisation, production is a primary function, supported by the other areas such as finance, personnel, and marketing. Other functions such as research and development and design may play important roles depending on the type and range of products the organisation manufactures.

Distribution industry
Such an organisation is not directly involved in the production process though may be involved in the movement of manufactured goods. For example, retailers, wholesalers, and distribution companies. In such an organisation the primary function will be marketing and sales, with the support of functions such as purchasing, finance/accounting and personnel.

Public services
These organisations often provide a range of services for the general public. For example, local council services, police and fire services. The primary function of such organisations is 'public service' in its various forms, backed up by functions such as training, finance, personnel and public relations.

Financial sector
Such organisations provide a range of financial services to public, industry and commerce. For example, banks, building societies, financial advisors, insurance companies, and the Stock Market all can be considered in this category. The primary functions of these organisations are marketing/sales and finance reinforced by research, training and personnel.

Educational services
Institutions, particularly in the further and higher education sectors, are increasingly being expected to operate as business enterprises. Their primary function is education, training and research. These are supported by other functions such as personnel, finance, and marketing.

In the following sections we will consider the primary functional areas of production, marketing/sales, finance and personnel in relation to their information needs and resulting information systems.

Self-assessment questions _____

I   Consider your own company, or an organisation with which you are familiar. What are its primary functions? What secondary functions are included in this organisation?

2   Consider a large utilities organisation such as your local water company. Try to list all the functions that you would expect to see in such an organisation. Are some functions more important than others? If so, list them in order of importance.

Marketing and sales

For many businesses the marketing/sales function is of primary importance to ensure continued success. Marketing involves a wide range of activities including the planning and development of new products, and the promotion of existing products. As such the marketing role involves communication with a variety of individuals and companies external to the business. These contacts include existing and potential customers, clients, suppliers and competitors. Figure 9.3 illustrates some of the main activities involved in the marketing and sales functions.

Figure 9.3   Activities in marketing and sales

The activities shown in Figure 9.3 are described in the following sections. A **marketing information system** may be used to support these activities requiring information in a variety of formats.

Sales analysis
In this area information is collected on current and past sales of items in the company's product range. In many cases the entry of such data can be automated such as by the use of point-of-sale input systems. Using such data can assist in the estimates of future sales. It can be useful to catagorise sales data in a variety of ways such as:

- **By product.**   The sales of each item in the product range will be recorded separately to enable specific product-based reports and forecasts to be produced.
- **By region.**   For advertising purposes it may be useful to monitor the location of sales and investigate whether any patterns exist. For instance to determine whether some areas achieve higher sales than others.

- **By salesperson.**   The results of each salesperson will be recorded to monitor an individual's effectiveness in comparison with the total salesforce. This may have implications for the employee's pay and position within the company.

Sales forecasting

Forecasts of demand are vital in many organisations. Short-term forecasts can be used to determine production schedules and purchasing tactics. Longer-term forecasts can be used to influence strategic decisions on product development and diversification. Such forecasts are based on a range of information including:

- **Sales history.**   Details of past performance in specific products can be used in statistical forecasting methods.
- **Competition.**   Knowledge of the performance of competitors, and total potential sales in specific product sectors.
- **Promotional activities.**   The range of marketing and promotional activities planned will clearly affect the sales forecasts.

The knowledge of external information cannot be ignored in any forecasting situation. Indeed in many cases, external information is far more important than details on past performance. For example, knowledge of competitors' activities, product ranges, pricing policies, as well as more global economic trends may be vital for reasonable sales forecasts to be obtained.

Product analysis

An investigation of each item in the product range may reveal useful patterns emerging. The sales performance of each product can be considered. Why is this particular product performing well or badly? How does the pricing of this item compare with similar products on the market? Are there features of the product that can be improved? Are new products required to replace existing items or supplement the existing range? Such questions may involve comparison of existing products, reference to external marketing sources, or additional investigations.

Product analysis will provide support for existing products, facilitate improvements in items or services where necessary, and assist in the planning and monitoring of new products.

Market Research

Market research involves the collection and analysis of a range of data to investigate current and future business opportunities. Market research data includes the following:

- **Customer information.**   Details on current customers and trends in buying patterns obtained from existing sales data.
- **Potential customers.**   Information on potential clients can be obtained from customer surveys, and consumer reports.
- **Product design.**   Analysis of customer's opinions on items in an existing product range. Consideration of changes in product design and services necessary to preserve and build upon the existing customer base.
- **Competitors.**   Details on present and potential competition in given sectors can be helpful in determining future marketing and sales strategies. Such details may include information on competitor's product ranges, marketing tactics, and customer profiles.

- **Demographic trends.** External information can be obtained from published databases and reports on the population distribution and movements. This enables possible targeting for specific customers such as those in particular socio-economic groups, or given age bands.
- **Economic data.** Wider economic indicators such as inflation rates, prices, wages and manufacturing costs can be vital in developing long-term strategies and current pricing policies.

Such information can be used in many areas within the marketing and sales function. For instance, sales forecasting, advertising and product development will all require information from market research activities.

Self-assessment questions _____

1 Consider any company or organisation with which you are familiar. Describe the main marketing activities that take place in this organisation. What information does it need to carry out and monitor these activities?

2 Market research is considered to be an important component of the Marketing function within an organisation. What role does Market Research perform, and how does it support the sales staff?

Marketing information systems

A marketing information system must provide support for the range of activities described in the previous sections. Such a system will enable information to be collected and analysed quickly and efficiently. In order to make effective decisions, accurate information must be provided to the marketing manager. This is a function that requires up-to-date information since trends can change extremely quickly. Information on current sales are vital, and it is often not sufficient to rely on sales reports from previous months or quarters. The Marketing Department uses data and information obtained from a variety of sources. Figure 9.4 illustrates the flow of information between components within marketing/sales and external sources.

The primary components of a marketing information system will include communication, data handling, data analysis, and reporting. Some features of a marketing system are described in the following sections.

Databases
A range of appropriate files will be used to form the backbone of a **marketing database**. The following files will generally be required within an organisation:

- **Customer files.** These files will contain relevant details on past, current and potential customers and clients. Basic information on these customers would be stored such as company name, customer code, contact name, address, telephone number, credit rating, appropriate product ranges and previous orders.
- **Product files.** Information will be stored on all items in the product range promoted by the organisation. Such details will include item name, item number, product categorisation, location and possibly price.

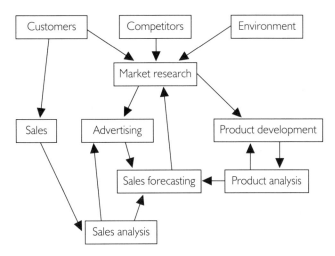

Figure 9.4   Marketing information flows

- **Sales files.**   Information will be kept on sales results for each product range. Records in these files will include item name, number sold, date, invoice reference, salesperson, and possible additional marketing details such as who made the initial contact, and how the customer found out about the product.
- **Competitors.**   Data should be available on current and potential competitors in specific product areas. These files may include competitor's name (either individuals or companies), contact address and telephone numbers, sector of market, and, if available, details on performance, marketing strategies, and future plans.

These files will contain a minimum amount of common information in order to establish links between them. For instance, a product name or code may be contained on a number of separate files such as the sales file, product file, and customer files. Thus, an order from a customer can be linked to specific items, descriptions of those items given and sales information updated if required.

Other internal files are likely to be kept on market research data such as results of promotional campaigns, feedback on existing products, and reactions to new services.

Much of the information required in a marketing information system will incorporate external data. Thus, the use of **external databases** such as those described in the Applications section of Chapter 6, can be vital to provide information that is relevant, up-to-date, and reliable. The linking of internal and external databases will be an important element of the total marketing system.

Data entry
Much of the information described in the previous section will require inputting in the usual way via keyboard entry methods. However, it is useful to note some of the ways of speeding up **data acquisition** in these circumstances by using the following approaches:

- **Point-of-sale.**   Many companies, particularly in retailing, use the electronic point-of-sale methods of data entry. For example, each item is identified by a bar-code. A bar-code reader is used at the point of sale to record the transaction, provide a receipt for the customer, update stock records, and provide immediate amendments to the sales files.

- **Invoices.** Any information on sales need only be entered once into the organisation's information system. Often order details are entered for the payment/invoice system operated in the Accounts Department. Such information can then be used by the Marketing Department to update sales files and product details.

- **Remote entry.** It is increasingly common for systems to allow sales staff to enter details of sales and transactions from remote terminals. For instance, the sales person may have a small lap-top computer into which sales details are entered whilst negotiating with clients. At the end of the day, or at a convenient time, this data is uploaded onto the organisation's computer system by linking into the telephone network. Again, such information can be incorporated into the range of data files required in the total marketing system.

Data analysis

The marketing information system will incorporate methods of analysing the vast array of available data. In particular, the sales forecasting process may involve complex data analysis using statistical or economic forecasting methods. Thus, the information system must be able to convert available data into the format required by these forecasting systems. Other data analysis methods will be used in interpreting market research information. Statistical analysis techniques can be used to determine relationships between data such as age profiles of customers, segmentation of the market, and effectiveness of the various promotional activities. Such analyses may lead to the development of new products and the improvement of existing services. Other packages linked to the information system may be used to analyse the data in specific ways. For example, spreadsheets could be used to investigate the likely customer response of sales strategies, and effects on likely revenue of specific product changes.

Reporting

The information system will be required to generate information in the correct format and in the required detail for different levels of management within the marketing function. Thus the Marketing Director will require summary reports providing an overview of the salient points. Alternatively, the Market Analyst will require more detailed information from market research concerning specific products or trends. The success of the information system will depend partly on the degree of flexibility offered in reporting information. So-called **report generators** can be used for this purpose. Standard reports will be produced such as information on daily, weekly or monthly sales figures. Such reports may need to be broken down into product ranges, geographical areas or customer categories. Furthermore, details on performance of individual sales personnel and regional sales figures may be required. Similarly, reports on effectiveness of advertising and promotional campaigns will be required. Other reports on external data such as competitors' current performance and future estimates may be needed.

Communication

An important component of any information system is efficient communication. The term is used here in its wider sense as defined in Chapter 6 in this text. Communication can involve individuals or groups talking to each other, or it can imply the transmission and receiving of data and information. The marketing information system will facilitate all of these elements. It is vital that individual files such as those containing details on sales, products and customers, are linked together so that data can be related when required. This database will enable information to be located centrally, and accessed by a variety of users when required. It is also necessary that such data can be transferred to other systems for further manipulation. For instance, transferring data from the sales file into a data analysis package for evaluating trends and forecasting figures. Providing the data formats for all software are **compatible**, there need not be problems in such interaction between the various systems.

Self-assessment questions

1   A marketing database will contain a range of computer files containing details in specific areas. For example, an important file in the database will contain details on the organisation's customers. Describe other files which may be used in the marketing and sales areas.

2   Consider the contents of a customer file. Each record in this file will contain details on a single customer including company name, address, and telephone numbers. List out other details which you would expect to find in a customer file. Give examples of how each of these details could be used in the marketing and sales functions.

Manufacturing and operations

The use of computers in manufacturing has expanded since early developments in the technology. Computer systems may be used to control machinery, and the term 'automation' is often used to describe such situations. Computers can also be used to assist in the activities required to develop the product and plan **manufacturing schedules**. Thus, computer systems can be used in the complete production cycle, from the early product concepts, through the design stage, through to the manufacture of the completed product. **Computer integrated manufacturing (CIM)** is an attempt to integrate these activities to enable both a quicker response to the market and a reduction in costs.

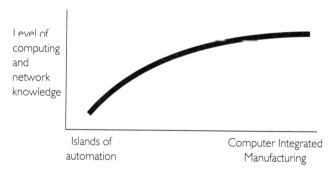

Figure 9.5

Currently, manufacturing companies may have developed computer applications to varying degrees between the two ends of the automation spectrum. Figure 9.5 illustrates how some manufacturers may have adopted an 'islands of automation' approach where individual situations have been automated while others have installed a totally integrated system. The required amount of computing and network knowledge is greatly increased if using a CIM system.

Islands of automation	Integrated manufacturing
1. Product concept	1. Product concept
2. Detail design and drawings	2. Detail design
3. Process planning	
4. Machining operations	
5. Inspection operations	
6. Production scheduling	
7. Warehousing	3. Warehousing

Table 9.1   Stages of interaction

Table 9.1 shows the various areas within manufacturing and operations that might be employed at the two extremes of applying automation. As can be seen, an integrated system has fewer stages within the whole process. This is due to making use of computers to communicate with other computers that in turn control machinery.

Later sections consider the two extremes in detail and describes each of the applications more fully.

Islands of automation
Many organisations have developed computing expertise in a variety of manufacturing activities over a period of time. Often this occurs simultaneously in different departments but this can be an expensive exercise. Therefore we find automation being adopted piecemeal, subject to cost and budget constraints.

- **Design.**   The product concepts and design will be developed either through market research or with the customer when an order is negotiated. Use of a **computer aided design (CAD)** or graphics system can help to improve the production of initial designs. A modern CAD system should allow not only representation of the product's physical characteristics, but also carry out calculations such as stress analysis. Purpose-built CAD systems are available in many areas such as architecture, mechanical engineering, and civil engineering.
- **Drawing.**   Once the general concept of the product has been developed the design must be interpreted into component parts with limits, fits and tolerances. This is

done by a manufacturing or production engineer and a draughtsman. A **computer-aided drawing** system will aid in rapid production of drawings though often the CAD system can be used.

- **Planning.**   In conjunction with a computer-aided drawing system a **computer-aided process planning** system (CAPP) is useful. This will enable process choices to be made rapidly as well as the fast production of planning sheets. These tell the operator at what speed to run the machine and list the tools necessary to produce the component.

- **Machine control.**   The process production sheet may be used by the machine setter to program a **computer numerical control (CNC)** machine to manufacture the component.

- **Inspection.**   The process production sheet can also be used to program a coordinate measuring machine to inspect the parts after manufacture to ensure that they are within the **design tolerances.**

- **Scheduling.**   The planning and scheduling of production starts with either an order from a customer or the manufacture of items to go into stock in anticipation of sales. The **master production schedule (MPS)** is the first stage in planning and is a compilation of customer orders and sales forecasts. The MPS integrated with material requirements will give a **purchasing schedule. Material requirements planning (MRP)** is a standard software package able to carry out this task. If the manufacture of components is necessary **Manufacturing Resource Planning** (MRP II) software is available to integrate capacity requirements with MRP.

- **Warehousing.**   Automated warehouses, i.e. the storage and location of components and sub-assemblies in warehouse or storage areas, have been common in some industries for many years particularly in the retail trade.

Computer integrated manufacturing

In this approach the same processes described in the previous section are totally integrated. Thus human intervention is not required between the design stage and completion of the manufacture.

In design, the product concepts and the design of the product will be developed in just the same way as the island of automation situation. The use of a computer-aided design (CAD) or graphics system will have the same role to play.

In Manufacture, the general concept of the product and the design must be interpreted into component parts with limits, fits and tolerances. This is done in the same way as before but with a very different computer system. Instead of a computer-aided drawing system for rapid production of drawings the computer system translates the detail design into a program suitable for the machine on which the component will be manufactured. This program will need to be stored in the computer system ready for the date to be manufactured. **Direct numerical control (DNC)** is a term used to describe this situation, i.e. a single computer, storing and loading a programme to a CNC machine when necessary. The addition of a robot to transfer materials between machines and controlled by the central computer gives a computer-aided manufacturing system.

A major difficulty with this situation is ensuring satisfactory communication between computers, i.e. design computer, planning computer and machine control computer. **CAD/CAM** is a term often used to describe the integration of design and manufacture but there is much debate as to the meaning of these terms (see Browne, Harhan and Shivnan in Further Reading). Implied within this system is not only design and manufacturing but also the scheduling of when these activities should occur.

In warehousing, the use of automated warehouses will be much the same as in the islands of automation situation.

Manufacturing information systems

A manufacturing information system provides support for all of the foregoing activities. Such a system must enable data to be collected and analysed quickly and efficiently. This will produce accurate information upon which the manufacturing manager can make effective decisions.

Databases

A number of files will be in use within manufacturing and be utilised by the MRP or MRP II system to establish schedules and exception lists. A report generator or 4GL will probably also be used. Requirements include:

- **Product file.** This file contains all of the company's products. These details will include a product description and part number, list of styles, colours, sizes, list of components for each product. This file will also hold the information mentioned in the marketing information systems.
- **Sub-assembly file.** Sub-assembly name, description and part number are held in this file as well as details of the product(s) that it is used on.
- **Component file.** Each component produced used by the company will be contained in individual **records**. Each record contains details such as component name, description and part number, drawing location, raw material, list of operations and for each operation – machine description, speed settings, tools required and their location, time to set up the machine, time to produce one item. The sub-assembly(s) or product(s) that the component is used on is also indicated.
- **Tool file.** Each tool's name and part number, location, drawing location, components manufactured with each tool will be recorded.
- **Machine file.** This file is often integrated with the Accountant's **asset register** and will contain such things as machine name, description and number, location, date purchased, maintenance history.
- **Employee file.** The employee file can be used to record the activities of each employee and is often of joint interest with the Personnel Department.
- **Sales file.** This is described in the section on Marketing Information Systems.

Self-assessment questions _____

I   Identify how many records would be necessary in a database for the components that constitute the chair on which you are sitting.

Personnel (human resource) management

The personnel function is a significant area involving management of the most important resource within an organisation, namely 'people'. However, in contrast with other
areas, the personnel function can be structured in a variety of ways. For instance, in
many organisations there will be a large Personnel Department, possibly controlled by
a Personnel Director. Conversely, in other companies the personnel role may be
devolved to managers within the other functional areas. In such a case, there need not
be a separate Personnel Department, and specialist personnel roles may be kept to a
minimum. The descriptions of the Personnel function given in this section assume the
existence of a separate Personnel Department or section. However, it should be recognised that not all companies, particularly smaller ones, will conform to this model.
Nevertheless, the personnel tasks described here will be relevant whichever organisational structure is considered.

Primary activities in the personnel function are illustrated in Figure 9.6 and are
described in detail in the following sections. Such activities can be integrated by the use
of a **personnel information system.** The elements of such a system will be described
later in this section.

Figure 9.6   Activities in the personnel function

Recruitment and selection

One of the primary tasks of the personnel function is the management of the recruitment and selection process. The main steps in this process are:

Defining the job
Specifying details of the vacancy to be filled may involve simple reference to a **job
description** or analysis of the job. **Job analysis** will involve identification of the main
tasks and duties, and consideration of how such tasks are performed.

Selection criteria

Producing a list of aptitudes and traits of the ideal candidate for the job under consideration involves writing the profile of the perfect applicant which is usually called the **person specification**. The person specification would include a range of attributes such as:

- Attainments – educational and training, or previous experience required;
- Special aptitudes – what special skills are required for the job?
- Interests – personal interests of relevance to the job;
- Physical characteristics – health, strength and appearance relevant to the job.

These points would be considered in relation to both desirable and essential attributes for the post.

Attracting applicants

Encouraging potential job-holders to apply for the post. This would involve decisions on when and where to advertise, possible liaison with external agencies, and consideration of the pay and benefits package to be offered.

Selection

Processing of all applications for the post advertised. This would include a number of tasks such as:

- Sift through applications and produce a short list of those candidates who satisfy the criteria stated in the person specification.
- Plan the assessment process using appropriate selection techniques such as interviews, aptitude tests, intelligence tests, personality tests and assessment centres.
- Make final selection based on these techniques.
- Ensure additional requirements are confirmed such as satisfactory medical examination and references.
- Make job offer to selected candidate.

Salaries and benefits planning

This involves careful consideration of the current salaries system and a detailed appraisal of employee benefits to ensure that the package on offer is appropriate with reference to internal and external factors. The Personnel Department would usually be responsible for managing the salaries and benefits of employees. Tasks in this category include the following.

Salaries

Consideration of current salary scales, involves, for example, comparison of employees on different levels within the organisation. Also establishing pay differentials to distinguish employees on different levels in the hierarchy; devising plans for the progression of employees between grades and salary levels; consideration of incremental salary systems; reviewing salaries for individual employees; use of additional payments, and overtime pay.

Benefits

An appropriate level of employee benefits together with basic salary rates are important in recruiting and retaining staff. There are a range of benefits that can be offered to employees including:

- company cars
- private health schemes
- company pension schemes
- profit sharing
- relocation allowances and home loans
- company share schemes.

The Personnel Department would manage these benefits and could make recommendations on changes to existing benefits or the introduction of new ones.

Comparison

One of the responsibilities of the personnel function would be to compare the current pay and benefits package with outside companies and organisations. It is important for an organisation to know what its competitors are offering so that the appropriate workforce can be recruited and conserved. For example, an organisation may decide that it wants to keep the pay and benefits of its employees in the upper half of comparable companies. A comparison with the external labour market can be done with reference to a number of sources such as:

- published statistics such as the official Department of Employment data
- published reports on pay surveys
- employment agencies
- job advertisements
- liaison with other companies
- conducting own surveys.

Appraisals and performance

The Personnel Department will be involved in the evaluation of performance of employees. This evaluation may involve a range of methods including a periodic **performance appraisal** scheme. The primary objectives of the appraisal system are:

- review past performance
- improve individual's performances
- provide a mechanism for development plans
- improve communication between levels of management.

The appraisals involve line managers setting objectives, or tasks to be completed by their subordinates, with specific time frames agreed. The regular appraisal will involve determining whether the previous objectives have been met and formulating fresh objectives for the forthcoming period. Such an appraisal system is usually managed and administered by the Personnel Department.

Employee relations

An important aspect of the personnel function is the promotion and monitoring of successful relationships between employees and employer. The objectives of good employee relations are to encourage employees to identify with the organisation in order to improve output and enhance the organisations' efficiency. The employee relations area covers a wide range of tasks including:

- **Communication.**   The establishment of effective two-way communication channels between all levels in the organisation.
- **Negotiations.**   To participate in contractual negotiations concerning terms and conditions of employment. To agree with employee representatives (such as Trades Unions, Staff Associations, or other bodies) on pay and benefits.
- **Policies.**   To define and communicate policies on a range of areas such as equal opportunities, redundancy, early retirement, dismissal and grievance procedures.
- **Individual problems.**   To handle individual requests, grievances, and ensure that the correct procedures are carried out with reference to disciplinary policy and practice.

Employee Relations will involve liaison between a range of different parties including employer, employee, manager, Trades Unions, Government and legal bodies.

Organisational analysis

In this category the **organisational structure** is considered supported by the analysis and evaluation of current jobs. Each of these elements is described in the following sections:

Job analysis
The process of determining the major tasks and duties involved in an existing or proposed role. In addition to a description of the main duties there will be an analysis of the relationship between the job-holder and other key members of staff. For instance, the job analysis will specify the job-holder's line manager, and subordinates and level of responsibility and autonomy. Such an analysis will be conducted using a range of techniques such as reference to existing documentation, interviews with existing job-holder and appropriate manager(s), job questionnaires, and observation of the job being carried out. The end result of the job analysis will be the production of a job description.

Job evaluation
This involves the comparison of jobs within an organisation in order to determine a 'hierarchy' of tasks. This should then enable a more consistent approach to be established in relation to pay and benefits. Essentially, an attempt is made to rank the jobs in order of precedence. This is often achieved by the use of **benchmark positions.** For example, a group of jobs at different levels in the organisation are chosen. These roles are evaluated, and all other jobs are compared with them and slotted into the appropriate position in the ranking. The result of the evaluation will be a hierarchy of job roles that can form the basis of a reasoned pay structure.

Organisational structure
Knowledge of the organisational structure is important in a number of areas in the personnel function. For instance, it can form part of the process involved in job analysis and evaluation. It also has other applications in personnel areas such as **human resource planning** and **training & development.** The structure of an organisation can be defined in many ways. In Chapter 2 (Figures 2.1 to 2.4) a range of organisational structures for increasingly complex companies have been illustrated. An organisations' structure can be defined in terms of a variety of categories such as:

- Functional areas (e.g. personnel, production, and finance departments)
- Geographical areas (e.g. UK, Europe and Far East Divisions)

- Product or service areas (e.g. electrical, textiles, and commodities groups).

The current trend is towards 'flatter' structures with fewer levels in the organisational hierarchy. One of the roles of the personnel function is to advise on the current organisational structures and recommend changes or alternatives when appropriate.

Human resource planning

This Personnel role involves consideration of current and future demands for labour. The following procedures are often applied:

- **Analysis of current work-force.**   Knowledge of existing employees and their expertise and potentials.
- **Analysis of turnover.**   Estimates of numbers of existing staff that will leave in a given time-span. This can involve complex statistical models or simpler quantitative and qualitative techniques.
- **Analysis of requirements.**   Knowledge of existing and future plans of the organisation and the implications on recruitment, in particular for the demand of those with specified skills.
- **Comparison.**   Matching the future estimates with potential requirements and making appropriate recommendations on the best courses of action to ensure the required expertise is available at the right time.
- **Succession planning.**   Consideration of where existing staff will be in the organisation in the future, and whether any of these staff will be able to fill future vacancies as they occur.

Human resource planning can incorporate extremely complex mathematical models. However, in most organisations, the numbers of employees at the appropriate levels are not large enough to provide precise forecasts using this approach. Nevertheless, it is useful to be aware of a range of quantitative data such as the following:

- age distribution of employees, possibly broken down into specific levels or functions
- analysis of Length of Service of existing employees
- employee turnover rates
- numbers of lost working days due to absence, sickness, holiday, etc.

Training & development

Training and development is an important role usually undertaken by those in the Personnel Department. The main purpose of this role is to ensure that existing staff are able to perform effectively in their current jobs, and where required, be able to pursue other roles in the organisation. Training and development can take a number of forms such as:

- **Initial training.**   This often takes the form of an **induction course** to introduce new employees into the company and familiarise them with relevant information.
- **Skills training.**   This will be provided to give the necessary skills for an employee to carry out his/her current role effectively, or to provide new skills for a proposed job.
- **Skills development.**   Upgrading or upskilling an employee's skills in a given area. This may be necessary because of changes in working practices, or organisational changes, or providing the opportunity for employees to advance in the present organisational hierarchy.

- **Team building.** This involves providing the appropriate vehicle in order to improve an individual's ability to work in teams. This may be appropriate to help existing teams improve their performance, or where new teams are being established.
- **Motivational development.** This may involve attempting to enhance an employee's motivation, such as improve employees' attitudes to work in order to enhance output or improve the working environment.

Training and development can be carried out in many ways such as the participation in the following activities:

- formal courses
- short courses
- open learning
- seminars
- projects
- secondments
- team working
- role playing
- job shadowing.

The personnel staff involved in this area may be required to assess training needs, establish training objectives, design training content, select appropriate training methods, select suitable candidates and perform the associated training administration duties.

Personnel services

An additional range of basic services are provided to employees and managed from within the Personnel Department. Such services include assistance and management in the following areas:

- **Health and safety** – providing advise on health and safety matters. This is particularly important in a manufacturing organisation where a Health and Safety Manager may be employed to ensure that the company conforms to National and European regulations.
- **Catering** – the provision of staff canteen and/or refreshment facilities. This may involve the internal management of catering facilities or the appointment and management of external caterers.
- **Medical services** – provision of medical facilities and medical/nursing staff. Training of supplementary staff e.g. 'first-aiders'.
- **Counselling** – providing help on request to employees with reference to personal, work and financial problems.

Self-assessment questions

1   Describe the main functions of a Personnel Department. Consider the duties of personnel specialists in your company, or any organisation you are familiar with.

2   How are the areas of organisational analysis, performance appraisal, and human resource planning inter-related in personnel operations? Give an example of where activities in these three areas would overlap.

Personnel information systems

The personnel information system enables integration of the main tasks previously described. Traditionally, the administration of employee records would have been the primary role of a personnel information system. Such systems have developed in recent years, particularly with the advent of more powerful microcomputers and sophisticated software systems. Employee files still constitute a major role in the information system, but increasing breadth and depth in content of such files has led to more complex applications of such data. The following information is normally stored within a personnel system.

Employee files

These files will contain details on individual members of staff. The following information is likely to be kept on individual employees:

- **Basic data.**   Employee's name, employee number, age, gender, ethnic origin and address.
- **Work details.**   Employee's NI number, role at work, location, contact number, job title, present earnings, bonus details, position on earnings scale, department and line manager's identification.
- **Career history.**   Length of service, date joined company, positions within company, previous employment, previous earnings.
- **Training details.**   Qualifications held, courses attended, results of training, training required, current skills
- **Analysis.**   Appraisal details, development potential, possible future roles, absence details, disciplinary records, previous performances and awards.

A computer-based personnel file containing this range of data can provide easy and quick access to up-to-date information on individual employees. In addition to basic record keeping the personnel information system can form the basis for a range of applications as illustrated in Figure 9.7. These applications are outlined in the following sections.

Figure 9.7   Applications of personnel databases

Recruitment and selection

Details of applicants for specific jobs can be entered on the system. These details can then be used to track the candidates through the recruitment and selection process. The system can be used to provide initial screening of applicants, producing a short list of those satisfying pre-defined criteria. The generation of appropriate correspondence such as rejection letters, requests for attendance to testing sessions, interviews and assessment centres, and job offers, can all be automated using such a system. Computer-based assessment methods such as aptitude tests, psychometric tests and personality profiling can be used as part of this process, with results automatically transferred onto the applicant's files. Finally, the details on successful candidates can be transferred to the employee files when appropriate.

Salaries and benefits planning

The analysis of current pay and benefits packages can be produced from within the personnel information system. For instance, the effect of changes to salaries on the total staff budget can be analysed by the use of computer systems. Current pay statistics can be manipulated to consider possible alternatives in the **pay structure** and **pay rates** for individual grades within the organisation. Such analyses can be extremely complex. For instance, a simple calculation would be required when awarding everyone a 3% pay increase, resulting in the total pay bill increasing by 3%. However, the actual calculations may be much more difficult. For example, if different grades are awarded varying increases, or incremental scales are in operation, or additional payments given based on levels of performance, then the final calculations become complicated. A computerised information system will enable such calculations to be performed with ease. This information can be used to assist those involved in pay negotiations to accurately assess the cost of proposed changes and to stay within agreed staff budgets. The system can also be used to globally update the pay and benefits of employees instead of the necessity to change information on each individual's records.

Absence records

Details on the absence records of employees will be kept on the personnel files. Such records will include categorisation of the type of absences incurred such as sickness, holidays and unscheduled absences. Such information can be used in management reports, and for costing purposes such as the administration of **statutory sick pay (SSP)**.

Job analysis

A number of systems are available to assist in job analysis and evaluation. Such routines use a database containing the range of job descriptions, and person specifications. Organisation charts can be constructed using these systems. Specific jobs can be analysed to provide consistent definitions of the tasks and duties involved, together with a profile of the ideal employee to perform this role. Such systems are able to analyse the relationships between the assessments from different managers and construct an overview of the descriptions and specifications required. These analyses can then be used in areas such as recruitment and selection, organisation design, performance appraisals, and training and development.

Human resource planning

The personnel information system can be used to analyse the existing workforce and forecast future requirements based on current plans and developments. The personnel database will include details on individual employees in terms of their potential for advancement in the organisation. Furthermore, vital positions within the organisation will be identified such as the posts that are critical to the achievement of the company's objectives, or posts providing ideal development opportunities for key staff. Computer modelling can consider complex human resource models and will involve the analysis of staff turnover, age distributions, wastage rates and employee profiles. Such models can use the existing organisation's structure to evaluate the effect of changes in the staffing levels, staff flows within the system, succession plans and recruitment policies.

Training and development

The personnel information system will assist in the analysis of training and development needs within an organisation. This can be achieved by a comparison of the existing employees' skills compared with the current and future person specifications. Disparities may then be apparent which may be rectified by appropriate training and development activities. **Training records** can be used in other areas such as succession planning. The training needs of employees may be identified from the appraisal systems, and therefore there should be a link between the appraisal and training records.

Training administration can be performed with the assistance of computerised records. Delegate lists will be constructed. Delegates can be informed of proposed courses and events with times and dates. Course bookings, attendance of delegates, and training costs can be recorded. Training effectiveness, and provision of additional training can be managed.

Communication

A vital component in the personnel information system is good communication linking various management levels to all the functional areas. Information contained on the system must be easily accessible by appropriate staff including non-personnel specialists. Security systems are essential since much of the data contained on the personnel system is sensitive. Password systems should provide different levels of access to relevant information.

Self-assessment questions _____

1 At the core of a Personnel Information System is the employee database. Describe the basic details that you would expect to be kept on each employee in this database.

2 You are the line manager of an employee who you are about to appraise. What details would you wish to obtain concerning this employee that may already be on the employee file? Give examples of this information.

Finance and accounting

The financial and accounting information systems within an organisation are often the most advanced systems used. Traditionally, earlier computer systems concentrated on the accounting applications. Such development resulted because of the mass of data to be processed in addition to the repetitive nature of some of the activities associated with basic accounting systems. Early examples of computer-based applications included **payroll administration** and **invoice handling systems.** Modern financial systems provide sophisticated management information in addition to performing basic **accounting operations.** Figure 9.8 illustrates some of the primary activities in an organisation's financial and accounting processes.

Figure 9.8 Activities in Finance & Accounting

The primary aims of such systems are to record, monitor, report and forecast the flow of resources through an organisation. The following financial and/or accounting activities are common to most organisations.

Order processing
This process records and monitors the progress of an order received from a customer or client. The main steps in this would include:

- **Order receipt.**   Details of orders received from customers are recorded.
- **Customer screening.**   The customer is checked to ensure credit-worthiness, method of payment and any additional relevant details.
- **Invoice preparation.**   An invoice is produced and sent following services or goods being provided.
- **Payment.**   When payment is received the amount outstanding from the customer is reduced by the appropriate value.
- **Overdue payments.**   If any account is overdue by more than a pre-defined duration then procedures are invoked to encourage payment. For example, sending reminders, copies of invoices, offering incentives and ultimately threatening legal action.

Accounts Receivable and Payable
The **accounts receivable** records are kept on any outstanding amounts owed by customers. These records would be used in the order processing procedures to check

customers' credit limit, produce invoices, and obtain reports on any overdue accounts. Similarly, **Accounts Payable** records provide details on any outstanding amounts owed to suppliers. They will enable the payment of any outstanding debts with minimal delays, and provide information on **cash flows.**

Payroll

Such systems manage the whole process of payment of salaries, wages and other bonuses and allowances. Payroll systems enable accurate payment of wages and salaries, and the production of pay slips and annual pay summaries for employees. Such a system would also provide management reports, and information for external bodies (such as the Inland Revenue) when required.

General ledger

The general ledger systems provide a way of recording and summarising the financial information used in the other systems such as accounts receivable, accounts payable, and payroll. The general ledger is used to produce a variety of financial statements such as **balance sheets** and income accounts.

Management accounting

This element is involved with the consideration of internal **budgets** and **expenditures.** Thus, budgets are decided upon and spending controlled within individual departments or sectors within an organisation. Performance reports will be prepared for managers summarising a range of details such as budgeted costs, revenues and expenditures.

Financial reporting

The general ledger will be used to produce a variety of financial reports for management within the organisation, including those already listed. Other detailed reports and financial statements may be produced to summarise the income, costs and profitability within different sectors in the organisation.

Financial planning

This process involves evaluation of the current financial position of the organisation. This information, together with external information such as economic trends, inflation figures, and exchange rates, will be used to obtain forecasts of future performance. These forecasts can then be used to produce financial plans in order to enhance the company's competitiveness and improve it's commercial position. Such information would be applied in the development of a **corporate plan** outlining ways in which the organisation's objectives can be attained in terms of investment, growth, productivity, and market share.

Self-assessment questions

1 Describe the primary roles of an accounting system with reference to a company. Give examples of where accounting and financial methods should be used.

2 Consider a local college or university near you. Such an institution will use accounting procedures to record and control a range of transactions. Give examples of such transactions.

Financial and accounting information systems

The financial and accounting information system will incorporate links between the components described in the previous section. Many of these elements are little more than transaction processing systems. However, these systems also provide information that can be incorporated into a management information system for use in tactical and strategic planning and monitoring. These financial systems will provide a degree of control and feedback for other systems in the organisation as described in Chapter 3 of this text. Figure 9.9 shows the relationship between a number of components in the financial and accounting system.

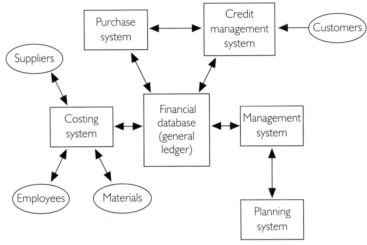

Figure 9.9   Components in a financial and accounting system

The primary elements illustrated in Figure 9.9 are:

- the **purchase system**
- the **credit management system**
- the **costing system**
- the **management system**
- the **planning system.**

These interrelated systems perform the functions outlined in the previous sections. Transactions are processed such as:

- receiving orders
- sending invoices
- receiving payment
- sending receipts
- sending orders to suppliers
- arranging payment for suppliers
- paying other expenses
- paying staff.

Such transactions are recorded in the Ledger and then used for **management accounts, financial reports** and **financial planning** leading to **corporate planning.**

Such a system involves the use of an integrated database including the financial accounts previously described. An integrated accounting information system is therefore likely to include the following elements:

Purchase system

Such a computer-based accounts payable system would consist of interrelated files including those indicated below:

- **Suppliers files.** Keeping records of suppliers of goods and services. These files will contain information such as a record of past orders obtained from suppliers.
- **Orders files.** These will contain records of orders to suppliers and enable the tracking of such orders. For example, to check for those orders where no goods have been received, or for goods received where payment has not been made.
- **Accounts files.** Information on outstanding accounts is stored. Thus details of amounts owing to specific suppliers, and age of overdue accounts, can be obtained.

The system will assist in automating much of the purchase process such as:

- production of order form
- processing of invoice received
- processing of payment
- updating appropriate files such as accounts payable
- updating the general ledger account.

Credit management system

Credit management will include the **accounts receivable system.** The following interrelated files will be used in this system:

- **Customer files.** Details on past and present customers and clients. Information such as credit ratings, payment arrangements, and special discounts offered may be contained in these files.
- **Orders files.** Information on **orders received** from customers and position of orders such as whether completed or not.
- **Invoice files.** Details on position of **invoices produced,** such as whether paid, method of payment, and age of outstanding debt.

The system will assist in the following tasks:

- processing of customer orders
- transmission of order to appropriate section in the organisation, e.g. manufacturing
- updating sales and cash receipts accounts
- updating customer files and related files.

Costing system

Such a system would monitor and control the costs involved in a particular job or project and would make use of the following files:

- **Job files.** Providing details of the activities and costs associated with each job. These costs could involve the purchase of materials, payment of staff, capital costs, and additional expenses.
- **Supplier/contractor files.** This would contain details of previous contractors and

information on tenders submitted. This could be used to make decisions on the best contractor to perform the work required.

● **Payroll.**   Costs of existing staff are stored, including hourly rates, salaries, overtime rates, and bonus conditions.

The process of costing will involve access to other data files such as **employee files** for information on staff costs for the payroll system, and **production files** for details on manufacturing and materials costs. The costing system would assist in the following areas:

● decisions on appropriate contractors for each job
● tracking of current jobs in progress
● monitoring additional costs
● linking to purchase and credit management systems
● budgetary control.

Management system
This system would provide a range of **financial reports** such as balance sheets, income and funds statements. The management system is based on information contained in the **general ledger.** Such information must be reproduced in the most appropriate format for different levels of management within the organisation. For instance, the Managing Director requires global financial details providing overviews of the performance of each sector in the organisation in areas such as income, expenditure and forecasts. Conversely, the departmental manager requires details such as costs, revenue and budget variance in his/her department as well as a comparison of the department's performance with others. The management system must provide this by an ability to produce a variety of report formats giving varying degrees of detail as required.

Planning system
This system uses data obtained from the management system in order to produce forecasts and estimates of future performance. 'What If' analysis can be performed in this area in which a variety of strategies are simulated and the results in terms of financial variables are obtained. Based on these simulations, the manager can make informed decisions on current tactics and **corporate strategies.**

Integrating the financial and accounting system

In many organisations the financial system will form the backbone of the overall management information system. As previously described it is essential to link the financial and accounting information system to other functional areas if only for costing and budgeting purposes. Such a system will be linked into other information systems in the organisation as shown in Figure 9.10.

Figure 9.10 illustrates the financial and accounting system at the hub of the overall information system. Other functional areas require information from, and add information to, the financial system. Other important links are also illustrated such as the primary entities including customers/clients, suppliers/contractors, and external bodies such as financial institutions, tax and auditing authorities.

Figure 9.10 Integrated information systems

Self-assessment questions

1   Identify the main components of a financial and accounting information system. How are these components linked together?

2   Describe the types of data that are taken from other systems in the organisation for use in the financial and accounting systems.

Summary

Information systems are used to support an extensive range of functional areas in business. Increasingly, such systems are enabling integration of the business processes that take place. The type of business or organisation will clearly affect the specific functional areas involved. For instance, manufacturing organisations, service industries, financial sectors and public services will all have different primary functional areas and consequently varying information needs. However, many of the functions are common to all sectors. The primary functional areas that have been described in this chapter are as follows:

● **Marketing and sales.**   Information systems can be used in this area to assist in sales analysis, demand forecasting, product analysis, advertising evaluation and market research. The basis of such a system would be the marketing database consisting of a range of information on customers, products, competitors and sales.

● **Manufacturing and operations.**   Information systems have been developed in many areas in this function. For example, the increasing use of computer-aided design, integrated manufacturing, resource planning and automated warehouses are just some of the many areas of application. Databases used to support such systems will include details on products, sub-assemblies, components, tools and machines, as well as requiring details from other areas such as personnel and sales files.

- **Human resource management.**   Systems can be used to improve a company's effectiveness in areas such as recruitment and selection, performance, human resource planning and organisational analysis. The foundations of a human resource system are the personnel files containing employee details such as name, employee number, address, as well as details on pay, benefits, career history, training and performance records.
- **Finance and accounting.**   These systems incorporate transaction processing management requiring records of purchases, accounts, payroll, costing and sales, in addition to management accounting and planning modules. Basic data files used include those containing details of suppliers, customers, orders, invoices and accounts.

An organisation's information system can integrate these functional areas simply by the sharing of common data. This facilitates improved communication flows between the functions and can provide a more extensive, global view of the organisation resulting in the generation of enhanced management information.

Questions for discussion

1   An accounting information system is little more than a computerised transaction processing system. Discuss this statement, and give reasons why it may not be true.

2   Discuss the statement: 'Computer applications for many small and medium sized companies are restricted to basic accounting processes'. Give reasons why you agree or disagree with this statement.

3   Discuss the role of information systems in human resource planning.

4   A corporate information system consists of a number of distinct systems catering for the needs of the main functional areas. Discuss the range of functional areas that would be included for a large industrial organisation. Describe how these systems are linked together to form a corporate system.

5   The structure of organisations can vary considerably dependent on the type of business and range of services being offered. The four primary functional areas have been described in this chapter in relation to a production company. Consider the main functions involved in the following businesses, and describe the information requirements for each type given:

(a) hotel group
(b) insurance company
(c) estate agency chain
(d) airline company
(e) university
(f) local education authority
(g) recording company.

6   Discuss how the information from a company's sales system can be used in the marketing function. How can such a system help the marketing manager?

7   Discuss the advantages and disadvantages of using a computer-integrated manufac-

turing system within an organisation in a company that has only a few 'islands of automation'.

8 A manufacturing information system requires a number of files that can be shared with other departments. Discuss who should have the responsibility for the management and administration of these joint files.

Problems

1 How can a financial information system assist the manager in decision-making?

2 Describe how electronic point-of-sale systems can assist the operation of an accounting information system. Give practical examples of the use of such systems.

3 How can a computer-based personnel information system assist the recruitment and selection process within an organisation?

4 Describe the primary roles of information systems in the personnel function. Give examples of each role with reference to a specific company e.g. a large hotel chain in the UK.

5 Consider the payroll function in an organisation. A computerised payroll system will require a range of data on all employees in order to calculate their gross pay and net pay rates. Describe the data requirements of such a system and list out the main steps involved in the overall payroll process up to the actual payment of remuneration.

6 Describe the main elements in a marketing information system. Outline the advantages of a computer-based system over a manual system. Describe additional marketing facilities that could be incorporated in a computerised information system.

7 Describe how a bar-code system can be of use to the planning and control of manufacturing.

8 Produce a diagram to represent the information flows within a manufacturing company.

Case-study 9.1: Electrogoods Megastores information system

Electrogoods plc is a large chain of retailers dealing exclusively in a complete range of home electrical goods such as televisions, music systems, micro-computers, washing machines and 'fridges. The company owns twenty-four sites throughout the UK operated on the lines of 'retail clubs'. Each site houses a megastore containing the electrical goods at discounted prices. Customers must join the Electrogoods club before being able to buy any items. The cost of membership is £15 per year per person. This entitles the member to purchase goods at significantly less than the recommended retail price. Electrogoods claims to undercut any other store and offers a pay-back scheme if it is found that a product purchased at one of the stores can be bought cheaper elsewhere in the area.

Each of the sites consists of a General Manager, Assistant Manager, sales staff, technical and stores staff, as well as clerical and secretarial assistance. The number of staff at each site varies between 30 and 64 employees. A separate head office consists of an additional forty staff including the senior management team.

- Staff at the head office deal with purchasing, pricing and distribution for all the retail outlets.
- All purchasing of goods from manufacturers is performed centrally.
- Electrogoods does not have any central distribution sites, and all orders are delivered directly to each of the megastores.
- The current information system at Electrogoods enables communication between all stores and the head office.
- Managers at the head office use this system to make decisions on issues such as the choice of product ranges to be sold, pricing policies and promotional strategies.

I   Describe how such an information system will be used in relation to the main functional areas in this business. What links are there between these functional areas?

2   List at least six basic data files that you would expect to be used in the Electrogoods information system. Describe the main contents of these files and show how they can be linked together.

3   What type of information would the senior managers require in order to make decisions relating to:

(a) purchasing of new stock

(b) pricing of new and existing stock

(c) long-term marketing strategies.

4   Describe any external information that could be used to assist senior managers in their decisions such as those described in 3 above. How could such information be incorporated into the overall company's information system?

Case-study 9.2:   Information system for the Ecco Oil Company

The Ecco Oil Company (EOC) is a multinational company involved in the sale of oil and petrol in countries throughout Europe and North America. EOC is based in London, with regional offices at Frankfurt, Milan, Madrid and Vancouver. The UK fuel sales are managed and administered from the London office. The main functions of EOC are the purchase and sale of various types of fuel. EOC buys fuel direct from the producers. Because of the volatility of this market, it negotiates new contracts on price and quantities required on a monthly basis with each of the producers. Thus there is a significant amount of flexibility in the source of EOCs fuel. The contracts director, Alice Rathborne, has overall control of this aspect of EOCs business. The director controls a number of staff including the purchasing manager, legal and administrative staff. One of Alice's primary tasks is to ensure that EOC achieves the best commodity price and contract conditions from the range of producers used.

In the UK, EOC:

- owns over 100 petrol stations spread throughout the country;
- franchises a further 50 outlets which means that privately owned garages can sell the Ecco products.

The sales director, Ali Rahmad, gets involved in decisions about where to set up new retail sites, and the redesign of existing sites.

1   Consider the range of information that Ali Rahmad requires in making decisions about potential new sites for Ecco petrol stations.

2   Describe the personal, work-team, and corporate information systems that Alice Rathborne may be involved in. Give examples of each type.

3   Describe, with practical examples, the range of decision support tools that Alice or Ali might use to help them in their current roles.

4   How will information systems be used to ensure that the Ecco Oil Company remains competitive, and where possible stays ahead of its business rivals in the service it offers its customers?

5   Ali and Alice have to report to their parent company on future strategies that EOC might adopt in the UK. Discuss the procedure that they would go through in doing this and the role that information systems might play in carrying it out.

6   Alice has been asked by the board of EOC (UK) to examine possible information systems strategies open to them. This has occurred at a particularly apposite time as Alice has been contemplating how to arrange closer contacts with suppliers and Ali has felt the need to establish more detailed sales reports about EOC petrol stations and competitive stations nearby. Write a report to discussing the strategies open to the company.

Case-study 9.3:   Computer applications in operations
Horizon Garden Supplies (HGS) produce a range of concrete garden accessories ranging from five-seater benches to small gnomes. These are sold to garden centres throughout the country by a small sales force. Each member of the sales team is based in one of the ten regions into which the sales manager has split the country. The company also produces a free catalogue that is sent to prospective customers who have requested it after responding to advertising. The catalogue contains items of extra quality or some other form of uniqueness that cannot be purchased from a garden centre.

The company promises in its catalogue next day dispatch, but increasingly find that they are out of stock of certain items. A similar problem arises occasionally with garden centre orders. They are often dispatched incomplete and will only be completely fulfilled two weeks later. On the other hand the auditor has mentioned the high value of stocks within the business. The works manager has asked for an injection of money to purchase more production equipment and storage racks whilst the work force of 45 people often complain that their wages have been calculated incorrectly.

1   Discuss the potential uses of a computer system within the company.

References for this text

1 Thompson, J.L., *Strategic Management* (Chapter 2) Chapman & Hall 1990
2 Robson, W., *Strategic Management and Information Systems* (Chapter 5) Pitman, 1994

Further reading

Blewett F. and Jarvis R., *Microcomputers in Accounting,* Van Nostrand Reinhold, 1989

Browne, Harhan and Shivnan, *Production Management Systems,* Adison-Wesley, 1988

Cushing B.E. and Romney M.B., *Accounting Information Systems,* Adison-Wesley, 1990

Evans A., *Computerizing Personnel Systems,* IPM, 1986

Gallagher M.L., *Computers and Human Resource Management,* Butterworth-Heinemann, 1991

Gelinas U.J., Oram A.E. and Wiggins W.P., *Accounting Information Systems,* PWS-Kent Publishing Co, 1990

Harry M., *Information Systems in Business,* (Chapter 6) Pitman, 1994

Hicks J.O., *Information Systems in Business: An Introduction,* West Publishing Company, 1990

Kroenke D. and Hatch R., *Management Information Systems,* (Chapters 2, 5–15) McGraw-Hill Publishing Co., 1994

Kroenke D. and Hatch R., *Management Information Systems,* (Chapter 11) McGraw-Hill, 1994

Laudon K.C. and Laudon J.P., *Management Information Systems* 3rd ed, Macmillan Publishing Company, 1994

Mandell S.L., *Computers and Information Processing* 6th ed, (Chapters 1, 3) West Publishing Company, 1992

O'Brien J.A., *Management Information Systems: A Managerial End User Perspective* (pp. 494 – 505) Irwin Publishers, 1993

Peppard, J., *IT Strategy for Business,* Pitman 1993

Rhodes P.C., *Decision Support Systems: Theory and Practice,* Alfred Waller Ltd,1993

Senn J.A., *Information Systems in Management,* 4th ed. Wadsworth, 1990

Sprague R.H and Watson H.J., *Decision Support Systems* Prentice-Hall International, 1993

Smith K., *Corporate Accounting Systems* Adison-Wesley, 1988

Tom P.L., *Managing Information as a Corporate Resource* Harper-Collins, (Chapter 12) 1991

10 Developing an IT strategy

Objectives

By the end of this chapter, you should be able to:

- describe how companies achieve competitive advantage through the value chain
- understand the sources of competitive advantage
- explain how companies use IT applications to strengthen the value chain and gain competitive advantage
- appreciate the role of IT in the process of strategic alignment
- understand how IT may transform a business
- answer the case-study at the end of the chapter.

Introduction

The previous chapter illustrated how companies can make use of software applications to meet the decision needs of particular parts of the business, whether at the strategic, tactical or operational level. This chapter moves beyond the use of IT to solve individual information problems to the broader question of how IT may be deployed by companies as a whole to fulfil their strategic goals and achieve competitive advantage.

Parsons has identified a range of strategic responses to IT which can be grouped into two basic types:

- The **laissez faire approach,** where senior management may have little interest in, or commitment to, IT. They may regard IT as a necessary evil to which resources are grudgingly allocated in response to immediate pressures.
- The **scarce resource strategy** where there are strict, primarily financial, controls on investment. Since IT benefits are not always easily quantified in this way, this approach can be an effective brake on development.
- The **free market strategy** in which individual IT users develop their own localised systems. Such an approach has the advantage of tailor-made solutions to individual needs, but the result is an uncoordinated and mismatched patchwork of systems with little strategic perspective. This approach is a characteristic 'emergent' strategy for businesses coming to terms with IT for the first time.
- The **planned approach** in which IT and the information needs of a business are seen as a strategic issue by senior managers. The most adventurous may adapt a leading edge strategy focusing on employing the latest technology. Whether or not they do so, senior managers may decide on a monopoly or a centrally planned strategy. If they adopt the first, investment and development are centrally controlled and

directed. The second is characterised by greater flexibility, providing company-wide standards and guidelines, but devolving responsibility for investment and particular IT solutions much more suited to individual users. Martin, the American IT guru, has espoused this combination of top-down planning and localised design as the way forward for large corporations.

The company that grows from local exploitation of individual IT applications to the strategic deployment of IT throughout the business makes a fundamental leap forward in harnessing IT for competitive advantage. As we shall see, this leap is in itself only one step in a dialogue with IT which can end in the transformation of the business itself. This process of strategic alignment is one of the most important issues in the use of IT. However, before we look at this process, we need first to understand its starting point in the search for competitive advantage. An understanding of this search requires a brief analysis of competitive strategy.

Strategy and the value chain

It is beyond the scope of this book to look in detail at the whole strategic process. A full analysis would need to consider:

- how a business defines its role in relation to its stakeholders and markets
- its strengths and weaknesses within its chosen environment
- its competitive advantage and the range of strategic options needed to achieve such advantage
- how to implement and measure the strategy it then chooses.

As we shall see later in the chapter, IT impacts on all these stages and can even redefine the whole strategic process itself.

In this chapter, we will concentrate on one of the ways a company can define and strengthen **competitive advantage** once it has defined the business it is in and the challenges it faces. **Value chain analysis** has been widely adopted as a way of identifying how the basic activities of a business contribute to its competitive advantage. Michael Porter has described the value chain shown in Figure 10.1. Porter divides businesses into two fundamental components:

- primary activities concerned directly with adding value to its products or services for the customer;

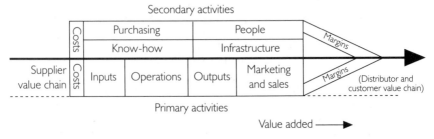

Figure 10.1   The value chain (M. Porter)

- secondary activities which, whilst they don't add directly to the value chain, play a crucial role in supporting those activities.

Competitive advantage may be defined as the amount of value a business can add to the product and services it creates to make customers prefer them to its rivals at the right margin.

Support activities broadly comprise the following:

- **Purchasing** – the businesses resources and skills in acquiring the materials needed for carrying out the whole range of primary activities, whether it be materials, machinery or marketing.
- **People** – the recruitment, motivation and development of the people in the business.
- **Know-how** – the processes and knowledge underlying each primary activity, whether it be the technology used in manufacturing operations, or the expertise in selling effectively.
- **Infrastructure** – the systems for planning, organising and controlling a business' primary and secondary activity, for instance, the calibre of its quality or cost control systems.

Primary activities involve the following:

- **Inputs.** The activities concerned with the acquisition, storage and distribution of the **raw materials** required for the manufacture of the product or service.
- **Operations.** The processes involved in converting the raw materials into the finished **product or service.**
- **Outputs.** The means for storing and distributing the product, or **supplying** the product or service, to the customer.
- **Marketing and sales.** The channels used to access and attract customers to purchase the product or service. This category could also include: service – those activities concerned with enhancing or maintaining the value of a product/service, for example, a maintenance and repair service; market research – the means used to identify customers' needs and expectations so that the product/service and the way it is manufactured, distributed, marketed and serviced, meets customer requirements.

Competitive advantage lies in the way businesses can blend their primary and secondary activities most effectively to add value for customers and themselves. As an example, a company might apply its purchasing skills, technological know-how and strong financial controls in its infrastructure to reduce its input, operational and output costs. Its added value in its cost-effectiveness would give it **competitive advantage** in price over its competitors.

Porter identified **cost leadership** as one of three fundamental ways in which a business could manipulate its value chain to achieve competitive advantage. The second was **differentiation,** the business's identification of a unique product or service benefit fundamentally different from, and superior to, those offered by rival businesses. As an example, a business might concentrate on adding value to its input, operations and output activities to make its speed of delivery unique amongst its competitors. Federal Express's use of IT to create a fast-cycle distribution business superior to its competitors will be discussed later in the chapter. The final means of establishing competitive advantage is a **focus strategy** in which a business targets a specific segment of customers and tailors its strategy to meet their needs better than its rivals, securing its niche in the market. The case of Carters of Faringdon, seeking to monopolise its corner of the retail market within a specific locality, which we will discuss later, provides an example of a focus strategy at work.

This use of the value chain in defining these kinds of competitive advantage is, of course, not an isolated process. As the diagram illustrates, a firm's value chain may well be only one in a series of separate value chains, including the firm's suppliers and the distribution channels it may use in reaching the customer, for example through retail outlets. Its strategy must take into account these other chains, for example the pressures on suppliers to force up prices to protect or improve their own added value, or the capacity of retailers to reach a target market effectively.

As was made clear at the beginning of the chapter, value chain analysis must also take place within the overall strategic process. It must, for example, be sensitive to the nature of market conditions and customer and stakeholder expectations, and to the prevailing state of competition in a business's chosen market. As an example, an emphasis on cost leadership in an already low margin business may be entirely inappropriate in a market overloaded with cheap competing products. In this case, an emphasis on differentiation or focus may provide a more sustainable source of competitive advantage with more acceptable returns for stakeholders.

IT, the value chain and competitive advantage

In the following cases, we will look at how various types of business have deployed IT to achieve competitive advantage by strengthening one or more key activities in the value chain. They broadly follow the order of primary activities from input to output and service. These examples provide a starting point for tackling the case-study exercise at the end of the chapter. They conclude with the case of a company which used IT to generate a new kind of business, Federal Express.

In each case, the company's use of IT is first highlighted and then its role in achieving competitive advantage analysed to illustrate the strategic potential of IT.

Illustration 10.1:   From input to output – the case of McKesson

McKesson is a major US drug wholesaler buying from large pharmaceutical suppliers and distributing to small local drug stores. It has been using its Economot IT system since the 1970s to strengthen its, and its clients, position against competition from the big chain stores with their potential for greater customer choice. McKesson's initial IT response included supplying its client stores with free hand-held terminals, later updated to scanners. Shopkeepers could then carry the scanner around the store, using bar-codes on each shelf to key-in orders for replacement stock more rapidly and accurately. These orders were then transmitted via telephone cables for immediate fullfilment by McKesson, who later developed the capacity to supply the goods packed in shelf order and priced to include the shopkeeper's mark-up. At a later stage, McKesson integrated its purchasing system electronically into the order systems of its large suppliers, generating an automatic ordering system for the supply of drugs to be passed onto local stores.

McKesson has even used IT to simplify customer purchasing. Most customers have health insurance which involves reclaiming the initial cost of a prescription. For a nominal fee, McKesson offered customers a credit card which allowed the company to supply the prescription free, and claim the cost directly from the insurance company, thereby taking the hassle of reclaiming prescription costs away from the customer. The service was even developed to hold medical records on behalf of customers so that, if they purchased a drug, they could check it would not react with any other medication they were taking.

In its use of IT, McKesson was able to add value at various key stages in the value chain. Beginning at the input side, McKesson succeeded in tying its suppliers more closely into its systems, making them less likely to shift allegiance, given the convenience of an automated system, whilst at the same time speeding up delivery and saving significant personnel costs in its purchasing department. On the operations side, IT provided more effective stock control and rapid delivery, again improving costs and level of service at the same time.

In its output and service activities, McKesson added value further on in the chain by making its clients both more efficient in their stock-holding for customers through easier ordering, more rapid, individually-tailored distribution, and enhancing the service they could provide customers. As a result, McKesson strengthened its supply chain and made its client stores more dependent on and loyal to the company. McKesson was thus able to secure competitive advantage in both cost and service over its rivals.

Illustration 10.2   Adding operational value and beyond – Benetton
Benetton is a major international clothing company, manufacturing its own brand of sports and fashion garments and franchising independent retailers via a network of agents. It has made a major investment in IT, for example, deploying CAD and CAM to improve the speed and costs of its production operations. The CAD system automatically translates a new design into a full range of standard sizes, and communicates the information to a CAM system deploying automated fabric cutting machines. By reversing the traditional approach and dying clothes *after* they have been sewn, Benetton is also able to react more flexibly to changing fashions in colours keeping stock levels and waste to a minimum.

At the distribution end, orders for retailers are taken in by agents who dial Benetton's EDI network from DOS or Unix-based microcomputers. The order-handling system collects the order, routes it electronically to the relevant factory and arranges for distribution. The system also handles the invoicing and allows agents to monitor all aspects of their client retailers' accounts enabling them, for example, to restrict deliveries to retailers exceeding their credit limits. The system allows Benetton to monitor the performance of its agents closely.

Finally, Benetton also uses the electronic point-of-sale (EPOS) system within key shops to track early sales of new designs (which are bar-coded). Information on style, colour and size is collated and analysed electronically to isolate which new items are most popular. Agents can then be informed so that they can brief retailers and anticipate demand.

Whilst Benetton has not been immune to trading pressures in a notoriously volatile market, its use of IT has enhanced its value chain to give it significant competitive advantage. As an example, its automated order-processing and manufacturing operations have enabled it to speed the whole process from design to distribution from a three/six-month cycle to as little as eleven/fifteen days. This speed of operations and output activities gives the company competitive advantage by allowing it to respond quickly to changes in fashion and levels of demand, meeting customer needs better, whilst minimising its stock costs and level of risk. The efficiency of the ordering system is also valuable on the input side in allowing Benetton to forecast its production requirements quickly, enabling it to plan the most cost-effective purchase of raw materials.

IT has also given Benetton the opportunity to strengthen its sales and service activities, tying its distributor 'customers' into its franchised network by the speed of service and resulting competitive advantage it gives to them. In addition, Benetton's ability to forecast demand provides another valuable service to its retail customers, securing their continued commitment and loyalty, whilst ensuring that both parties are closest and most responsive to the consumer at the end of the chain.

Illustration 10.3: Adding value in output – Carters of Faringdon
Founded in the 19th century, Carters is a family-owned and run grocery store in the town of Faringdon, Oxfordshire. With 12,000 square feet of store space, it is the only store of comparable size in the area. Carters has been using IT since 1984. It began by contracting the Warwick Bepos Group, an ICL added value reseller, to supply the back office package, *Storemaster*. Offering 15,000 lines, *Storemaster* handles stock control, sales order processing, financial ledgers, generation of purchase orders, reports by department and profit analysis by orders, sales or suppliers.

The next major step has been the installation of EPOS machinery. EPOS terminals from ICL Retail Systems were evaluated and, as a result, ICL 9518/200 terminals with flat bed scanners have been installed on the eight checkout lanes and in the cigarette kiosk, plus another terminal in the cash office. Those on the checkout lanes have a weigh scale link and can read credit cards. Updated *Storemaster* software supports EPOS functions, providing all the information necessary for effective day-to-day store management. (*Independent Retailer*, June 1993)

In the case of Carters of Faringdon, IT has been crucial in adding value to both its primary and secondary activities. A key operational and service issue has been the need to squeeze the right range of goods for its customers, including some slower-selling lines, into a relatively small shelf area. As John Carter explains,

'Probably the main difference between us and a big multiple (one of the larger retail chains) is that we are stocking as many lines in 12,000 square feet as they are in 25,000 square feet'.

Storemaster allows the family to monitor sales closely, adjusting the range to fit customer preferences, allowing rapid and frequent restocking to keep shelves full as well as the capacity to pinpoint the profitability of scanned items and the gross profit of the whole store on a regular basis. The EPOS system has also raised levels of customer service by speeding up transactions at the checkout, providing an automatic cheque-printing facility so that customers no longer have to write out cheques, as well as the capacity to process credit card purchases (which Carters started to accept in 1990) more rapidly.

Investing in IT has thus enabled Carters to build on the firm's traditional strength in retaining loyalty through a high quality of local service, including a delivery service for customers. As John Carter comments,

'I am not a technical man, but one of the strengths of this company is that we have always tried to keep abreast of changing trends within the supermarket industry. Our customers now get exactly the same treatment from us as they get from the major multiples, plus personal service'.

By adding value to its output, service and infrastructural activities, Carters has retained its local competitive advantage and strengthened its position in warding off potential encroachment from another independent retailer or one of the major chains.

Illustration 10.4: Getting the marketing right – the cable business

An increasing number of cable companies are making use of IT-based geodemographic classification systems such as Mosaic and CableAble, both from CCN. These systems, based on the division of the country into postcodes, which can then be linked to particular social groups, allow users to define and target particular customer types more closely.

Nynex is a cable company owning 16 franchises in the UK (a franchise is a geographical area granted by Government licence). Traditionally, it has relied on blanket direct mail followed up by its salesforce to locate potential cable subscribers. To improve this process, Nynex is building a database to target its marketing on areas dominated by customers with the greatest potential. John Palmer, marketing manager of information systems at Nynex, was given the task of developing the database. Palmer decided that 'a customer-orientated system designed for marketing use' was required. He needed to know who Nynex's potential customers were, their spending habits and typifying characteristics. He enlisted the help of an information services company, CACI, to collate and analyse existing customer information on Nynex's database and to match it to an analysis of each franchise using such tools as local maps and the electoral register to identify differing customer types and levels of spending power. Matching the two, allowed Nynex to estimate the potential of, and put a value on, every prospective customer, made up of a 'positive revenue factor', the amount of money that might be spent by the customer, balanced by the relative cost factor – the amount Nynex would have to spend to supply the service to the customer. Such information could then be used to target those areas with greatest potential for sales and cable-laying activity. (*Marketing Week*, 27.01.95)

For cable companies, a critical success factor has been the need to get the cable network established so that they can offer a service to potential customers. To quote Barry

Winter of CACI, 'the priority is to get the roads up and the cables down... the actual sales of the services is a little secondary at present'. This has to be balanced against the huge cost of laying the cable: about £40 a metre. As a result, a primary value-adding activity is in market research and marketing, in concentrating cable-laying in areas with the highest percentage of likely customers. Nynex's database allows it to target prospective customers with the highest revenue potential down to individual households. To quote John Palmer,

'It allows us to compare the values of neighbouring networks and, on a larger scale, it allows us to see where the most attractive areas are within a franchise.'

IT has given Nynex competitive advantage in maximising its return on investment in relation to other franchise holders, putting it in a stronger position to attract further investment and to extend its franchise network in the future.

Illustration 10.5:   An IT-generated business – Federal Express

Federal Express is a $6billion business with 60% of the US overnight package delivery business. It currently handles over 1.5 million packages sent to 127 countries. It was built in the 1970s on the guarantee that any package dispatched within the US would arrive by 10.30 am the next day. This promise has been built on the systematic use of IT throughout the business. In order to achieve this, a good communication and information system has proved as important as a good transport system. The company has its own planes and vehicles and has spent a considerable amount of money on information technology.

Firstly, to give good initial customer contact, centrally located telephonists answer calls from potential customers. Computers give precise information on the nearest collection point to any enquirer. As soon as Federal Express receives the parcel at a collection point a bar-code is put on it giving details of its destination. This is used to control the parcel throughout its journey. The bar-code can be read by a hand-held scanning pen called a super-tracker. A parcel tracking system called *Cosmos* scans the bar-code on the parcel at each stage on the journey and reroutes it. *Cosmos* is much more than a tracking system; it generates information to control and monitor activity levels and provides the information for planning vehicle and flight operations.

All vehicles have an in-cab computer and this, together with the super-tracker, means that any parcel the company is delivering can be traced within thirty minutes – wherever it may be in the world at the time.

Federal Express pioneered the now widely-used hub and spoke system. The system has a central hub where most of the sorting is carried out and through which all parcels flow. Spokes radiate from the hub to various regional airports and from the airports the parcels are taken to their specific destinations. Thus, the parcels move in along one spoke to the hub, where they are rerouted and sent to their destination along another spoke.

More recently, the company has been experimenting with IT to establish even closer and more flexible links with its customers, including the electronic transmission of automatic package pickup instructions from customers and the electronic posting of shipping bills to them. Its aim, to quote one of its senior executives, is 'to find ways to smoothly make electronic connections with major accounts'. The result will be a 'virtual' organisation closely tied into its major customers, increasing the level of service and tying its customers more closely to the company. (*Computerworld* 25.2.91)

Federal Express is one of the most dramatic cases of a business which sprang directly from the potential of IT. The company saw that competitive advantage in the distribution business lay in a combination of speed, reliability and cost for the customer. IT provided the speed and versatility of communication to coordinate the most efficient and cost-effective movement of goods. Reliability was provided by introducing a computerised routing system which had the additional benefit of being able to pinpoint the whereabouts of any parcel within half-an-hour. It also made the hub and spoke system feasible.

In reflecting on the use of IT for competitive advantage, Federal Express's Chief Executive Officer commented:

'The application of information and telecom technology has to be very incremental and very user-friendly. Its main goal must be to improve quickly... whether the quality of employees' work or the quality of information to customers. We don't do what lots of people have tried to do – use technology to save labour or be a Big Brother to employees.'

His comments underline the importance of using IT not so much as a mechanism for control or cost-cutting, but more as a way of adding value to the process chain.

IT and strategic alignment

So far we have looked at the ways IT can provide a company with competitive advantage by adding to the value chain. If this process is to occur in a conscious, planned, way, it depends on a business having a clear understanding of its strategic position and a clear set of strategic goals defining the competitive advantage it needs to aquire in its chosen market. Once its strategy is clear, it can begin to explore the IT options available and what they could contribute to achieving competitive advantage.

However, the most successful businesses exploiting IT have not done so by simply adding a layer of IT on top of their existing systems. They have realised that a full exploitation of IT requires a flexibility of approach which can have a profound impact on the rest of the business. This flexibility may be contrasted with those companies that have lacked this ability to adapt and have failed to reap the competitive potential of IT. Indeed, evidence in the US and elsewhere suggest that, at the beginning of the 90s at least, increased investment in IT seemed to be coinciding with *lower* overall productivity and growth (Scott Morton 1991). In many cases, IT systems either failed to function properly or did not recoup the original investment by adding value in better costs and business performance. In some cases, rather than falling, headcounts actually rose with the introduction of IT.

In part, this reflected the first applications of IT to speed up such traditionally labour and paper-intensive parts of the business as transaction processing and the accounts function. More fundamentally, it reflected a failure which is illustrated dramatically by a classic piece of research done on the American car Industry in the 1980s.

Illustration 10.6:   Organisation and technology in the American automobile industry

During the 1980s, a team from the Massachusetts Institute of Technology analysed the impact of new technology in the US automobile industry. The MIT team chose a number of sites which had introduced varying levels of automation and compared them with the degree of accompanying organisational change. The key results for four of the sites are summarised in the graph and table in Figure 10.2

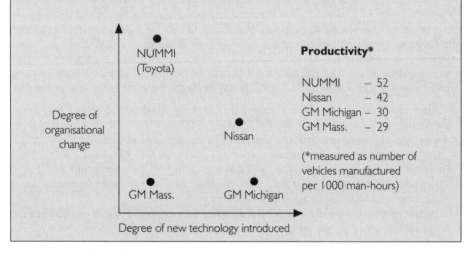

Figure 10.2   Manufacturing productivity compared with organisational change and technological advancement (Source: Scott Morton, p. 225)

It is not surprising that the least automated site, General Motors, Massachusetts, should have the lowest productivity. What is more remarkable is how small an increase in productivity was achieved by its far more highly-automated sister-plant in Michigan. This contrast becomes even more marked when one compares the productivity of the Michigan plant first with the Nissan plant which introduced a comparable level of technology, together with some organisational change, and then with the Toyota plant, which combined a relatively low level of investment in technological innovation with a high level of organisational change, achieving a level of productivity 24% better than Nissan and 79% better than the General Motors Massachusetts plant.

IT and business change

This research illuminates very clearly some of the themes discussed in Chapter 2: that the way businesses are organised can have a profound effect on their effectiveness and that the failure to adapt an organisation to meet changing needs can put it at a serious disadvantage. The advent of IT places exceptional demands on a business and highlights this inflexibility. This impact has been summarised as follows:

'IT offers the capability to redefine the boundaries of markets and structural characteristics, alter the fundamental rules and basis of competition, redefine business scope, and provide a new set of competitive weapons.' (Scott Morton: p. 125).

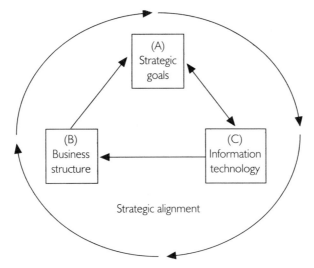

Figure 10.3   The process of strategic alignment

To put it another way, the impact of IT is not a simple, one-way process. It is, rather, a continuous process of dialogue, a process of strategic alignment in which IT may redefine a business's original strategy and organisation. This process of strategic alignment can be illustrated as in Figure 10.3. A business may begin with an initial set of strategic goals (A) which determine its key IT requirements (B) and an appropriate organisational structure (C). However, the deployment of IT may generate new market opportunities and require an altered organisation structure which then requires the redefinition of business goals.

One model of this dynamic, changing relationship between strategy, IT and organisation is shown in Figure 10.4.

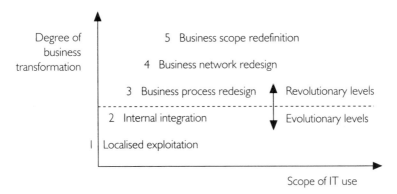

Figure 10.4   Evolutionary and revolutionary changes as a function of IT usage (Source: Scott Morton, p. 127)

This model shows the various stages a business may go through in exploiting IT for competitive advantage. It may begin with **localised exploitation** of a particular IT application within an isolated part of the business, for instance, one of the applications discussed in the previous chapter, or the use of an enhanced marketing database by the cable company Nyrex. This approach may sometimes be characteristic of companies relatively new to IT and adopting a *laissez faire* approach in which individual users and departments develop local IT solutions to particular problems. This sporadic use may improve the speed and efficiency of a particular process, particularly at an operational or tactical level, but it is unlikely to result in any transformation of the process or the business itself.

From this tentative start, the business may move to **internal integration:** a fuller, more systematic application of IT to all parts of the business. The case of Carters of Faringdon illustrates this stage with IT solutions applied comprehensively to such activities as stock control, transaction processing and management reporting. This more systematic use of IT not only increases the efficiency of individual operations, it integrates them within a common IT platform. Within many businesses, this integration takes place through a common sales database which links customer transactions to such areas as stock control, marketing activity and financial reporting. At this stage, the degree of change still remains evolutionary with no radical transformation of existing business processes.

It is only when a business reaches stage three and **business process redesign** that it moves into a more revolutionary mode and IT begins to change the business itself. Benetton provides an example in the transformation and integration of traditional design and production processes through the application of CAD and CAM, whilst McKesson's shift to direct electronic links with suppliers led to a substantial reduction in the scale and role of its purchasing department.

McKesson in particular provides a rich example of the penultimate stage of **business network redesign** in which not only are the traditional boundaries and processes within the business redefined and redesigned, but the boundaries of the business itself changed to create a 'virtual organisation'. In McKesson's case, its IT links with suppliers and drug stores blur the division between it and them so that drug store proprietors and even suppliers are effectively integrated into the McKesson network.

The final stage is the most revolutionary, the impact of IT not only in transforming a business's internal processes and broadening its organisational boundaries, but in **business scope redefinition,** the alteration of the markets and *raison d'etre* of an organisation. Perhaps the most famous example of this final stage is American Airlines, discussed in Illustration 10.7.

Illustration 10.7:   IT transformation of a business – American Airlines

A key issue in the airlines business is the speed and effectiveness of booking flights. Up to the 1950s, the system was largely manual. An airlines reservation office would monitor available seats and once a travel agent wished to make a booking, it would telephone the office to check on availability. When the number of available seats on a flight dropped below a minimum, the office would notify the travel agents to stop booking. The system was slow, labour-intensive and inefficient with frequent overbooking, as well as under-booking, of flights because of time-lags and the level of paperwork.

As early as 1954, American Airlines and IBM developed a simple automated proto-type booking system, but it was ten years later that the SABRE system was developed, with the first trial in a limited number of travel agents in 1967. In 1976, in response to the piloting of its rival United Airlines' Apollo system, American Airlines began to install free terminals for its SABRE system into travel agents. It expected it might gain an extra $3m a year over installation costs since, whilst it included information from all airlines, American Airlines flights were always shown first and were therefore more likely to be booked. In fact, before installation was complete, it had to revise its estimate up to over $20m, a return on investment of over 500%. By 1985, profits were an estimated $143m. SABRE helped American Airlines to overtake its rival United in market share.

What few had foreseen was the potential of IT, not merely to improve efficiency, but to change the rules of competition and redefine the scope of an individual business. American Airlines discovered that, by being first, they were able to use SABRE as a way of promoting their own flights. They consolidated this position by tying travel agents into their system. Rivals found it difficult to persuade travel agents to change once they had SABRE installed. Even more significantly, SABRE created an entirely new market for American Airlines: the marketing of information, for example, by selling preferential screen space to other airlines. Such was the success of the system that the Chief Executive, Robert Crandell, once remarked that: 'if forced to choose, he would rather sell the airline and keep SABRE!'

Summary

This chapter has built on the previous chapter in looking at how IT can be used, not only to solve individual problems in business, but to provide it with competitive advantage. Full exploitation of IT to meet the key decision needs of a business requires the business to understand two things: the sources of its competitive advantage in its chosen markets, and the potential of IT to enhance that advantage. The third consideration is the need for a flexible response to the impact of IT on a businesses organisation and strategy. As we shall see in the next chapter, understanding the human organisational implications of IT is crucial to its successful and most productive application.

Problems

1 Describe how Euro Insurance (Chapter 9 illustration) might 'add value' to the customer.

2 Assess where Euro Insurance's competitive advantage might lie.

3 How do the IT applications used by Euro Insurance contribute to getting competitive advantage? What other applications should they consider?

4 Where do you think Euro Insurance lies in the scale of business change? Could the company reorganise further to make fuller use of IT for competitive advantage?

References for this text

Johnston, R. and Laurence, P., Beyond vertical integration – the rise of value-adding partnership, in *Harvard Business Review,* July – August 1988

Porter, Michael *Competitive Advantage,*1985

Scott Morton, M., (Ed.) *The Corporation of the 1990s: Information Technology and Organisational Transformation,* Oxford University Press, 1991

Zottola, L., The united systems of Benetton, in *Computerworld,* April 1990

Further reading

Cashmore, C. and Lyall, R., *Business Information: Systems and Strategies,* Prentice-Hall, 1991

Johnson, G. and Scholes, K., *Exploring Corporate Strategy: Text and Cases,* 3rd Edition, Prentice-Hall, 1991

Peppard, J., *IT Strategy for Business,* Pitman, 1993

Robson, W., *Strategic Management and Information Systems: An Integrated Approach,* Pitman, 1993

11 Implementing an IT strategy

Objectives

Introduction

> By the end of this chapter, you should be able to:
> - identify the key stages in implementing an IT strategy
> - understand the key problems at each stage
> - answer the case-studies at the end of each chapter.

In the last chapter, we looked at the strategic use of IT in business and the potential implications of the strategic alignment process on the business itself. This broader strategic framework provides the essential context for implementing an IT strategy, the theme of this chapter. Without such a framework, introducing IT is likely, at best, to be a piecemeal affair with only local benefits and, at worst, a costly and counter-productive experience which makes no contribution to competitive advantage.

There are a number of established methodologies such as **structured systems analysis and design methodology** (SSADM) which have been developed for the implementation of IT systems. These will be discussed within the overall approach outlined here. This approach is based around a major case-study, Sun Alliance International, which we will use to discuss and illustrate the range of issues associated with implementation.

The stages involved in the growth of any information system can be regarded as forming a continuous process. They commence with a recognition of a problem, development of a method of solution, use of this solution, and improving the method of solution whenever appropriate. The improvement of such a system then leads on to a reassessment of the problem and the cycle repeats itself again. Figure 11.1 shows the simple model used to illustrate the **life-cycle** of information systems.

In this chapter, we will consider the overall approaches to the design, development and application of computerised information systems using the life-cycle model.

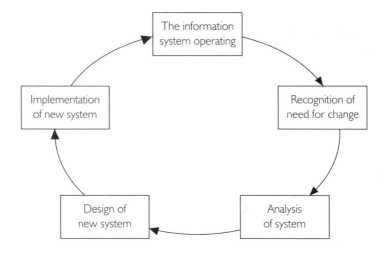

Figure 11.1   Life-cycle of information systems

The strategic context

As has been noted, IT strategy begins with the strategy selected for the business as a whole. One approach is for a business to identify and analyse its value chain for ways of adding value to achieve competitive advantage.

A **strategic analysis** of this kind isolates the parts of the business which need improvement and the kind of changes required. Within this context, the business can begin to investigate the potential role of IT in offering a solution, the kinds of solution it needs and the broad benchmarks by which an IT solution can be judged. In the case of Sun Alliance International, the strategic issues it faced are explained in Illustration 11.1.

Illustration 11.1:   The strategic challenge facing Sun Alliance International
In the 1980s, Sun Alliance faced mounting pressures from the market place. Deregulation led to over-supply and rate cutting which, coupled with the recession and a major increase in the number and scale of claims, prompted the highest ever losses in the UK insurance market.

These pressures hit Sun Alliance International, the company within Sun Alliance providing an insurance specifically for business, indeed, the largest insurer of UK-based commercial risks. Its customer base consisted of some direct corporate clients, but mainly brokers (or agents) acting on behalf of clients with whom it liaised via ten regional centres and a network of smaller offices. Brokers judged Sun Alliance

International's performance on the added value it could provide through the speed and flexibility of its response to specific insurance needs, its ability to generate a tailor-made and cost-effective solution for the customer, the efficiency of its claims service and its day-to-day customer service.

In the face of sharper competition and lower rates, Sun Alliance International identified the following key elements in sustaining and improving competitive advantage:

- it needed to cut costs by closing its 20 smaller centres without compromising support for its sales force or its levels of customer service, especially to its broker clients.
- it needed to be able to concentrate fewer resources on the most profitable parts of the business.
- it needed to be able to identify customer needs better and improve its levels of service to them.

The elements identified by Sun Alliance International suggested two key issues involving communication and information. Without the support of the smaller local centres, the sales force would need alternative ways of linking effectively into Sun Alliance International.

If Sun Alliance International was to target its customers better and to provide an improved service, it would need better control of its information in analysing its clients and their needs. This analysis pointed to a database solution supported by a flexible communications network to enable the sales reps to exploit it.

Developing an information system

There are many approaches that can be used to develop an information system for a business. However, most of these approaches have common elements which can be regarded as the main phases in the life-cycle. Whether developing a system for a small business, or producing a total Management Information System for a large organisation, the overall approach is similar. In this section, we will consider the main steps involved and summarise the overall approaches. Later sections in this chapter will consider each step in more detail and refer to methodologies where appropriate. One simple way of considering the stages involved in developing an information system is outlined by Capron and Perron (1993). The main stages involved are described by Capron and Perron as:

- Preliminary investigation
- Analysis
- Design
- Development
- Implementation.

In this text, a sixth stage called Maintenance will be considered separately. These six stages constitute the main elements to be considered in the systems development life-cycle and are illustrated in Figure 11.2.

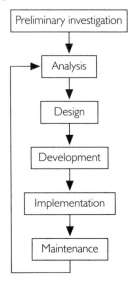

Figure 11.2   Stages in information systems development

Preliminary investigation

The preliminary investigation stage would involve the initial statement of the problem. This may result from a manager in a company complaining about not receiving the right information, or receiving it at the wrong time, or in the wrong format. A preliminary investigation may then highlight the problem areas, define the scope of the problem and specify objectives.

Analysis

The analysis stage, usually called **systems analysis,** deals with looking at the current systems in operation. Systems analysis would involve collecting all the relevant information available and analysing the main issues and problems. After this stage, we should be in a good position to consider possible methods of solution for the problems defined.

Design

Following detailed analysis, the design stage (**systems design**) can take place. During this phase, a variety of solutions to the problems will be considered and compared. At this stage, a range of factors are appraised in terms of how the final information system will evolve. Factors such as output requirements (e.g. what sort of reports are required), input requirements (e.g. how information is to be entered), organisation of files and hardware requirements will all need to be considered in the design stage.

Development

The development stage (**systems development**) involves the actual production of the systems designed in earlier stages. This will include developing any new software (writing programs) and ensuring that these programs operate effectively (testing).

Implementation

The implementation stage involves getting the system fully operational. New equipment may need to be installed, staff will be trained to use the new systems, documentation must be produced. The system will be evaluated to ensure that everything is operating according to the design and existing systems will be gradually phased out.

Maintenance

The maintenance stage includes monitoring of the system, producing modifications and additions to the system when required. This important stage will then take us back into the earlier phases since any new addition to the system will need to be properly analysed and designed.

The following sections will consider each of these stages in more detail. It should be stressed that such a life-cycle is equally appropriate when producing an upgrading for an existing system as it is when developing a totally new system. The only difference is that the point at which the life-cycle is entered (illustrated in Figure 11.2.) will vary. For example, the development of a totally new system will clearly commence with the problem definition stage. Alternatively, the upgrade of an existing system will initially involve considering the maintenance stage, since it is at this stage that the potential for new systems and upgrades will become apparent.

Self-assessment questions _____

1   List the main stages involved in the development of a new information system for a company with which you are familiar.

2   You wish to develop a new system at your workplace to produce weekly reports on sales figures. Briefly describe, in terms of the system's development life-cycle, the steps you will need to go through in order to develop such a system.

Preliminary investigation

During this initial stage in the system development life-cycle, the problems are studied in brief. This may take the form of a **feasibility study** in which an inquiry is carried out to ascertain whether the system development is necessary and appropriate. A team may need to be set up in order to conduct this feasibility study. The team would consist of a combination of systems experts and users. It is vital that prospective users of the system are involved from a very early stage in the system's development.

The feasibility study will consider a number of issues, including the following.

What is the problem?

In many cases the actual problem or problems are not clearly defined. These will need to be clarified before moving forward with the project. This would involve consideration of the problems occurring with any existing system to discover where improvements need to be made. For example, the manager of a sales department notices that a number of orders have gone missing over the past few months. This has resulted in some confusion, delays in delivery and poor customer relations. The problem here may be the poor management of incoming orders, though different interpretations could be drawn.

What is the scope?

Care must be taken to clearly define the scope of the problem. In systems terminology, we would need to define the **boundary** of the problem. If this is not done then information systems can expand beyond what is required. For instance, a problem has been defined in one department within an organisation and therefore the scope may simply be contained within that department. It may be unnecessary to develop a company-wide system to solve the problems of a single department. Consider the previous problem of sales orders going missing. It may be that the scope of the problem is confined to the sales department. Alternatively, in order to solve the problem, current working practices in other departments, such as marketing and accounts, may need to be considered. When defining the scope it will be necessary to consider the project time-scales. It is possible that a wide definition of the scope may result in a five-year project when an immediate solution is required.

What are the objectives?

At this stage, we should consider the problem and its scope in order to determine what is actually required. A set of objectives will be produced stated in general terms. For example, the objectives related to the problem of lost orders may include: improve order form handling and upgrade communication with reference to orders between departments such as sales, accounts and production. More specific details based on these objectives will be determined later in the overall development life-cycle.

Following the preliminary investigation, a decision will need to be made on whether or not to continue with the project, or whether to review and redefine the projects' objectives. This initial process in the case of Sun Alliance International is developed in Illustration 11.2.

Illustration 11.2:   Sun Alliance International. Step 1: Identifying an IT solution
Sun Alliance International's first step was to involve *both* business managers and IT specialists at an early stage. A joint approach blending systems and technical know-how with the strategic focus of marketing and sales management meant that the development of an IT solution did not lose its essential strategic focus.
That projected IT solution came to be known as ADaM, short for Agency Development and Management, emphasising the strategic focus of the system in meeting agents' (or brokers') needs via Sun Alliance International's sales force. The first step was to agree a broad specification for the system consistent with Sun Alliance International's business needs. Such a specification included the following elements:

- **customised:** the system needed to be adaptable enough to fit Sun Alliance International's precise requirements.
- **relational:** a relational database was needed to handle the volume of information, its range and the need to manipulate it in a variety of ways. It would need to be

large enough to handle the needs of at least 50 users to begin with and to be capable of handling more as needed.
- **compatible:** the system had to interface satisfactorily with the company's existing mainframe which held the core information on brokers and data on performance.
- **cost-effective:** the cost could not outweigh the savings Sun Alliance International needed to make
- **complete:** the system had to be advanced enough to be on line within six months, the deadline for closing the smaller offices.

Self-assessment questions

1 Summarise the main elements involved in specifying the requirements of a new information system for your company.

2 You have been asked to manage the initial stages of the development of a new computer system in the accounts department. How would you proceed to start the project? What would your initial steps be and how would you achieve them?

Systems analysis

This stage of developing an information system will commence following approval of the findings from the preliminary investigation. In this stage, any existing systems are considered and analysed. This will involve clarifying the definition of the project's scope and objectives, collecting data on current operations, documenting any systems in operation (whether computer-based or manual), and analysing the results to provide details on the new system's requirements.

It will be at this point that more detailed research will be done amongst potential users. A range of techniques can be utilised to record data, including the use of such tools as data flow and entity diagrams discussed in Chapter 3. They can help to build a model of how a new system might work and the requirements it must fulfil to meet the businesses needs.

A statement of requirements is vital before the next stage (design) can commence. A number of areas should be considered when producing the **requirements specification.** One important element is to determine any constraints that exist for the new system. For instance, limits on the funds available for the design, development and maintenance costs of the new system will clearly affect the scope of the project as defined from the preliminary investigation.

The requirements for the new system will include a range of factors outlining the user's needs, such as the following:

- **Input methods:** how the data will be input, in what format and at which locations, i.e. whether centralised or de-centralised.
- **Output methods:** the types of output required, such as report formats, regular updated summaries, *ad hoc* reports, screen displays and locations required.
- **Communications:** types of links between systems, integration of computers.

- **Timing:** requirements on timescales, response rates, frequency of usage, whether any bottle-necks may occur.
- **Security:** the level of security required. There will inevitably be a variation in the required security levels for both users and programs; some requiring a higher level of security than others.

Such requirements will be included in a report for management. The report is likely to contain the following elements: a review of the preliminary investigation, a statement of the constraints identified, a review of possible alternatives to the system, and estimates of costs involved in further development.

At the end of the analysis stage, a decision will be made about whether or not to continue with the system development. If the project is approved, then the next stage (design) will be started.

Make or buy issues

A key issue implicit in Sun Alliance International's case is the early choice that needs to be made between creating an entirely new system, buying in and developing an existing software package or enhancing the existing system. The first of these has the advantage of giving the end user the possibility of owning a unique system tailored exactly to the business' requirements and, potentially, maximising competitive advantage. It has the drawback of the high level of cost, time and risk involved in developing a completely new and untried system. Where it has a good chance of meeting the strategic requirements set out at the beginning, a company is likely to prefer enhancing its current system or tailoring an off-the-shelf package. Enhancing the existing system has the advantage of least potential disruption and making the most of something users will already be familiar with. It will be disadvantageous to the degree that the existing system is ill-suited to the real strategic needs of the business. Tailoring a commercially-available package also has the advantage of making use of a known quantity, the reliability of which has already been tested in the market. Its disadvantage lies in a reduced potential competitive advantage in using a publicly-available solution. In the case of Sun Alliance International, the limitations of the existing system and their own technical resources, together with constraints of cost and time, pointed them towards customising an existing package. One of the case-study exercises at the end of the chapter provides a different perspective to consider.

If a decision is made to use an outside agency, whether as a software developer, a supplier of an 'off-the-shelf' package, or as (frequently) a combination of both, the right choice can be critical for success. A business may be heavily dependent on the software house for technical advice on both hardware and software, and the likely duration and cost of the project, the complex area of translating a set of business requirements into a **technical systems specification,** the writing or adapting of the software, and ongoing maintenance of and improvement to the system. An inefficient, uncommitted, or unscrupulous supplier would leader to a rapid escalation in cost, delays and technical problems.

As well as taking up references from previous customers and parent organisations (many suppliers are officially vetted by major hardware and software companies), a company needs to assess the suppliers degree of experience of its business, the quality and fit of its product, and its willingness to make that extra commitment to understand

and fulfil the company's requirements. Sun Alliance International ultimately chose a new company, Integrated Sales Systems (ISS) over some established names, partly because its *Oxygen* software came close to fitting Sun Alliance International's requirements and partly because, as a new company, they were keen to cultivate a major corporate customer and demonstrated the commitment and flexibility to match. An alternative choice is included in one of the case-studies at the end of the chapter.

Illustration 11.3:   Sun Alliance International, Step 2: The analysis phase

Sun Alliance International began by asking Integrated Sales Systems to provide a first prototype of agency development and management, using their core *Oxygen* database, *before* the contract was signed. This was compared to the existing paper system to test the quality of the database and Sun Alliance International's capacity of meet the challenge.

The next step was to compare the *Oxygen* database in detail against a statement of requirements and to provide a detailed specification for new programming. Once the key points were clear, the development team consulted potential users to check it still fitted their requirements.

In parallel with software development, a team looked at the interface of the system with the mainframe, for example, the mechanisms for downloading data between the two. Another looked at broader communication issues such as the provision of PCs, modems and a central database server to link sales reps to the database and head office staff via a LAN.

Self-assessment questions

I   You have been asked to analyse the processes involved in the receipt and booking of travel requests by customers in a travel agent. What methods would you use to record these processes?

2   The systems analysis stage is usually completed with a basic requirements specification. What would you consider to be important for inclusion on such a list?

Systems design

During the design stage, the new system is planned to meet the requirements highlighted in the analysis stage. It should be stressed that this does not simply involve the computerisation of existing manual systems. On the contrary, it is likely that the new design will incorporate changes to procedures in order to produce an efficient, effective information system. The new system must be designed with reference to the following considerations:

● **Usability.**   The system must be able to perform the various functions defined from the analysis stage. It needs to be a practical system, which will be suitable for the targeted users. Thus, generally systems must not assume a high degree of computer expertise from the users.

- **Cost.**   Clearly, this is an important factor which will constrain the design within certain parameters. These constraints would have been highlighted in the analysis stage of the system development.
- **Expandability.**   The system should be designed recognising that requirements are likely to change and evolve over time. Thus, the system must be flexible enough to be able to expand to satisfy any future requirements. A term used for this approach is '**future proofing**' – ensuring that future requirements will be catered for without causing obsolescence.
- **Security.**   A range of security measures should be incorporated into the design in order to guard against **computer fraud** and access to classified data. The level of security required will determine the hardware and software that will be necessary. These issues are discussed in more detail in a later section on data security and controls.
- **Reliability.** The system will need to be in operation constantly and thus must be as close to 100% reliable as is reasonably possible. The design will need to take this into account by means of suitable backup systems for hardware, software and communications links between systems.

There are a number of different activities which will need to be designed into the system. The main activities are input, output, data file construction, processing and testing facilities. Each of these elements are briefly described below.

- **Input requirements:** the way in which data will be input, such as using keyboard entry or the use of appropriate forms. Will **input screens** need to be designed? What type of data is required in order to satisfy the requirements?
- **Output requirements:** what type of information is required? What reports are required and in which format? Will only regular, planned reports be needed, or *ad hoc* reports required? Will **output screens** need to be designed? Will different users require the information in different formats?
- **Files:** what data is required to be stored in order to satisfy any output requirements? What will the structure of the files be? For instance, what will the individual records within the files contain? How will these files be linked together and related to existing systems already in operation?
- **Processes:** how will the data files be used? What processes will take place (eg comparison of data, validating information, arithmetic operations, updating of files and sorting records)?
- **Testing:** the testing of the final system will need to be planned ahead of implementation. Testing procedures need to be designed into the overall project otherwise problems will inevitably occur. This will involve designing test data in order to check the various processes in the system.

Such considerations will require resolution in the design process in order to achieve an effective information system. As we have seen, the Sun Alliance International example also makes use of prototyping at the earliest stage possible. Developing a prototype can be a crucial counterbalance to the generation of a detailed set of requirements. It is often at this stage that potential users, invariably not IT specialists, find the greatest difficulty in describing the precise deficiencies of the current system. In specifying their detailed requirements for a new system, they may find it difficult to visualise their needs, whilst the IT specialists, who will not have the functional expertise of users, will have similar difficulty in interpreting and translating those requirements. By providing something to criticise and compare with the current system, a prototype, whether a trial version of some elements of the new system, or a first stab at the whole system, makes it easier for users to contribute to the process and to identify and resolve technical problems.

The issue of the involvement of users with software houses and their products at an early stage in the development process is also a vital consideration in a successful implementation programme. As has already been mentioned, the leadership and involvement of managers with an awareness of, and involvement in, the key strategic issues facing the business is essential in ensuring it meets its business goals. Similarly, the involvement of users is a key issue which we will discuss in greater detail in the next section.

At this stage, it is possible to outline in more detail the nature of Sun Alliance International's proposed Agency Development and Management system:

Illustration 11.4:   Sun Alliance International, The ADaM System: key features

Hardware

Each rep was equipped with a Notebook computer containing the ADaM system and database, a compact modem, a BT business telephone line for both voice, e-mail and data transfer linked to the mainframe computer (to allow rep enquiries) and an answerphone and carphone.

Information from reps was initially stored on his/her PC and, at regular intervals, passed to the central database server for transfer onto relevant parts of the database. In turn, information was transferred to databases held by local sales managers.

Software

- **Agency records.**   Included basic information (e.g. addresses), key contact details and profiles, the value of businesses with individual agents, profiles on agents' businesses activities and a history of contacts with Sun Alliance International.
- **Organiser.**   This piece of software allows users to select and sort information from the agency records and elsewhere. As an example, in planning a sales visit, a rep is able to call up all customers providing income over a certain level within a certain post code.
- **Task Management.**   This software allows users to arrange their own and others' workload, listing individual tasks, monitoring completion dates and even providing an automatic date for a follow-up contact.
- **Reports.**   Standard report formats designed for most operational needs are built into the system, which a user can tailor to specific requirements, whether productivity levels amongst sales reps, or the top 20 agency accounts.

Systems development

This stage involves the use of technical expertise to produce the programs necessary to satisfy the design criteria previously established. **System development** involves the following areas:

- **Design specifications:** detailed specifications are produced from the system design before further work can commence.
- **Programming:** this is the real 'production' stage. During this important stage all the programs are written giving computer instructions to implement the detailed specifications.

- **Testing:**   prior to full operation, the system will require thorough testing. During this stage, any errors (so-called 'bugs') in the system will be located and corrected, ensuring a smooth transition to full operation.
- **Documentation:**   much of the documentation should have been created at the design stage, such as **systems flow charts** and **structure charts**. Further documentation on the specific processes involved will be produced, such as flow charts, descriptions of the programming logic and information on data contained in files.

System implementation

System implementation involves a number of phases aimed at obtaining a fully operational system. All the programming work and preliminary testing will have been completed prior to this stage. The following elements will be conducted during this stage:

Training

This important stage involves ensuring that all prospective users of the system have the appropriate levels of knowledge in order to operate the system efficiently. This will include the 'end-users' (such as managers and other non-technical staff), in addition to the computer specialists (computer manager, programming and operating staff) who will be involved in the operation of the systems. Training material will be produced in addition to the system documentation such as user manuals and course material. Courses will be run for individuals and groups to ensure familiarity with the system.

Hardware

Depending on the scale of the new system, new hardware may need to be installed. Existing computers and other equipment may need to be replaced or phased out. This will involve additional testing of the required hardware systems.

System Conversion

Existing systems will need to be removed and replaced by the new system. This can be achieved in a number of ways, such as:

- **Direct conversion** means that the original system is removed and replaced by the new system in one operation. This method is unusual as there are no safeguards if the new system fails.
- **Phased conversion** involves a slow conversion from the old to the new system. Some elements of the new system replace the old and are tested before changing further elements. Step-by-step the new system will be implemented.
- **Parallel conversion** involves both new an old system running alongside each other for a period of time. In this way, the new system can be thoroughly tested with the old system in full operation as a back-up if anything goes wrong. Only when the new system has proved to be effective will the old system be removed. Theoretically, this is the best method to adopt, though in many cases it may not be practicable to staff the two systems side-by-side.

Figure 11.3 shows the different methods of conversion from existing to new information systems.

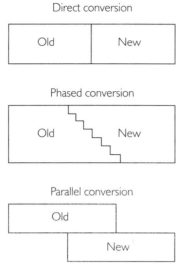

Figure 11.3   Conversion approaches for new systems

Review

The final phase in implementation is to review all the previous steps to ensure that the new system is fully operational and satisfies the objectives defined in the earlier stages. This involves checking that all the procedures are working correctly, staff have been fully trained, correct outputs produced, old processes have been eliminated and no 'bugs' are apparent.

Modifications

At this late stage, it may be necessary to make relatively minor changes to the system to cater for any problems highlighted in the Review phase.

Illustration 11.5:   Sun Alliance International, Step 3: Piloting

Sun Alliance International incorporated a pilot phase before the system went live, partly to test the system, but also to gauge users' responses to the hardware and software and to test differing hardware options. Four salesmen, two of their managers and three HQ personnel were invited to a two-day briefing workshop to assess levels of skill and concern about what would be a new way of doing business for them. The workshop identified the key training issues as well as a fair number of technical problems to iron out. It was also used to build confidence in and enthusiasm for the system.

Step 4: Phase 1 release

The release of the system was focused around two workshops for users. The first, over three days, involved the 14 sales managers directly responsible for the sales reps. The management team was seen as critical to getting full commitment to working with the system and maximising its benefits. The workshops were divided equally between training on the system itself and managing the process of change. Two-day workshops were held for the sales force at which equipment was distributed, the

> infrastructure of telephones and telephone lines having already been installed. Arrangements were also made to pair-up remote users to provide some degree of self-encouragement and support. The initial period of implementation was closely monitored to deal with technical problems and to list potential enhancements.

It is noticeable that much of the pilot test at Sun Alliance International was concerned with human resources issues and not just technical training. This is an issue of huge importance, but has often been neglected by businesses which focus narrowly on getting the technical issues right only to find their work unravelling in the face of a poorly trained, inappropriately organised, demotivated and suspicious workforce, either unable or unwilling to make the system work.

Self-assessment questions

1 Consider a computer system at your workplace or college. Are there any faults or limitations with the system? What would you do to rectify these faults?

2 Describe how you would attempt to improve the current system

Who to involve in systems development

In order to produce an efficient information system it is essential that the right staff are involved from the beginning of the project. User involvement is vital from an early stage in order to produce an effective system. In the traditional systems development life-cycle, a combination of technical experts and users are required at each stage. At the beginning of the project it is usual to set up a Project Team to manage the systems development. The Project Team is likely to consist of computing professionals such as analysts and programmers, as well as representatives from the 'users' such as departmental or functional managers. This team will oversee the whole project and will attempt to ensure that the 'users' demands are satisfied by the resulting system. The degree of user involvement will vary throughout the project lifetime. Figure 11.4. shows the changes in user involvement at different stages in the development process.

The illustration shows how the users are heavily involved in the early stages. Indeed, at the outset, when the initial problems are being clarified and the need for a new information system established, there may be no technical staff involved. Managers in a business may see a need for a new information system or an improvement in the existing systems. Technical staff will be introduced as part of the Project Team in order to investigate the feasibility of the proposals. Computer specialists become increasingly involved in the analysis, design and development stages. User involvement in the development stage, though important, is minimal, and will largely involve helping in testing and evaluation of the systems. Users become more involved in the Implementation stage, being trained to use the new systems. In the maintenance stage, users are in control, with minimum ongoing support from the computer specialists.

Computer staff

A range of technical computer staff may be involved in the design, development, operation and maintenance of any computerised information system. The current trend is

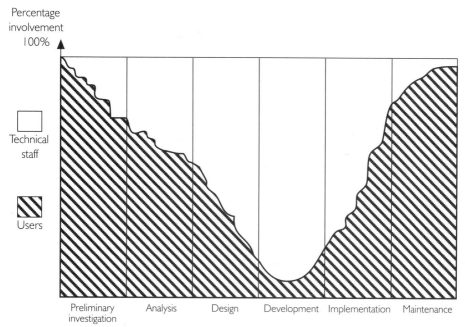

Percentage
involvement
100%

Technical
staff

Users

Preliminary   Analysis   Design   Development   Implementation   Maintenance
investigation

Figure 11.4   Comparison of user vs. technical staff involvement in information systems development stages

for such staff to be dispersed through the organisation, but often they are located in a separate section or department entitled Computing or Information Systems or Information Services or IT Services or Management Services. Depending on the size and complexity of the organisation, and the degree to which computer-based systems have been incorporated, the computing staff will include some or all of the following:

- **IT Manager:** the IT Manager has overall responsibility for all the computing staff. This role includes the management of systems development and operations and maintenance of existing systems. Generally, this person will have experience in a number of the positions within the department such as programmer and analyst.
- **Systems analysts:** systems analysts are involved in the analysis of existing systems, consideration of the feasibility of computer applications, and design of appropriate computer systems. The systems analyst is likely to manage a team of programmers during the implementation of a system.
- **Communications staff:** such staff will be involved in the management of communications and network systems in the organisation. Depending on the size of organisation, this could involve roles including Network Manager, Network Administrator, and communications technicians.
- **Programmers:** the programmers are primarily involved in implementing computer-based systems. The so-called applications programmers translate design specifications into **programming code**. Such code will require **testing** and **de-bugging** before full implementation. Some programmers spend all their time in maintenance, modifying existing programs in order to improve/upgrade or rectify errors in systems.

● **Operations Manager:** the Operations Manager controls all the activities involved in running the systems. This will include managing the maintenance of computer systems, installation of new systems, as well as the normal day-to-day computer operations.

● **Technicians:** such staff will be involved in the installation of computer equipment and the maintenance of hardware systems. These staff will work under the Operations Manager.

● **Information Officer:** this role will involve liaison with users, providing details on available databases, new software and hardware systems. The Information Officer may also access these systems to provide information for non-expert users when required.

● **User support:** the user support team will provide assistance to all employees in the use and application of current systems. This may involve organising formal **training courses,** offering **help-line services,** and one-to-one **trouble shooting** sessions.

The previous chapter made clear that the full exploitation of IT requires the capacity to rethink business processes, organisation and even the scope of the business itself. The same requirement affects the impact of IT on people and people on IT. The introduction of IT can be an intensely destabilising experience. It removes existing skills and replaces them with new and unfamiliar ones. The speed and flexibility it provides also change employees' level of skill and content of work, whilst the greater degree of communication it provides can erode established organisational boundaries.

Illustration 11.6:   Sun Alliance International, Step 5: Training issues

A good illustration of this kind of input can be seen in the reaction of Sun Alliance International's salesforce to the new system. A minority had no keyboarding experience at all and needed elementary training, but even those with the relevant experience were initially cautious. As well as a natural concern at the unknown, the sales force was confronted with a new style of working. Instead of the support of a local office and a familiar pile of paperwork, reps would now be much more self-sufficient, relying instead on ADaM for support. They would need to be more proactive and analytical in making full use of the greater range of client information at their disposal, as well as the task management software, for example, in planning their own workload more efficiently. On the whole, levels of responsibility would rise with reps more directly responsible for their operations and the inputting of key data. Some of the reps were also concerned that the greater scope for monitoring their performance turned the system into a potential 'Big Brother'.

Sun Alliance International thus faced a range of challenges which they met in two ways.

● Firstly, at the prototype stage, users were involved to try to ensure that the system was as closely focused around their needs and abilities as possible. User involvement was also exploited to inform and reassure staff. Opening up the development process both removed the secrecy that would unsettle staff and, by consulting them, gave them a stronger sense of involvement in the system.

● The second approach was extensive training to impart both skills and confidence in the system. Sun Alliance International realised the importance of getting the key influencers, the sales managers, on its side, as well as providing as much support as possible, for example, in the pairing of sales reps in remote areas to provide a degree of mutual support. It also placed considerable emphasis on explaining the benefits of the system to the reps to encourage ownership and encouraging them to experiment with the system.

Sun Alliance International's approach illustrates the importance of sensitive handling of the human resource dimension of introducing any significant IT innovations in a business, especially when they were accompanied, as in this case, by significant organisational change within the business.

This investment in training provides a major hidden cost in IT development. It has been estimated that training costs can range from 20–30% of hardware costs for a major system (for instance, the introduction of computer-integrated manufacturing into an industrial plant) to as much as 100% of the cost of a PC in training a single user.

Self-assessment questions

1 Consider a company/organisation with which you are familiar. Does this company include a computing or IT department? If so, find out the main job titles of the staff in this department.

2 What function does each of these jobs actually serve?

Maintenance

Once fully operational, the system will need to be maintained. Maintenance will involve the correction of errors in the system that have previously been undiscovered. However, the principal component of this stage involves the continual enhancement of the system. Such **enhancements** could be necessary for many reasons, including the changing needs of the users. Inevitably, users will require extra facilities and processes to be included in the system. This may lead to further analysis, design and implementation, thus completing the circle in the development life-cycle illustrated in Figure 11.2 earlier in this chapter.

Illustration 11.7: Sun Alliance International, Step 6: Evaluation
Once the system was up and running, Sun Alliance International was able to evaluate its success against strategic objectives:

● Customer service: despite loss of office support, the sales force has been able to maintain and improve information on clients, enabling them to respond more rapidly to their needs. Quicker and more reliable communication between the sales, marketing and other parts of the organisation, has also assisted a more prompt and effective service.

- Cost-effectiveness: phase 1 was achieved whilst making the economics needed to improve performance. Information transfer and the production of management information has become quicker and less labour-intensive, saving staff time.
- Management: the system now allows a much better analysis of performance and target-setting. It has also allowed better collection and analysis of data collected by reps on competitor activity.

Step 7: Phase 2 and beyond
Six months after implementation, the sales force was brought together to review the system and to receive training on updates to the system. This base was used to plan extending the system to all managers and other sales personnel, totalling around 170. On the hardware side, various improvements were made, including equipping new users with Toshiba 4865X Notebook PCs and providing higher specification modems, to improve the speed and reliability of loading data from sales reps onto the system.

Self-assessment questions

I   Describe the main elements involved in producing a system following the design stage. Who would you expect to be most involved in this stage?

2   What is the difference between implementing and maintaining a computer system?

Further development methods

As stated at the introduction in this chapter, the life-cycle approach describes a traditional method of systems development. Clearly not all systems development will be conducted exactly as described in this approach. However, regardless of the approach adopted, the main components of analysis, design and implementation must be performed. This section briefly looks at other methods of information systems development and some of the tools that are used. In particular the process of prototyping, using CASE tools, SSADM, object orientation, and the soft systems methodology will be reviewed.

Prototyping

One of the main problems with using the traditional development life-cycle approach is that very early on a detailed **analysis of requirements** must be conducted. At such an early stage users of proposed systems may find extreme difficulty in specifying their requirements. Some will only be able to describe what currently happens, whereas others may try to predict their new requirements with varying degrees of success. It is much easier for a user to criticize a system in current use, and thus come up with possible improvements, rather than starting with a 'blank sheet'. The prototyping approach enables some of the elements of the new system to be developed, and shown to prospective users prior to the complete system being developed.

A prototype is a model of the overall system. Such a model could contain just some of the elements required in the final system, or alternatively could be used by a small selection of the targetted users. For example, a prototype could be tested by one department, such as Sales, before developing the full system for use by all departments. Figure 11.5 shows an illustration of the prototyping approach. This diagram shows that following the development, testing and acceptance of the prototype, the full system can be designed and implemented.

In practice there may be several stages of prototypes, building up gradually towards the full operational system.

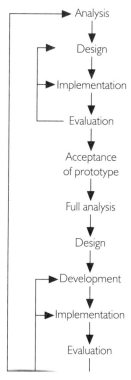

Figure 11.5   Systems development using prototyping

The primary advantage of the prototyping approach is that users are involved at an early stage in the design. By having an early involvement in development, users are more likely to accept the final system and thus be more satisfied with the results. Other advantages include the ability to find errors and rectify them quickly. The prototyping approach is often less expensive than the traditional approach where all the specifications are determined at an early stage.

CASE tools

Computer Aided Software Engineering (CASE) tools provide a relatively quick and easy method of designing and developing systems. CASE tools are programs that enable the analyst to produce and modify designs on the screen, and can be used to automate many of the elements in the development life-cycle. For example, CASE tools can be used to produce **data flow diagrams.** The analyst can change an element on one DFD (such as a process or source or sink), and the design can be automatically re-drawn to take account of the changes. Furthermore, other related DFDs can be automatically updated.

CASE tools can also be used to create other diagrams such as **structure charts,** create **programming code** direct from the designs, and generate **test data** for reviewing the resulting system. Such tools can assist with the speedy development of prototypes prior to full system development.

Self-assessment questions _____

1 Describe the differences between prototyping and the traditional life-cycle approach to systems development. Would you agree that users could be more involved if the prototyping approach is adopted?

2 How do CASE tools help the Prototyping approach in the development of computer systems?

Structured systems analysis and design methodology (SSADM)

This method is in widespread use in the UK and was originally produced for use in the Civil Service for information systems development. This structured approach is split into a number of phases similar to the traditional life-cycle approach already summarised. The following shows the main phases of this methodology:

- **Feasibility study.** Definition of the problem. Terms of reference defined for the project.
- **Analysis of present system.** Looking at current data flows. Production of a list of problems of current system and requirements.
- **Requirements specification.** More detailed look at requirements. Data structures are defined.
- **Selection of physical options.** Consideration of appropriate hardware choices.
- **Data and process design.** Data structures and corresponding processes are designed.
- **Physical design.** The implementation of the system designs previously established.

SSADM is an extremely structured, prescriptive method of development. As such this method must be managed with extreme caution and requires expert involvement in its application. The method relies on a clear specification of requirements which in practice may not be available. SSADM uses a range of basic tools to perform the various stages including **data flow diagrams** and **entity diagrams.** This design methodology is often more appropriate for larger organisations, or large systems development in order to justify the high investment in training and staff costs involved. SSADM is one of a range of 'structured' approaches to system development. Other similar approaches include the Jackson Structured Development methods. Jackson introduced a range of structured programming techniques in the mid 1970s (Jackson, 1975) and incorporated such techniques in the development process in the early 1980s (Jackson, 1983).

Object-oriented development

It should be noted that a range of new development procedures have been introduced using the object oriented concepts. Object-oriented programming methods have become increasingly important in recent years with programming languages such as 'C++' being popular. It is beyond the scope of this text to consider object oriented approaches in any detail. However, it should be recognised that these new methodologies exist and are likely to become more important in the future. The reason for the increasing popularity of such methods is the ease with which systems can be developed. Object orientation enables relationships between 'objects' to be defined and amended easily. Thus a systems developer can use these techniques to produce and amend the information system design with far greater ease than if using more traditional approaches. Such methods also allow 'learning' to take place during the development process so that early mistakes in the design can be rectified, and not repeated, in later modules.

Soft systems methodology

The soft systems methodology (SSM) provides a range of techniques to analyse problems and situations that are extremely vague or fuzzy. These so-called 'unstructured' (or 'soft') problems invariably occur when people are involved. Staff within an organisation will have different ideas on what the current problems are, will differ in their ideas for potential solutions, and may disagree on specific requirements. Such disunity of ideas provides added difficulties for the traditional method of systems development. The development life-cycle assumes that the problem under investigation can be clearly defined and analysed. This is often not the case, indeed the actual nature of the problem in many situations needs to be clarified. SSM developed by Checkland in the early 1980s attempts to resolve such fuzzy problems. It should be stressed that this methodology is not used solely for information systems development. SSM can be used to analyse business problems without the need for computerisation. It can be used as a starting point to clarify the problems that require attention in the overall information system. This clarification may then lead to a detailed analysis of the system and a consideration of alternative solutions.

In this section we will consider the elements of soft systems methodology in more detail and look at their relevance in systems development. The methodology consists of the following stages.

1. Situation unstructured
'Soft' issues are those which are not easy to define. Individuals in an organisation will all have different views on a particular problem. Such a situation can be analysed by

means of a **rich picture** which is used to illustrate a wide range of information relating to a given problem area. The Rich Picture is developed in consultation with a range of those people involved.

2. Situation analysed

The situation is analysed by reference to the rich picture. A number of important themes will be clarified such as employee's fears, conflict between sectors in the company, external competition and marketing.

3. Relevant systems

A **root definition** is produced to specify the properties of a relevant system. The Root Definition encourages questions along the following areas:

- **Customers.**   Who does the system serve?
- **Actors.**   Who actually uses the system?
- **Transformation.**   What processes does the system perform? How does it transform inputs to outputs?
- *Weltenschauung.*   What is the world-view of this system? From which viewpoint is the system being analysed?
- **Owners.**   Who owns the system?
- **Environment.**   How does the system relate to the environment? What effect does the environment have on the system and what effect does the system have on the environment?

Using these areas (the so-called **CATWOE test**) will ensure that the root definition is meaningful and unambiguous. The production of a root definition is iterative. The root definition is continually changed and refined following discussions with the various parties concerned. The root definition concentrates on *what* the system is rather than on *how* it functions.

4. Conceptual models

A conceptual model is built based on the root definition. Such a model defines what the relevant system should do. The conceptual model is often produced in the form of a diagram showing the activities to be carried out.

5. Comparison

In this phase of the soft systems approach, the models produced are compared with the real-life situation. Any features that are particularly different between the models and the present situation are identified and listed. This may then provide a framework for implementing any necessary change in the systems.

6. Debate and implementation

Following the comparison phase there may be some clearly defined issues that have been identified. Thus the original soft problem has been clarified, and the standard approaches to systems development such as the life-cycle or prototyping, can be utilised. Alternatively, the soft systems approach could have identified other themes or issues that are more important. Priorities can be established for the overall system before unecessary development work is carried out.

7. Ongoing development

To summarise, the soft systems methodology attempts to resolve issues involved in vague (soft) problems. Too many information systems are developed without due consideration of the problems and relevant issues. There is always a temptation to rush to develop a system and imposing solutions on a 'problem' before carefully analysing what the problems really are. This can lead to expensive and inappropriate systems being developed. The soft systems approach can be used to clarify the situation and investigate areas of debate before proceeding to the requirements specification and on to the system design stage. The latter stages of development can then involve a more traditional hard approach such as the life-cycle or prototyping methods.

Self-assessment questions

1   In what circumstances would a soft systems methodology be used in developing a new computerised information system?

2   Describe the main phases of SSM. How do these phases fit in to the traditional life-cycle approach to system development?

Software acquisition

The procedures adopted in acquiring software range between the extremes of 'make' or 'buy'. In other words, a decision needs to be made about whether to start with a clean sheet and develop a new system specifically aimed at your own requirements or alternatively, purchase an existing off-the-shelf package. This section considers the advantages and disadvantages of both these options and investigates compromise solutions between these extremes.

Bespoke systems

In this scenario a company will attempt to 'make' a totally new system, designed to meet its requirements. This will involve the use of the company's own computer staff and/or external consultants to produce the necessary programs. The complexities involved in the development of new systems have already been explored. It follows that the 'make' option should only be used if all other avenues of software acquisition have been exhausted. The disadvantages of using this approach are as follows:

- **High costs.**   The design and development of bespoke software is the most expensive option. The total development costs are incurred by a single company instead of spreading the expenses across a range of companies. Thus, the bespoke software route is the costliest and least attractive of the acquisition options.
- **Lack of expertise.**   There may not be the appropriate expertise available neither in-house nor externally to develop the required systems. To develop such systems may require a combination of skills using both technical and subject expertise that may be difficult to find. This type of problem is often overcome by the use of project teams involving individuals who together provide the necessary skills.
- **Time-consuming.**   The design and development of new software involves a long time span. For large systems this often means requiring several years for completion. Such development cannot be rushed without damaging the effectiveness of the resulting system.

- **Maintenance and testing.** This process can seem to be never-ending. The location and correction of bugs in the system can extend over a period of many years, and indeed may seem to be a continuous process. This can result in a lack of support and commitment from the participants and employees which may be difficult to counteract.

The production of bespoke software is considered to be a high risk option. The costs and time-scales may significantly overrun with ongoing changes in the requirements within the organisation. It would be very difficult for an organisation to abandon such a project after considerable investment in both time and money. Therefore having started such a process the project tends to be continued even when costs rise astronomically. The organisation becomes embedded in the development long after the disadvantages outweigh the benefits.

However, there are a number of advantages of developing in-house software including those described below:

- **Control.** Developing the system allows the company total control on all aspects of the development stages and the final product. This results in a closer involvement by potential users and an improved awareness of employees over all phases of development.
- **Functionality.** The bespoke system will enable the company to get exactly what it wants. Assuming that the early stages of analysis and specification of requirements are performed effectively, the resulting design and development stages should produce a package which satisfies all the organisation's needs.
- **Minimum changes.** Producing a system that matches in with existing requirements will mean that no changes to existing operations and procedures are necessary. The system could be produced to fit exactly into existing procedures. (This of course may not be an advantage! The production of a new system allows an organisation to take a fresh look at existing procedures and encourages improvements to be introduced where appropriate.)
- **Support.** The production of in-house software will enable corresponding software documentation, user manuals, training and ongoing support to be specifically directed and tailored to the needs of the company's employees. This should result in improved user performance and cooperation in using the new system.
- **Competitive edge.** The unique software obtained using this approach may result in additional system facilities being available. For example, providing extra and more efficient information facilities for the company's customers and clients. Thus the new system may provide a competitive edge that would not be the case with other acquisition methods.

Such advantages are in many cases not totally convincing. For instance, the functionality aspect of bespoke software is probably the most powerful argument in its favour. However, in many cases companies have discovered that having spent large sums of money over many years, that the end result still does not cater for all needs. To attempt to achieve 100% functionality, by producing a package that includes *every* conceivable requirement, is usually impractical and not achievable.

Off-the-shelf software
The decision to 'buy' a software solution in order to satisfy an identified requirement is by far the most common method of acquisition. Such software ranges from the off-

the-shelf **application packages** such as spreadsheets and databases to dedicated software produced and distributed for vertical markets such as medical centres, estate agencies and travel agents. Software produced for specific (or vertical) markets is more likely to satisfy the needs of organisations in those markets. Conversely, off-the-shelf packages produced for a mass market may be less likely to fit in to the specific needs of a company. However, with these differences in mind, the advantages and disadvantages of the 'buy' option are outlined in the following sections.

To understand the reason for the popularity of the 'buy' option consider the following advantages:

- **Cost.**   The cost of application packages is significantly less than for bespoke software. This is largely because the costs of development have been shared by all the customers of such software. Thus a package that costs a few hundred pounds to buy off-the-shelf may have cost hundreds of thousands to develop. The development costs have simply been spread over the range of users of the product.
- **Speed.** The time taken to install purchased software is insignificant compared to development time-scales. Therefore following the initial purchase the software can be in use almost immediately.
- **Reliability.** Purchased software has already undergone significant and extensive testing. Most, if not all, the bugs should have already been found and corrected before the package becomes available for sale. Also, the package would have been tried and tested by a range of previous purchasers. Therefore the software has already proved to be efficient and reliable thus alleviating many potential problems the company may have after installation.
- **Updates.**   Popular software is regularly updated to rectify any problems in the system as well as improve the facilities offered. Existing customers of the software are often offered the new versions at a significantly reduced rate. Thus a company can be assured that the software being used is reasonably up-to-date and is comparable with other available software.
- **Portability.** Generally, off-the-shelf packages are portable between different types of hardware. Thus, purchase of a new computer need not automatically involve the acquisition of different software. It may be necessary for a different version of the package to be used but this would not drastically affect the users of such systems.

The arguments on cost, speed and reliability make the option to purchase almost irresistable. However, there are a number of drawbacks to the purchase of standard applications software including the following:

- **User dissatisfaction.**   The package may not perform exactly as required. It is unlikely that an off-the-shelf package will fit exactly the requirements specified following the initial needs analysis. For example, the package may be too slow, the reports produced in the wrong format, or data files not large enough to handle the required data. User dissatisfaction is by far the most likely reason why an off-the-shelf package is not fully utilised. The purchase of such a package will usually involve some compromises. Thus a package that satisfies 95% of the requirements may be considered adequate. Furthermore, adoption of such a package may involve some changes to existing procedures creating new problems for the workforce.
- **Compatibility.**   It may be that the package that best fits the requirements is not compatible with existing software. Data stored on an existing system may need to

be used on the new package. Some link or interface between the varied systems may be required which could involve additional software development.

- **Efficiency.**   Most of the popular off-the-shelf packages are designed to meet the needs of a wide audience. Therefore, the generality of such packages may mean that they are less efficient for specific needs than a package which simply caters for selected requirements. This inefficiency may involve additional data storage space being required or extra time needed in entering data or setting up reports.

- **Security.**   The security systems on many off-the-shelf packages are not as effective as may be required. Such security mechanisms would include password access to different modules of the package, and levels of access to data. For example, some users may be allowed into a system to change data and modify reports, whereas others may just be allowed to view existing information. The level of security procedures available on many packages is inadequate compared with comparable bespoke systems. For some organisations this problem may not be important, whereas for others security may be a vital requirement.

Make or buy questions
The final decision on whether to make or buy will involve a range of factors already summarised. To simplify this process a number of questions should be asked including:

1. Is there a commercially available package to meet your needs?

2. If not, can any package be modified to meet your needs?

3. Is the package compatible with existing systems?

4. Do you have the expertise within the company to develop the required software?

5. How much time do you have available before you require the system to be implemented?

The answers to these questions will enable you to make an initial decision concerning the make or buy issue. However, as previously stated, the end result will almost inevitably involve compromise between costs, time-scales and functionality of the software required

Self-assessment questions _____

I   You are a manager of the Logistics Department in a production company. You require new software to assist in the production planning processes. You already have the hardware necessary. How would you proceed in choosing and obtaining the required system?

2   Buying existing software is by far the best option for most business applications. Comment on this statement.

Purchasing software

In this section we will consider the techniques used in the evaluation and selection of software. It has already been stated that the purchase of software is the most common method of acquisition. However the method used in choosing software will be a significant factor in the effectiveness of the resulting package. The actual procedures adopted will depend on the size and complexity of the required system. Clearly, the approach to choosing a package is different for the manager who states; 'I need a spreadsheet for my micro to do some basic data analysis, compared with, 'I need a new package on the central computer system to integrate the stock control and accounting procedures'. However, in general terms the following steps should be undertaken when acquiring software.

Analysis of needs

This stage has already been covered in an earlier chapter. Resulting from this analysis of needs will come a **requirements specification.** This will summarise all the requirements of the software. This can be simplified into a list of the key performance requirements. For example, the following factors may appear on such a specification:

- **Input methods** – using a menu-driven approach, or icon interface;
- **Data entry procedures** – screen designs required, and interfaces with other packages;
- **Output methods** – screen displays of data, standard and *ad hoc* reports, and communication between different computer systems;
- **File design** – specification of size and types of files to be used, and format of data to be saved.

Evaluation of software

It is likely that you will need to produce a short-list of software that fits your requirements as defined in the previous section. Each package on the short-list can then be investigated in more detail with reference to a comprehensive list of evaluation criteria such as the following:

- **Performance.** Consider the speed of operation and data handling capabilities. Can the software cope with the amount of data you wish to store and manipulate?
- **Cost.** How does the cost compare with other similar systems? You may need to look at single-user, multi-user or site licence charges.
- **Flexibility.** Can the package be altered if required to cope with additional requirements later? How easy is it to modify the software?
- **Security.** Does the package provide facilities for security to cope with illegal access to data and error handling procedures?
- **Documentation.** Is the software well documented? Are there comprehensive user manuals and introductory tutorials available?
- **Useability.** Is the package easy to use? Are the screens well designed? Is on-screen help available in context when required? Are there quick ways around the systems for experienced users?
- **Popularity.** How common is the package? How many other users are there? Is there a user group in your area?
- **Vendor.** Can you vouch for the suppliers of the package? Are they reputable? Are they likely to still be in business in five years time?
- **Support.** What level of user support is available? Will any training provided be included in the purchase price? Is a **helpline facility** available? What about any bugs found in the package? Is a special price to existing users offered for any new upgrades of the software?

- **Availability.** When can you receive the software? Is it available now?
- **Hardware.** Will the existing hardware run this package? Do you require any additions/enhancements to the hardware to make the software run efficiently?

These criteria can be used to consider all the packages. Table 11.1 illustrates two packages compared using a selection of the criteria listed. Each criterion is graded out of 10 in order to gain an objective comparison of the software under consideration.

Evaluation factors	Rating (out of 10)	
	Software A	Software B
Speed of procesing using test data	8	9
Useability (user-friendliness)	8	6
Documentation (manuals and tutorials)	7	7
Support (training and user help facilities)	6	5
Vendor (background and reputation)	9	7
Overall rating	38	34

Table 11.1: Evaluation of two packages using rating system

Many of the criteria such as vendor, support, popularity, cost, availability and hardware can be investigated with reference to business journals, computer magazines, newspaper articles, and promotional literature. Other criteria such as performance, useability and documentation can also be assessed from demonstrations of the package, talking to other similar users, and preferably trying out some of your own data.

Table 11.1 illustrates the differences between the two packages. There is little difference between the performance of the two packages in terms of speed although software B just has the edge. Documentation of both packages is of a similar standard. Software A is superior in terms of useability, support mechanisms provided, and the reputation of the vendor. Overall, we see that software A seems to be better, though neither package is totally suitable. In fact, if the speed performance of the package is weighted heavily then it may be decided that software B is the best package despite its obvious drawbacks. Cost would clearly be a factor in the final decision. It is even possible that on the basis of this analysis both packages would be rejected and the search for software continued.

Self-assessment questions

1 You require a new spreadsheet package for use at work and home. What criteria would you use in helping you choose the most appropriate package?

2 Give a weighting for each of the criterion you have listed, so that the total weight for all the criteria is 100. Now, try to rate a package that you are familiar with, by giving a score for each criterion. What problems do you encounter in this process?

Producing software

If **bespoke software production** is the chosen option then this probably implies that either no current available software performs in the required way or insufficient time has been spent on searching. Details of the actual steps involved in producing software have been given earlier in this chapter on the system development lifecycle. It is therefore not necessary at this stage to cover the same ground. However it is worth noting that there are still choices to be made before the design and development work actually takes place. The main choice involves whether to produce the software in-house or employ external consultants to carry out the necessary work. In order to make a decision on how the software will be produced a number of factors should be considered as summarised below.

In-house production

Clearly, this is only feasible if sufficient staff and resources are available. Unless there is considerable slack in the present system then the use of existing staff may not be possible. In-house production will involve existing staff having some or all of their responsibilities removed in order to schedule time for the new project. This may necessitate the delay in other projects or the reduction in current services such as user support. For larger development projects it will almost certainly involve the appointment of new staff to supplement the existing team. The rescheduling of work activities may not only affect the technical staff. For larger projects a project team will need to be established involving the commitment of a range of personnel including technical and non-technical staff. These potential users of the proposed system may be heavily involved in the development activities at various stages of the project. This should also be taken account of when scheduling the project work-load. The in-house approach to systems development is generally only possible with relatively large companies with well developed information systems departments or sections.

The advantages and disadvantages of the in-house production approach have already been summarised in an earlier section. However it is worth stressing the enormous expense involved in taking this path. The risks of overruns on time and costs are high, and as the project evolves it becomes increasingly difficult to pull out. There would be a significant amount of resources tied up in the project from its inception. This makes it almost impossible to 'cut and run' when the development seems to be leading nowhere.

External production

This method is not significantly different from the in-house approach in its advantages and disadvantages. However there are some essential differences. For example, being able to 'contract out' the development work means that the relevant expertise is only paid for when required. This can lead to a slight reduction in staff costs over the purely in-house process previously described. It should be noted that there is still a need to have expertise available permanently on-site. This is essential not only to provide internal knowledge on the organisation and systems in operation, but also to facilitate overall control of the project. One of the problems of using primarily external expertise is that management and supervision of scheduling becomes extremely difficult. It is important that the development project is coordinated by a team including internal and external members with overall control firmly with the organisation's management. It should also be recognised that the organisation's relationship with outside contractors is significantly different than with their permanent employees. Will the consultants still be available next year? What happens if problems occur with the system after implementation? How can you guarantee that there is sufficient expertise in-house to sort out any difficulties later if and when they arise? These problems need careful consideration and must be addressed before continuing too far with the system development.

Having determined that the development will require external contractors the main problem is to select the most appropriate personnel. This would often involve a tendering process to allow a number of external companies to bid for the work offered. The process of tendering will be explored in detail in the sections on hardware acquisition. The methods used in the tendering for software or hardware systems are similar and therefore a detailed description is not included here. However, it is important to note the main stages and how they are performed in relation to software production. The following steps should be followed:

1. Requirements identified. The **requirements specification** will be produced. It cannot be over-stressed that this is a vital stage without which it is almost impossible to achieve a satisfactory system. The software requirements could be listed in terms of essential and desirable items. For example, an essential item could be the screen display of records on a database. A desirable element could be the inclusion of a photographic image into each record displayed. It should be noted that even at this stage, external consultants could be employed to assist in order to develop a comprehensive specification. One factor in such a requirements specification is a consideration of the organisation's long-term objectives. This may then highlight future requirements and not simply satisfy current demands.

2. Request for proposals. A formal **proposal document** is produced to invite external companies/consultants to submit a **tender.** This document will include the requirements specification as outlined, together with a request for information on each external participant. It is important to obtain some details of the consultant's background including size and status of company, and previous experience in similar development areas. The request for proposal is then sent to a selection of potential candidates. Care must be taken over this selection. The list of potential consultants is usually constructed from previous contacts, reputation, exchange of information with other companies, and recommendations from hardware and software suppliers. It is usual in such a request to set a **deadline date** after which no proposals will be accepted.

3. Response from consultants. The time taken to respond to your request will be determined by the complexity of the required system and the experience of the individual consultants. The consultant may require visits to your site to discuss the requirements further. Initial responses will include written reports outlining suggested solutions, time-scales and estimated costs.

The initial proposals will be evaluated and a **short-list** of candidates produced. These candidates may be requested to provide more detailed information and possibly give an in-house presentation of their recommendations. It is likely that additional expert assistance is required in the decision process. A decision is made on a range of factors including:

- displayed understanding of the requirements
- previous experience and background
- best fit to the requirements
- budget considerations.

The best fit to the specified requirements may involve the production of an evaluation matrix as illustrated in Table 11.1. The candidates are compared and contrasted before a final decision is made on a single contractor.

Finally a contract with the consultant is negotiated. This is important and will give some protection to your business if the project is unsuccessful. It is usual for larger projects to include acceptance tests at various stages of the development. Continuation of the contract is conditional on these tests being satisfactory. Penalties can also be written into the contract to further safeguard your company's interests.

Following the above stages the project should be ready to start. At every stage it is advisable to work closely with the contractor, however rigorous your early selection procedures have been.

Tailoring software

The acquisition of software may not be a simple choice between 'make' or 'buy'. In many circumstances, a compromise solution is reached which incorporates the advantages of both. Such a solution involves tailoring software to meet users' needs. This involves amending or adding to an existing package in order to enhance its functionality. The following methods are most commonly used in tailoring a package:

Edit existing programs

This involves upgrading an existing package or piece of software by changing the programming procedures. If the actual programs are changed then it is an extremely complicated task involving expert technical staff in the same processes as software production. Furthermore, many packages cannot be changed in this way. To change the actual programs themselves requires access to the 'source code' for the package in order to edit lines of programming code. In most cases software producers do not allow access to this code for obvious commercial reasons. Thus, it may not be possible to change existing programs in-house. However, a possible alternative is to request the software producer to amend the existing package to incorporate additional facilities.

Amend procedures

This option simply involves the full utilisation of an existing package. Many current packages provide powerful facilities enabling the user to tailor functions (such as input and output) to suit their own requirements. For example, many database packages enable users to design unique **report formats, input screens** and **menu structures**. This enables a user, with technical support, to enhance the **functionality** of a package. Often off-the-shelf packages are under-utilised, with the majority of facilities remaining undiscovered. The full utilisation of such packages may be sufficient to satisfy requirements without the need for expensive development work.

Add-ons

It is common to improve the functionality of software by linking it with other packages or programs. Current trends in software production are towards integration of systems allowing **transfer of data** between packages. Therefore it may be possible to achieve the required functionality be linking software together. The use of two or more packages, with transfer of data between them may be sufficient to satisfy needs. Alternatively, it may be possible to produce additional programs to provide facilities not available in the package. The integration of several packages and in-house programs can provide an extremely powerful system.

Comparison of methods

In the previous sections we have considered the main methods adopted in the acquisition of software. The three methods previously described are:

- **To make.** Produce complete bespoke software systems.
- **To buy.** Purchase commercially available software or off-the-shelf packages.
- **To tailor.** Amend existing packages or combine with extra programs.

Table 11.2 gives a comparison of the main approaches to software acquisition. As shown, the most significant advantage of the 'make' option is to ensure full functionality. The 'buy' option is most popular because of the reduced costs and minimum timescales. The tailoring option is generally a compromise between the other approaches providing a good system at a low cost in a reasonable time-span. It is clear to see why this option is becoming increasingly common as a method of improving existing information systems.

Factors	Acquisition methods		
	Make	**Buy**	**Tailor**
Cost	Most expensive	Cheapest	Inexpensive
Functionality	Excellent	Can be poor	Good
Timescale	Longest	Immediate	Short time-span
Reliability	Uncertain	Reliable	Variable

Table 11.2: Comparison of software acquisition methods

Self-assessment questions

1 Describe the three main methods of acquiring software.

2 Consider the methods of software acquisition at your own company, or an organisation with which you are familiar. How has software been obtained? Has it all been purchased off-the-shelf or has any development work taken place?

Hardware acquisition

The acquisition of hardware follows a similar pattern to the acquisition of software. There is often a choice at this stage as to whether you wish to buy the hardware outright, or lease the equipment and thus spread the costs over a longer period of time. In either case the procedures used for the choice of system will be the same. Often the choice of hardware is determined by the software demands. In other cases, hardware and software are acquired in parallel as a total system. Essentially, the choice of hardware is driven by the requirements specified from the analysis stage. The following sections outline the basic steps required in the hardware acquisition process.

Analysis of needs

This stage will produce a range of hardware requirements in parallel with the software needs. Such requirements will include considerations on input and output methods, file design and database size, numbers and location of users, as well as existing hardware and software systems.

Evaluation of hardware

Hardware producers and suppliers may make extravagent claims in order to sell their own products. It is vital that these claims are checked and verified in some way. This will usually involve the use of sample data in demonstrations and test runs. The use of **benchmarking** to compare and evaluate the performance of systems is now commonplace. Another useful way of examining whether a system is suitable is to liaise with other users. Reputable companies should be able to supply you with a list of some local users in order for you to obtain reliable, independent feedback. A number of factors should be considered when selecting appropriate hardware. The following list gives some of the main factors that should be considered:

- **Performance.**   Test out the speed, capacity and data handling capabilities of the hardware under investigation. Can the system handle the required data? How will data be transferred into the system? How many users can the system handle? What internal and external storage devices are available?
- **Compatibility.**   Will the proposed hardware link in with any existing systems? Can it be linked to existing networks? Is there any additional hardware or software that will be required to ensure full compatibility?
- **Software.**   Can existing application software run efficiently using this hardware? Will this hardware be able to run software currently being developed?
- **Cost.**   How much does the hardware cost? Are there any additional costs necessary for implementation? What are the installation and maintenance costs associated with the hardware? Is it possible to lease rather than buy?
- **Reliability.**   Does the hardware have a track record of reliability? How long has it been commercially available? Can you check with other users of similar systems?
- **Expandability.**   Can the hardware be upgraded and enhanced at a later stage to cater for additional workloads if required? How expensive will it be to expand the system in this way?
- **Vendor.**   Can you vouch for the supplier of the hardware? Do they have a good

reputation? Are they likely to still be trading in a few years time? Are other vendors also able to supply this hardware?
- **Support.**   What type of support mechanisms are available if you buy the hardware? Is **training** provided on the management and use of the systems? What happens if breakdowns occur? What sort of **maintenance agreements** are there?

Such criteria can be considered on all the hardware systems under consideration. A simple check list can be produced to compare different systems in terms of each of these categories in the same way that software was compared earlier in this chapter. Table 11.3 illustrates the comparison of two hardware systems in relation to the categories outlined above.

Evaluation factors (weighting)	Rating	
	System X	System Y
Performance (40)	36	33
Compatibility (25)	22	23
Software (40)	40	40
Cost (20)	16	18
Reliability (30)	20	24
Expandability (15)	10	5
Vendor (10)	9	7
Support (20)	18	16
Overall rating (Total = 200)	171	166

Table 11.3: Comparison of hardware using simple checklist

Table 11.3 shows some essential differences between the two systems being compared. The table also assigns relative weights to the various categories under consideration. These weightings should not be considered as anything other than one example from many possibilities. The actual weightings assigned to each category will depend very largely on the scale and type of system required. Such weightings will also be affected by the degree of knowledge of the vendors and reliability, in addition to the budgetary restraints placed on the project.

Overall, Table 11.3 shows that system X appears to be best. Both systems score well on performance and compatibility, and neither system has any problems with running existing or proposed software. System Y is slightly cheaper resulting in a higher score for this category. System Y scores better on the reliability category. This may be that there is insufficient evidence to judge system X properly. This would be the case, for example if the system has been recently introduced and therefore has not established a reasonable track record with other users. Neither system scores particularly well on expandability, though X is significantly better than Y in this respect. Both systems score well on the vendor and support categories, with X just having the edge.

Selection of hardware
Overall then, system X seems to be the best option. However, there are a number of

potential drawbacks with this system. For example, whilst scoring higher than system Y the system does not satisfy all the performance criteria required. There is a question mark over the compatibility of system X with existing systems, and reliability is suspect. These limitations may be sufficient for us to reject the system automatically and continue looking for other possibilities. Alternatively, additional information could be sought concerning these systems under review.

Performance criteria

Clearly, the performance of the hardware will be of primary importance. In Chapter 4 we have considered details of choosing between microcomputer systems and Chapter 5 has illustrated differences between central computer systems. The performance criteria of computer systems involve similar categories whether involved in purchasing a microcomputer for a single user, or a central (mainframe) system catering for many hundreds of users. The obvious differences arise in the scale of performance requirements. The following list gives some of the main performance elements that should be investigated when purchasing any hardware together with an indication of the range of performances likely and differences between micro and central systems.

Internal storage capacity
The amount of data that can be stored within the computer system referred to as random access memory (RAM). This storage capacity can range between 1 MegaByte (1 million characters) for a small microcomputer, up to hundreds or even thousands of MegaBytes for the larger central systems.

Processing speed
The speed of the system measured is the number of instructions that can be performed in a unit of time. The standard measure is **MIPS** (millions of instructions per second). This ranges from 10–20 MIPS for a microcomputer up to over a thousand MIPS for some larger systems. Just to confuse the issue, different manufacturers may use their own unit of measurement! For example, Digital quote their processing speeds in VUPs (indicating VAX Units of Power). This can make things extremely difficult when attempting to compare systems from different producers. Microcomputer speeds are usually expressed in Megahertz (MHz). Typical speeds range from 25 MHz to 100 MHz for standard microcomputers.

External storage
The type and capacity of external storage should be considered. Magnetic and laser disks are common forms of external storage. The size of such storage ranges from 20 MByte (20 million characters) for smaller microcomputers and up to 2 GigaByte (2 thousand million characters) per disk for larger central systems.

Word length
The number of bits that can be handled together. This ranges from 16 bits for many microcomputers up to 64-bit processors. Many of the larger systems use 64-bit processors as standard.

Specification
Suppliers of hardware will be requested to tender in the same way as for software contracts. A specification of requirements will be sent to potential suppliers/producers and will include a range of data such as:

- **System details.**   Information on the systems to be computerised and the range of functions to be included.
- **Communication.**   Details of communication requirements, links between users, and geographical locations of remote sites.
- **Volumes.**   Amount and type of data to be handled. Number of users and workstations required. Priorities of work required
- **Processing type.**   Data processing requirements. The proportion of batch processing compared with on-line demands.
- **Security.**   The degree of security required, sensitivity of data, frequency of backups for data entry, and need for standby systems if required.
- **Reports.**   Quantity and frequency of reports required. The range of likely regular and ad-hoc reports required.
- **Maintenance?**   How will the systems be maintained? What guarantees are given, and what conditions are included in the contracts?

Further details on hardware specifications can be obtained by referring to Chapters 4 and 5.

Self-assessment questions _____

1   Consider a computer system with which you are familiar. Can you describe its performance in terms of speed, storage capacity, and any other factors?

2   How was the hardware initially selected? Ask the computer staff to find out who was involved in the acquisition.

Data controls and security

Control procedures must be designed to make sure that data integrity and data confidentiality are maintained. In any organisation, data is a vital resource, the loss of which may result in financial loss. The loss may arise directly (e.g. as a result of a mistake) or indirectly (e.g. where a competitor gains access to sensitive marketing data).

Physical security

In parallel with the development of sophisticated hardware and software, many comprehensive techniques have evolved to minimise the risks to data maintained at an installation.

The broad principles that should be applied to ensure that physical security is maintained over access to data files and the underlying programs which can manipulate that data include the following:

- Where possible, PCs/terminals can be physically locked using the **keyboard lock keys** and these keys should only be given to authorised personnel.
- **Password controls** should control initial access to the system.
- Programs should have their own password controls to cover **access** to applications.

- Where data is transmitted over some form of network, the data should not be transmitted in 'raw' format, but be encrypted (**encryption**).

Passwords

The British Computer Society's definition of a password is:

> 'a sequence of characters that must be presented to a computer system before it will allow access to the system or parts of that system.'

To be effective, the password needs to keep out unauthorised access. The limits to this form of control are that, firstly, an authorised user may divulge their password to an unauthorised user, possibly to bypass the administrative 'hassle' of getting new identities on the system. Secondly, most passwords chosen by authorised users have some form of association with them or are extremely simple to form and can be discovered by intelligent experimentation. Lastly, users may even write their password down either on the terminal itself or nearby, making the task of discovering it easy.

The system administrator needs to provide a number of options by which the end-user can generate their own password such that it will be easily remembered but difficult for anyone, even personal colleagues of the end-user, to decipher from their knowledge of the end-user. Examples might include dates of birthdays, plus personal initials of some sort.

Some systems include an automatic password generator, but experience has shown that, where these are used, users tend to write them down as they are virtually impossible to remember, leading to a resultant loss of security. In any event, all passwords should be changed on a regular basis (e.g. quarterly). Repeated attempts to log in using incorrect passwords should be noted and reported by the system so that users who have problems in this area can be given specific assistance.

The most common form of personal identification is the **PIN** (**personal identification number**) which acts as a form of password. Other, more sophisticated techniques that are coming into use include fingerprint recognition where the user's palm print is recorded using an optical scanner and this is compared with the user's every time access is requested. Eye retina 'prints' and voice 'prints' are being investigated and it is likely that by the end of the decade, if not before, these forms of checking will be the normal security control mechanism in addition to, or in place of, password controls.

Encryption

Currently, where data is transmitted by any means other than fibre-optic cable, a determined eavesdropper can easily gain access to the data using modern bugging equipment. Encrypting data to be transmitted, even across a simple office LAN is the only way to reduce significantly the risk of such unauthorised access. However, it should be stressed that there are very few completely secure encryption schemes.

Encryption is the use of a cipher code to transform original data so that when transmitted, the data appears to be nonsense until the 'key' code is applied to the data. Most methods require that both the sender and receiver know the same 'key' which immediately increases the likelihood that it will be disclosed to an unauthorised user. Current specific development is looking at what are known as 'public keys'. With these, the sender of the data uses a cipher which can be made available to the public at large, but the 'key' to the data is known only by the receiver and is the only way of deciphering the data. Mathematical algorithms are used so that the potential number of deciphering keys that can be generated from the public key is so large as to make it virtually impossible for an eavesdropper to decipher, even with the most sophisticated computer equipment currently available, or likely to be available in the near future.

Using 'public keys' removes the security risk of more than one individual knowing the deciphering key to the data.

Data back-up and storage

Users of computer systems must be aware that the medium on which data is stored for everyday use can be subject to failure and it is important that controls are put in place to ensure that the risks of that loss are minimised. The form of data back-up depends on the underlying design of the applications which access and update the data. Normally, one would expect one of the two following methods to be in use at a particular installation:

1. Where the data is maintained by batch processing, the grandfather/father/son method of backing-up will be used. The principle of this method is that, at any point in time, the last two back-ups made should be available plus all of the batches that have been processed since the older of the back-ups was made. These would be in the form of master and data tapes that would be separately labelled and stored. Once the grandfather tape becomes older than that, it can be reused as the latest tape for back-up purposes and becomes the son.

2. More likely, where the data is maintained on-line, data will be backed up each day along with separate audit printouts so that, if the normal storage medium fails, the information is available by which the system can be restored to the last point of data entry prior to the back-up being taken.

3. A third method is becoming more common and is associated with current **relational database management systems (RDBMS)** such as *Oracle, Ingres* and *Informix.* With these systems, it is possible to record every data input to the system as what is known as a transaction, either on a separate hard disk or to a tape drive. The RDBMS can then replay the transactions on top of a previous back-up allowing a system to be restored automatically to the last complete transaction should any part of the system fail. Whilst the RDBMS itself is maintained on-line, the process to back-up data is similar to the grandfather/father/son method.

Given that one of the risks that we are trying to counteract is the physical destruction of the installation, it is sensible to put in place controls to ensure that back-up data is stored in a fireproof environment on-site and, occasionally, some form of master back-up is removed from the installation site completely.

Operational controls

It is important to identify how errors might occur during the operation of a system. Errors will fall into the following classes:

1. **Data capture/classification errors:** these occur before data is ready for input to a system and arise because of incorrect classification of data (e.g. allocating a production cost as an administrative cost, for example).

2. **Transcription errors:** these arise during the preparation of data. Two examples are: data which has been written down previously, or which is passed on orally, may be incorrectly recorded on data input forms; and where data is converted from one format to another (e.g. from a DOS format disk to a UNIX system) and then used for the preparation of customer orders.

3. **Data communication faults:** if the system operates over a WAN, then the original input at the terminal/PC may become corrupted during transmission, either during on-line processing, or where the information is stored in a batch file and transmitted over the WAN later for processing. Similar issues need to be considered for LANs, but far fewer problems arise due to the greater level of resilience inherent in LANs.

4. **Data processing errors:** these can arise due to: programming error; system design; or data corruption on the system itself.

Since the above errors can occur, indeed because they are likely to occur throughout the life of a system to varying degrees of seriousness, we must take specific measures to identify when they occur and to ensure that corrections are made to the data, either before or after processing has occurred. The purpose of the controls is to ensure as far as possible that:

- the data being processed is complete
- it is authorised
- the results are accurate
- a complete audit trail of what was done is available.

Areas of control

The areas in which we could expect controls to be assigned to provide protection to the system are input activities, file processing activities and output activities.

Input activities:

- Data collection and preparation
- Data authorisation
- Data conversion (if appropriate)
- Data transmission
- Data correction
- Corrected data re-input.

File processing activities:

- Data validation and editing
- Data manipulation, sorting/merging
- Master file updating.

Output activities:

- Output control and reconciliation with predetermined data
- Information distribution.

Controls in these areas are vital and must deal with errors or problems as they arise instead of delaying their resolution to a later processing stage. This is because processing inaccurate data represents a waste of both computer time and human effort and may lead to further unforeseen errors occurring and misleading final results. The Systems Analyst must incorporate appropriate and effective controls within the system design. It cannot be left to someone else at a later stage in the systems development process. Within the three areas listed above, there are some fundamental principles that can be applied, including the following:

- Every item of data intended for processing must be processed.
- To be effective, any control must be simple to operate and be part of the overall system itself.
- The control should be built into the normal data flow within the overall information system.
- Wherever possible, the system should be designed to detect an error at the earliest moment in the data processing cycle.
- Similarly, the underlying system design should not be able to operate with incorrect data, unless such processing has to be accepted as part of the overall design.
- As with all controls, the cost of implementing them must be commensurate with the risks associated with incorrect data being processed.
- Specific consideration must be given to the prevention of fraud and not simply the avoidance of innocent errors.

Controls over data input

The place where the controls are implemented in this area will depend on the type of computer installation being considered. Table 11.4 deals with the different types of system operation depending on whether the management of the system is centralised, decentralised or distributed. It covers responsibility for implementing administrative controls and also identifies the likely location of manual controls external to the controls built into the applications themselves.

Equipment configuration \ Management control	Centralised	Decentralised
Centralised	All analysts, programmers, operations staff at central site.	Analysts, programmers work for various area divisions, make use of central resource through terminals.
Distributed	All analysts and programmers controlled by central site – assigned to different projects. Programs downloaded to distributed processors.	All program development done locally. Control through standards and procedures; central co-ordinating group optional.
Decentalised	Analysts and programmers assigned to project; local operations staff.	Complete local control over systems and operations staff.

Table 11.4

A control will be applied to a particular part of a given application or over a specific part of the processing cycle. It will be designed with completeness, authorisation, accuracy and compliance with audit needs as stated earlier. With regards the input of data, this will normally require that each source document is correctly and appropriately completed and securely transmitted to the computer either via a WAN or manually. The specific controls one might expect to see include:

- a pre-designed, **input form** that records the data to be input, ensuring that all coding required is completed;
- proper **authorisation controls** designed and implemented on any data to be input;
- use of **sequence checks** designed into the applications;
- a proper **training programme** for all staff inputting and/or preparing input data;
- an organised **filing system** for all input documents either separate from, or part of, the normal administrative filing of the organisation;
- batching of source documents, if appropriate, to the part of the processing cycle.

Certain controls are also required to ensure all data is correctly received by the computer:

- a **log** recording the receipt of data to be input, where the data is prepared separately;
- controls over **access** to the computer via the WAN and **reconciliations** where data is transmitted and updated via a batch file update process;
- **batch controls** for reconciliation purposes;
- where input is on-line, a **printout** of all input which can be reviewed for errors or other matters by a separate person.

These are the types of control we might expect to see as part of our input controls. The controls themselves will be designed using the following techniques: data validation and data verification.

Data validation

Type checks: every entry must comply with the prescribed format, e.g. dates may be defined as consisting of 2 digits, 3 alphabetic characters and 2 further digits such as 04APR93. Any other form of input will result in an error.

Non-existence checks: data fields requiring entry may have a separate validation table behind them such that the data being input must exist on that table; for example, a supplier account number must exist already before the system will accept that number on an invoice.

Checks for consistency: where data is originally entered and does not require on-going maintenance, the fact that it is still consistent with the original data input should be checked within an appropriate timescale.

Duplication/repetition checks: the system may check this; for example, for a particular invoice, the system could check that only this invoice has been received from a supplier with the supplier's invoice number input correctly.

Range checks: a minimum and maximum value could be established against which input could be checked.

Data verification

Data verification controls check to ensure that the data being presented to the system comes from a verified source. The sorts of verification that might occur include the following.

Batch total preparation: the preparers of the data for input may submit their own batch totals separately from the System Administrator for input so that any discrepancies with the data processed can be identified immediately. The failure to present these batch totals would prevent any data from being processed.

Separate validation run: before being processed, batch files uploaded via a WAN can have hash totals in-built to the file header, along with special passwords, all of which are checked by the application before processing can commence. The Banks Automated Clearing Service (BACS) system, which allows payments to be made directly from one bank account to another, operates on this basis.

Controls during data processing

The processing controls designed by the systems analyst will depend on the type of processing undertaken. Where data is maintained on-line, the application needs to check for the following conditions.

- 'The data input is correct' – this is normally on a field-by-field basis or screen-by-screen basis where block-mode terminals are in use.
- 'There is space on the system for the data' – prior to updating records, the application must check that all files required are in place and that there is room on the files for the data.
- 'Index values are correct' – indexes are created on on-line data to speed access and ensure uniqueness; where the data is updating an index, the system must check that it will do so validly or else the integrity of the data will be doubtful.
- 'The transaction can be completed' – the system must check that, should the operator confirm the data being input, it will be able to update all records required.
- 'The transaction has been completed' – after confirmation by the operator, the system must ensure that updating has, in fact, occurred; if this is not the case, then the system must be restored to the state it was before the transaction started, the operator informed that no updating has occurred and, if possible, notified why that was the case.

Where data is maintained by batch processing, additional checks must be built into the application. This can include:

- validation that master data, such as a supplier account number, exists on the system;
- pre-processing runs to verify the data;
- rejection of a complete batch of data where errors occur during processing, with an error report identifying why processing has failed;
- alternatively, processing of the valid entries on the batch file with an error report listing those items not processed;
- reconciliation of control totals such that the old balance, plus the total of the batch file processed, equals the new balance;
- recording occasions where an operator has made on-line amendments to a batch file where errors have been identified during pre-processing or actual processing;
- proper review, reconciliation and clearance of suspense files or accounts on the system.

As part of the design of any system, it is the analyst's responsibility to create or identify the different applications which should be used to provide security copies of data.

Controls on output

Controls are put in place over output to ensure that:

- the output expected from the computer is received by the user or user department;
- exception reports which are used as the basis of action are correctly used;
- error and data rejection reports are reviewed and actions taken to correct the errors;
- the output received reconciles with the input data provided;
- the users receiving data are authorised to do so and acknowledge receipt of it.

Types of control to be considered during design

- Printouts should be numbered starting from (1).
- Printouts should show the date and time they were produced, by whom and at whose request if the report has not been produced as part of the normal processing cycle.
- Exception reports should be considered for every aspect of the output required to see if long, detailed reports can be avoided.
- Sub-totals and final report totals should be included.
- Any reconciling information should be shown separately.
- The number of pages produced should be indicated beside the end of report marker.

Data transmission control

Where data is transmitted over a WAN, controls must be designed to ensure that any errors that occur during transmission are corrected. Transmission may be over a simple, analogue public telephone circuit or over a private switched network such as X.25.

Most errors occur with analogue-type signals where the digital information that computers use is translated into 'sound waves' for transmission over the public network. The subject is a very technical one which students are not required to study. What they must do, however, is identify that controls are necessary where data is transmitted in any form and that the less sophisticated the techniques used for transmitting data, the higher the level of separate controls that is often needed to be designed to identify errors and ensure that incorrect data is not processed.

Data control unit

In larger organisations where the system is centralised, there may be a data control section or unit that will undertake a large number of the controls with regard to the input, processing and output of data. Its responsibilities will cover the:

- scheduling of processing;
- accepting of new data and its verification;
- intermediate clerical tasks (e.g. establishing control totals);
- vetting of error or rejection reports and instigating corrective action;
- distribution of completed output to authorised recipients;
- maintenance of file security and data back-ups.

In smaller organisations, or where the systems are decentralised or distributed, there may be insufficient work for such a unit to exist. This should not stop proper controls over the data processing cycle existing and being implemented.

Reasons for failure of information systems

It is commonplace for employees in organisations to complain about their computer systems. Very rarely will a user be completely satisfied with the current information system. Comments such as the following are typical:

- 'I don't get all the information I need'
- 'I wish I had access to that data'
- 'Why does it always take so long to get what I need?'
- 'The reports I get don't tell me what I need to know'.

Why do computer systems rarely live up to our expectations? Part of the answer to this question may lie in the way the systems have been designed and developed. However perfect a system development methodology is, the resulting system is unlikely to satisfy everyone. The term 'failure' in this sense does not necessarily imply that the computer system does not function. This is rarely the case, though there are some notorious development disasters where this has occurred. (See Case-study 11.3 at the end of this chapter.) Failure of a system can simply imply that users are dissatisfied, and that expected benefits have not materialised. To consider why systems do not live up to expectations may lead to some of the pitfalls being avoided and consequently better systems being developed. Some of the causes of computer system 'failure' are as follows.

Poor management

A lack of concern or interest from the Senior management in an organisation can be disasterous in systems development. Often senior managers do not get involved in the design process. This can be for many reasons including lack of technical knowledge, computer 'phobia', and the widely held view that such processes should be left to the technical experts. Thus an important segment of the organisation is often excluded from direct involvement in the design process. Therefore a vital global view of the organisation is missing even if other management levels participate in the process. Policies, long term plans and strategies may consequently only be superficially incorporated into the information systems development.

Lack of participation

If users are not involved in the early stages of information system design then they are more likely to be dissatisfied with the resulting system. This lack of participation will manifest itself in different ways such as:

- poor specifications produced because of insufficient information obtained from prospective users and lack of consultation
- users apprehensive because of changes in their working practices, and in some cases reduction in security of work
- users resisting the new system because of lack of understanding of the benefits.

Involvement in the early stages of design and development leads on to acceptance and 'ownership' of the resulting system by the users. This usually leads on to greater satisfaction of the system in operation.

Poor planning and control

The importance of effective planning and control cannot be over-emphasised in an information system development project. The systems ideas of feedback and control mechanisms have been discussed in Chapter 3. Essentially, the project must have suitable control mechanisms and adequate procedures in place providing feedback when the project is not going according to plan. The Project Manager, or Project Team must have clearly defined objectives, and target dates for the project phases. This ensures that sufficient information is available in order to redistribute resources and reschedule work loads if required. Poor control may result in projects over-running deadlines and being over-budget. The total project must be managed effectively through all stages of development up to and including the implementation and maintenance phases where individuals will need training, induction and continual guidance and encouragement to achieve the best from the new system.

Self-assessment questions

1 Consider any computer system at your work-place or any situation with which you are familiar. Does the system perform effectively?

2 Are the staff fully satisfied with the operation of this system? If not, explain the possible reasons for the system's lack of performance and users' dissatisfaction.

Summary

This chapter has reviewed some standard methods of information system development. Regardless of the method used, care must be taken to ensure such development is 'needs-driven'; starting with the need and developing a system in order to satisfy that need. The system's development life-cycle has been described in some detail. This approach includes the stages of preliminary investigation, systems analysis, systems design, development, implementation and maintenance. Such a process should not be restricted to the computer specialist, and this chapter has stressed the importance of user involvement in the overall method.

The life-cycle method is a traditional approach to system development and should not be considered in isolation from the current methodologies. Individual elements within the life-cycle approach are valid and relevant even if other methodologies are adopted. One particular methodology that formalises the life-cycle ideas is the structured systems analysis and design methodology (SSADM). A more recent approach incorporating the use of Prototyping assists the information system development and enables a system to be produced much faster than the basic life-cycle technique. Prototyping has become more feasible with the introduction of a range of CASE (computer-aided software engineering) tools to assist in the product development. New approaches to system development include those incorporating the object oriented ideas.

The majority of design methodologies assume that problems are clearly defined and requirements can be easily specified. In many cases this is not true; problems are often vague and unstructured. These 'soft' problems are considered by the use of soft systems methodology (SSM) which concentrates a significant amount of time in the early stage of the life-cycle, analysing the problems, before attempting to define specifications and proceed into the detailed analysis stage.

Many reasons exist for the implementation of incomplete or unsatisfactory systems. Such reasons will include failure to abide by the basic system development procedures outlined in this chapter. Whatever design methodology is adopted there are essential elements in the process which, if missing, will increase the possibility of system failure. The following factors are vitally important:

● Management commitment – involvement of senior management in the process is essential to ensure that all levels of decision making are catered for.
● User participation – potential users must be involved at each stage of the process to ensure that the resulting system fully meets their requirements.
● Planning and control – the project must be carefully planned and scheduled and control mechanisms put in place to ensure that time-scales and budgets are adhered to, or schedules and estimates adjusted accordingly.

Questions for discussion _____

1   During the development of an information system at your work-place, you overhear one of the senior managers saying 'We are running behind schedule. We are still only in the middle of producing the programs that have all been designed. Why don't we spend less time on testing now and leave it to when we implement the whole system? The users can find any bugs in the system. We should be able to save weeks if we do this.' Comment on this statement. Discuss the implications of such a tactic.

2   'It is always better to buy a system in from another company, even if it only satisfies 90% of our needs. The alternative is just too expensive and time-consuming.' Discuss the implication of this comment in relation to the development of an information system.

3   Discuss the various ways of collecting data concerning current working practices in a company. Comment on the effectiveness and potential drawbacks of each method.

4   'Documentation can be left until all the systems have been designed and developed.' Would you agree with this statement? If not, give reasons.

5   A consultant has been bought in to your organisation to assist with the development of a new management information system. The consultant is very experienced and insists that the SSADM approach is all that is required in any development project. Would you agree with this? If not, under what circumstances would you think that other techniques may be appropriate?

6   'The best way of changing from the old system to a new one is to run both systems in parallel for a few months. That way you can iron out all the bugs in the new system whilst making sure that everything still runs smoothly.' Would you agree with this statement? Discuss this approach to changing over systems and describe alternative methods.

Problems

I   Describe the main steps used in the systems development process. Which step, if any, is most important to ensure the satisfactory running of the resulting system?

2   What questions should be asked during a system feasibility study? Who are likely to give you the required answers?

3   A project team should consist of an equal mix of computer specialists and users. Comment on this statement. Would you agree? What would be the advantages and drawbacks of having predominently computer specialists, or predominently users on such a team?

4   Would you agree that prototyping enables a company to have an information system up and running much quicker than other development methods? What are the disadvantages of using the prototyping approach?

5   The Accounts Manager has identified a 'definite' problem in the way sales orders are processed and invoices produced in his organisation. He recommends that a new computer system be produced to correct the existing drawbacks. He is willing to provide detailed specifications of the existing problems and a requirements list so that the main design stage in the systems development can start almost immediately. The offer sounds tempting. Would you, as Systems Development Manager, agree to the offer? If not, why not?

6   Explain the difference between systems analysis and system design. Can both stages be achieved by the same personnel? Give reasons for your answer.

Case-study 11.1:   Leisure services information system
The Leisure Services Department in a Local Authority controls a range of sports and leisure centres catering for the local population. Within a 25 mile radius there are three Sports Centres dealing with outdoor activities such as football, athletics, tennis, netball and hockey. Each Sports Centre employs at least six office staff including a manager, receptionist, bookings clerk, administrative and secretarial support. Additional staff would also be employed to care for the grounds, sports areas, and equipment. In the same locality, there are five Leisure Centres offering a range of activities such as swimming, squash, badminton, aerobics, bowling and snooker. The Leisure Centres usually employ more staff than the Sports Centres. Each Leisure Centre has a manager, assistant manager, reception and clerical staff, and a range of sports specialists who run training sessions, organise events, and provide supervision of all activities.

The Local Authority intends to install a new information system in the Leisure Services Department to assist in the management of the eight centres. The system will:

● enable the department's staff to monitor the performance of each centre in terms of a range of measurements such as number of customers, daily revenue, and range of services offered;

- be able to help monitor and control resources such as expenditure on capital items, maintenance and repair, in addition to staff costs, such as salaries, and overtime payments;
- enter details onto the system at each site, and be accessed at the central location;
- have a communications link between all of the centres in the locality.

You have been given the task of managing a project team to install such an information system.

1   Describe the steps that would need to be undertaken prior to installation of the system.

2   Outline the problems that you envisage may occur during the various stages of this project.

3   The Chief Executive has been quoted as saying: 'People are the most important single asset in any business.' How would you ensure that the employees in this case are fully supportive of the system you finally install?

4   What are the activities that should continue to take place even after the system has been installed and is fully operational?

Case-study 11.2:   University student management system

Eastcote University, based in the West Midlands, was opened in 1992. The University, sited on a brand new campus, presently consists of 300 academic and 400 administrative staff. A new computer-based information system is required to assist in the student registrations process and course management.

Eastcote University contains fifteen Academic Departments delivering a range of undergraduate and post-graduate courses. Staff within each department process student applications for these courses. This involves checking that the entrance requirements have been satisfied, confirming numbers of applications for particular courses, and determining availability of places. Refusals and offer letters are sent to applicants, and course lists of student names are prepared when required. Such processes would:

- involve computer terminals available for specified staff within each department;
- require access to central files containing details of class lists, registrations, and the progress of existing applications;
- provide centrally-controlled access to the University's accounting system for the payment and processing of course fees.

Currently, there are disagreements between academic staff involved in this process and the Central Registrations staff concerning the range and type of information required on such a system. For confidentiality and security reasons, the registrations staff consider that access of information for the academic staff should be restricted to those courses within their own department. Conversely, the academic staff state that they require all details on current applications so as not to duplicate work carried out by staff in other departments. The Finance Department also require that some data regarding the individual department's revenue is restricted to a limited number of specified staff.

A working group has been established to investigate the requirements of the new system prior to appointing specialists to develop the required systems.

1 How would this working group proceed in designing a system that will take into account these conflicting demands? Can the disagreements outlined in this case study be resolved?

2 It has been suggested that a small working system (prototype) be installed in the Central Registrations department to consider any drawbacks, and resolve any problems before attempting to implement the full system for the whole University. Do you think that this is a good idea? What are the advantages of using this approach? Can you see any problems that may develop after the prototype stage?

Case-study 11.3:   Wessex Regional Health Authority

A major information system development project was initiated in the late 1980s at the Wessex Regional Health Authority (WHRA). The Wessex region covers a large area in the South of England containing over 200 hospitals. The WHRA, with headquarters in Winchester, manages the health services for the whole region, including hospitals, local General Practitioners, and community services. The project (entitled RISP (Regional Information Systems Plan) outlined a massive information systems strategy that would link every hospital, ward, doctor, and nurse in the region. The idea was that a doctor on one hospital would have immediate on-lone access to the patients' files, containing information on past diagnoses, and other details such as drugs prescribes, and known allergies. Furthermore, information on costs, budgets and revenues would be available for the appropriate management levels in the Health Authority.

The RISP encountered a range of problems in its development, and by the early 1990s the whole project had been cancelled with very little of the planned systems being implemented. Many questions have been raised since then relating to the effectiveness of the senior management at the WHRA and the way in which external contractors were involved at various stages in the development process. The process of tendering for the initial contracts for the design of systems was dubious. For instance, the RISP project was put out to tender during 1986. A number of bids were received by the WHRA including those from DEC (Digital Equipment Corporation) and a consortium of IBM and the Andersen Consultancy group. The DEC bid was initially chosen as the best bid, and draft contracts were issued on this basis. The WHRA employed Andersen Consultants to provide advice on the tendering process. Clearly this may have created a conflict of interest where Andersens were advising WHRA on the overall process in addition to being involved as a partner in submitting a bid. Furthermore, there were close links between IBM and the WHRA such as one of the IBM board members also sat on the Health Authority board. The IBM consortium requested a reconsideration of their bid, which had originally been ranked as fourth in a technical evaluation. Eventually, in late 1986 the IBM bid was accepted. Controversially, decisions were made by the WHRA senior management team when a number of members were absent.

- The initial project estimate of £29 million rose to at least £43 million, with subsequent estimates put as high as £60–£80 millions.
- The contracts between the WHRA and a variety of suppliers were poorly constructed to the detriment of the Health Authority.
- The WHRA had little control on the contracts, and had no mechanisms for checking whether it was receiving good value for money from its suppliers. For instance, there were no penalty clauses in the original contracts for delayed or sub-standard supplies.
- Ex-employees of the Health Authority were able to bid for, and were awarded a number of contracts in the RISP programme.
- Suppliers sometimes effectively had open cheque books, and could charge any sum for services without question from the authority.
- A subsequent audit report advised on improving the contracts and tightening up on the controls.

A number of issues emerge relating to the failure of the RISP project. The project was incredibly ambitious, involving the development of a totally new system, not used by any other authority in the UK. A variety of the stakeholders (potential users) such as the medical staff did not accept that such a system would be cost effective, and were hostile to such a development. Many consultants complained that the money would be better spent on high-cost equipment such as scanners, or additional medical staff. The management at WHRA were inexperienced in the information systems area, and provided little control on the project, relying on external advice and support. After a number of years, the failing project continued to be funded, even after being effectively rejected. Finally, in 1990, following the appointment of a new general manager of the WHRA, the RISP project was abandoned. Only one integrated system covering the finance elements had been installed for the region.

1   What does this case study illustrate in the development of an information system?

2   How could some of the problems indicated be avoided?

3   As Project Manager of the RISP outline the main steps you would undertake in the initial stages of this development project.

Case-study 11.4:   Which IT strategy? – the case of Rose Limited
Rose Limited is a £20m business employing 200 people. For some time, it has been unhappy with its IT system, which has evolved since the 1970s. One of the Board members was asked to produce a report for managers on the options facing the company. A summary of some of his key findings, presented to a meeting of managers, is provided below:

1. What are our objectives?
A reliable, robust IT system which allows us:

- to run the core operations of the business in a way which satisfies customers, suppliers, our own and the parent company's needs;
- to gather data from the market in a way which allows us to identify customer needs and to satisfy those needs;

- thereby to develop competitive edge over other players;
- to adapt as technology changes and to have control of our own destiny;
- to maintain IT costs at or below 3% of company revenue.

2. What is our current situation?

The IT review has identified most areas of the system needing enhancement or redevelopment to meet these objectives, including market definition and analysis, product specification, production scheduling, order entry, electronic data interchange for ordering and invoicing, credit control and product returns. Operational effects include:

- poor customer service and documentation
- poor mangement information
- poor financial information
- excessive IT cost
- poor staff morale.

3. What are the options?

The options are:

- take full in-house control of IT development and ensure that it meets our needs in future;
- find external facilities management supplier to support IT development – using appropriate third-party packages for some operational elements;
- abandon current system and go to an industry-standard package.

Initial Findings:

- we do not have all the requisite skills to manage a big software development in-house and it seems inappropriate to acquire them;
- effective facilities management for our system is being offered by software consultants A;
- software company, B, is able to offer a full industry package which appears to cover most of our current needs.

4. What are they offering?

- Supplier A: Development of current IT system to provide a flexible, customer-built solution, including a relational database;
- Supplier B: A fully integrated, proven system covering most aspects of the business, operating on a flat file structure.

5. What are the costs?

	Suppler A	Supplier B
Capital cost	£470K	£460K
Optional extra charge (for aditional marketing enhancement)	£30K	–
Annual maintenance cost	£100K	£30K

6. What are the risks?

	SUPPLIER A	SUPPLIER B
1. Schedule	After systems analysis, developers realise that the tasks are much greater than allowed for in the three man-years, and we go into 199X with inadequate systems.	Tasks such as data conversion prove a greater issue than expected.
2. Costs	After systems analysis, tasks are shown to be greater than allowed for in budget. Progress impeded by lack of finance. Ongoing support proves too costly.	Costs of enhancing the new system to meet our marketing needs proves greater than expected.
3. Quality: reliability	Improvements fail to address the reliability of the system. Operations remain hampered by system failure.	
4. Quality: product	Pressure of other tasks during systems analysis means that staff do not include all necessary angles. Resulting product fails to meet emerging needs	Access to data proves more problematic than expected

I A final decision has not yet been made. What is your recommendation?

References for this text

1 Capron, H.L. and Perron, J.D., *Computers and Information Systems,* Benjamin Cummings Publishing Company, 1993
2 Jackson, M., *Principles of Program Design,* Academic Press, 1975
3 Jackson, M., *System Development* Prentice-Hall International, 1983

Further reading

Anderson, R., *Development of Business Information Systems,* Blackwell, 1992

Brown, A.W., *Object-Oriented Databases,* McGraw-Hill 1991

Checkland, P., *Systems Thinking, Systems Practice,* Wiley 1991

Clifton, H.D. & Sutcliffe, A.G., *Business Information Systems,* (Chapters 6, 7 and 8) Prentice-Hall, 1994

Curtis, G., *Business Information Systems,* Addison Wesley, 1995

Harry, M., *Information and Management Systems,* (Chapter 5) Pitman, 1990

Harry, M., *Information Systems in Business,* (Section 7) Pitman, 1994

Hick, J.O., *Information Systems in Business: An Introduction,* 2nd ed., (Chapters 6, 7, and 8) West Publishing Co, 1990

Lewis, P., *Information System Development,* (Chapter 4) Pitman, 1994

O'Brien, J., *Management Information Systems: A Managerial End-User Perspective,* (Pages 72-102) Irwin, 1993

Reynolds, G.W., *Information Systems for Managers,* 2nd ed., (Chapters 8 and 9) West Publishing Co, 1992

Senn, J.A., *Information Systems in Management,* 4th ed., (Chapter 16) Wadsworth Publishing, 1990

Index